Tartar City Woman

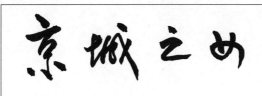

Tartar City Woman

Scenes from the life of Wang Hsin-ping, former citizen of China

Trevor Hay

MELBOURNE UNIVERSITY PRESS

1990

First published 1990
Printed in Australia by
Globe Press Pty Ltd, Brunswick, Victoria, for
Melbourne University Press, Carlton, Victoria 3053
U.S.A. and Canada: International Specialized Book Services, Inc.,
5602 N.E. Hassalo Street, Portland, Oregon 97213-3640

National Library of Australia Cataloguing-in-Publication entry

Hay, Trevor, 1946–
  Tartar City woman.

  Includes index.
  ISBN 0 522 84434 0.

  1. Wang, Hsin-ping, 1937– . 2. China—History—1949–
1976—Biography. I. Title.

951.05092

For my wife, Jennifer Hay, for her unfailing courage, dignity and loyalty

For my friend and teacher, Ron Price, who showed me the way, and then walked with me

For my father, George Hay, who taught me to listen carefully to a migrant's story

Contents

Illustrations

ABBREVIATIONS

C.Y.L.   Communist Youth League
P.L.A.   People's Liberation Army

Preface

'Tartar' is an old-fashioned, mysterious and intoxicating word, applied imprecisely to the bewildering variety of Central Asians, Cossacks, Turks, Mongols and Manchus who have inhabited Peking at various times. In old guide-books the northern walled town of the Manchus, including the Forbidden City, was referred to as the 'Tartar City', and another walled town to the south, outside the perimeters of power, was the 'Chinese City'. Although antique, these are still useful terms since they remind us that Peking was ruled by a conquering tribe. The wall between the northern and southern towns is gone now, and all that divides the Chinese from their rulers is Tian'anmen Square.

As for Wang Hsin-ping herself, I have called her a 'Tartar City Woman' because she lived just inside the south-west corner of the Tartar city wall, because her family were of the old ruling class, and because she is an exotic character, a fascinating misfit, who strayed into the Foreign Quarter with a strange and terrible tale to tell of goings-on in the Forbidden City. Hsin-ping is not an important historical figure, and played no key role in major events, but, as Chinese observe, even the fish in the moat fry when the City Gate catches fire.

Hsin-ping began telling me her tale many years ago, and in 1986 I began recording, as she narrated in Chinese. At first I made no attempt to interrupt her flow, or impose any particular order or sequence on her recollections. Then, during 1987, we went to Peking together and she shared some more memories with me. Finally I translated many hours of audio tapes into English, and went back and forth to see her, for clarification and detail. Hsin-ping is a wonderful mimic, and she frequently made the picture clearer by acting things out for me. The sessions often ended in unrestrained hilarity, and just as often in heart-rending tears. Of course her memory is imperfect and there are gaps in the story. I have not tried to press her about people or events she did not freely portray and, for the sake of the narrative, I have sometimes reconstructed coherent discourse from fragments; but in general the text reflects what Hsin-ping told me. I have noticed that Chinese people frequently do remember conversations in remarkable detail, perhaps because so much of modern Chinese political culture is a kind of polemic routine. It is often the case too, that what so-and-so said about something-or-other is a matter of life and death for somebody. I have added some background analysis of political campaigns in order to provide the reader with a context for the major episodes in Hsin-ping's life. Naturally, this is the product of an outsider's perspective rather than of Hsin-ping's perception of events at the time.

In the words of Hsin-ping's favourite poet, Du Fu, there have been many new ghosts to curse their fate since I started writing. Many 'foreign friends' have had a nasty shock about China. I hope it does not delude them into thinking that lies and labels are the exclusive hallmarks of Chinese—or communist—authoritarianism. In Australia alone, there are plenty of forceful reminders that democracy and justice are still searching for permanent residence, like all the other refugees.

TREVOR HAY
Melbourne, June 1990

Acknowledgements

Apart from constant support and advice, there are two things for which I am grateful to Dr Ronald Price of Latrobe University. Firstly, for all those Saturday mornings, and the lovely conversations *en route* to and from Hsin-ping's place, and secondly, for pushing me into the path of an oncoming word-processor. I would also like to thank Fang Xiangshu and Bi Lijun for their expert scrutiny of the manuscript and source materials, and Chen Shen for his fine calligraphy. I am grateful to my colleagues at the University of Melbourne's School of Early Childhood Studies for their patience and sympathy during the most difficult period of my life. In particular, I wish to thank David Cunnington for his painstaking preparation of the index, and Kevin Fell and Erika Price for their comments on the manuscript. I am grateful too for the support and encouragement of my friends in the Melbourne China Studies Group. I have benefitted greatly from the advice of Linda Jaivin, of the Australian National University, and I thank her for her cheerful and generous manner. My thanks also to Don Tinkler, educational consultant, for technical assistance and unstinting moral support and to Gabriel Lafitte for his help with the manuscript.

A Note on Transcription

In general, the system of transcription used in this book is *Hanyu Pinyin*—the Chinese spelling system currently in use in the People's Republic of China, and in international media agencies. That is, where a Chinese (Mandarin) word has been written, the *Hanyu Pinyin* system is used. Readers should note that that this does not preclude the use of anglicized forms such as 'Peking', 'Hong Kong', and 'Canton'. These and other forms, which may be familiar to readers (e.g. 'Chiang Kai-shek'), are sometimes used for place and personal names. In some cases, difficult judgements have to be made about whether a Chinese or anglicized form is more familiar to readers (e.g. 'Tientsin' or 'Tianjin', 'Nanking' or 'Nanjing'.

One rather embarrassing anomaly is the name of Wang Hsin-ping herself. Like many Chinese, she has an aversion to calling herself something with an 'x' in it, so instead of using either the *Hanyu Pinyin* form of her given name (Xinping), or the Wade-Giles form more familiar to an older generation (Hsin-p'ing), she prefers to have the best of both worlds and call herself Hsin-ping. It is, I might add, quite typical of her.

Prologue: Crossing the Bridge

In May 1975 I went to China for the first time. I had been reading avidly—Edgar Snow, Jack Belden, William Hinton—and was armed with a number of progressive attitudes, *circa* 1975, for dealing with the experience. I had grown up in a fearful, Cold War and Yellow Peril atmosphere, which I had been able to reject with all the confidence of the 1960s. I had also spent two years in the Australian Army as a result of Australia's perceptions of Asia, and that only strengthened my determination to tell China's side of the story, which still badly needed telling. I hadn't started using the word 'ethnocentric' regularly in conversation, but I was on my way. I had been studying Chinese for a couple of months, but I couldn't use chopsticks efficiently. In Hong Kong a friend took me into a restaurant, told the waiter I spoke Chinese and then taught me how to use chopsticks by practising with boiled peanuts on a glass tabletop. It was the first time I was to see that look of deferential contempt on a Chinese face.

For the first and last time I was 'fascinated' by a Chinese environment. I don't mean that I am no longer curious, or moved, or baffled, but I can't help thinking that 'fascination', like an adolescent crush, or a child's love of magic tricks, thrives on unwillingness to become familiar with realities. Everybody was talking about 'going in' to China next day. It sounded like a parachute drop behind enemy lines. The train sped through the New Territories and I absorbed the ugly jumble of the

1

place and the way Chinese and Western things seemed to lie down together, compatible in an incomprehensible sort of way—like an old married couple. When I returned from my trip I was able to tell a number of audiences that this was the first revealing comparison between the New Territories and China—the organized 'garden agriculture' of the People's Republic and the charming chaos of the New Territories.

After some hours the train stopped at Shenzhen. We crossed the river and I noticed gravestones sticking out from the hillside. The train always stopped here in those days and you got out and walked through Customs. Shenzhen was not a Special Economic Zone then but it certainly was a Special Psychological Zone. You knew that there was no turning back. I began clutching at my pockets for bits of paper and rummaging through my bag, as I always do when I'm nervous. For some reason the one thing I need to lay my fears to rest is never there.

We left the British Customs area, with its portraits of the Queen, and entered the Chinese side with its portraits of the 'Four Big Beards'—Lenin, Marx, Engels and Stalin. Mao was there too, of course, with no beard but a striking mole on his chin. A group of primary school children trooped past carrying red flags and singing at the tops of their voices. We were all mesmerized. Our safari had begun and we had seen our first big game.

Within days of our arrival, half the party had bought the blue jackets worn in China since Sun Yat-sen and now styled 'Mao' jackets. We began calling each other 'Chairman' this and that and generally went a bit silly, like kids allowed to sleep overnight in a strange house. We goggled at People's Liberation Army (P.L.A.) soldiers (most of us thought they were 'Red Guards'), and I suppose the sight of baggy green uniforms and caps with red stars on them provoked odd sensations in all of us. I thought of all those comics I had read as a kid, where slant-eyed midgets in quilted uniforms, looking rather like tea-cosies, fled in terror from cigar-chomping American sergeants. For some reason they fled in Chinese, with little balloons containing asterisks and exclamation marks above their heads. I recalled this with some indignation, thinking how racist we Westerners were. I had not yet seen Chinese comics. Crossing the bridge at Shenzhen was a powerful reminder that there was still an act of commitment associated with this experience. It was not like simply going on a journey. China had picked you for its team, and you stepped up eagerly, pleased that you weren't the last to be selected. We didn't know then that China would become an oriental fun parlour.

In those days you had to know something about the 'Maoist alternative' and you had to be at least associated with China experts before you were eligible to be picked for the team. Eagerness to demonstrate sympathy is often the greatest obstacle to understanding, and so it was that every incident, beginning with the lunch we had in the station at Shenzhen, became a rich source of anecdotes by means of which each person demonstrated his or her revealing insights into China. 'Can there really be such a thing as a truly egalitarian society?' was the truly daft question we asked ourselves. We decided that 'The Chinese', unlike ourselves, were motivated by moral rather than material incentives.

Six years later, teaching English in Nanking, I took as a lesson George Orwell's 'Marrakech':

> The people have brown faces—besides there are so many of them! Are they really the same flesh as yourself? Or are they merely a kind of undifferentiated brown stuff, about as individual as bees or coral insects? They rise out of the earth, they sweat and starve for a few years, and then they sink back into the nameless mounds of the graveyard and nobody notices that they are gone. And even the graves themselves soon fade back into the soil. Sometimes, out for a walk as you break your way through the prickly pear, you notice that it is rather bumpy underfoot, and only a certain regularity in the bumps tells you that you are walking over skeletons.

In fact we *were* walking over skeletons. In Orwell's story, he confessed that he had often looked at 'passing firewood' without noticing the human beast of burden underneath. My students did not quite see what he was getting at, so I used an illustration from their own environment. 'Every day out there in Ninghai Road you can see wooden carts with huge loads of steel pipes inching up the steep incline past the college gate, but how often do you notice the old women and young children pulling the carts?' They had never noticed them.

And so, from the comfort of our trains and buses, we too looked out on the passing firewood of socialist reconstruction, unable to see who was underneath. In our way we were every bit as blind as those old imperialists and colonialists we despised for resigning themselves to the spectacle of human misery with the thought that 'life is cheap in Asia'.

The trip went on for three weeks. The whole of China was fascinating, the people were so friendly ('aren't the children gorgeous?') and honest (one tour member had discarded an empty hair-oil bottle in Canton only to have it returned to him in Shanghai), and even the political sloganeering was kind of quaint (we saw kindergarten children throwing wooden blocks at effigies of Lin Biao and Confucius). Nobody would use a word like 'quaint' of course, and nobody betrayed the slightest sign of ethnocentricity. In fact, discussions, which took place over every meal, became a kind of party game, in which you got points for spotting 'Western value judgements'.

I distinguished myself after the trip by telling several audiences about the distortions of the Western news media. I cited the way Melbourne newspapers had reported on riots and strikes in Hangzhou. I had been in Hangzhou at the time and I had noticed nothing untoward. In fact Hangzhou had seemed like the most peaceful place on Earth—and so it was in our hotel by the idyllic West Lake—but there *were* riots and strikes going on nevertheless.

The group leader excited our ire on a number of occasions with disturbing displays of Western cultural superiority. He appeared sceptical when the chairman of a revolutionary committee in Suzhou told him there were no primary schools for us to visit. 'So what if they promised us a primary visit', we said, 'it's just plain discourteous to carry on like that'. We were all becoming addicted to courtesy and couldn't get enough of it—although this did not stop us from being very rude to each other.

On another occasion the leader probed indelicately about sex education in China. The group of eminent educational administrators with whom we were 'exchanging experience' had already explained several times that there was no need for this because sex was not a problem in China. For our leader to insist that there must be *some* problems was . . . discourteous. He said, 'But everybody has problems. It's only natural. Surely you must have some concerns about unwanted pregnancies and so on with such a large population as yours?' How could he keep going on like that? The Chinese have a different attitude to sex. They don't make such a big deal of it, they're not obsessed with Hollywood fantasy.

We all knew from our keen sensitivity to Western cultural bias that it was almost racist to imagine that the Chinese had similar problems to the rest of humanity and, in any case, it was obvious to all but the most blinkered observer that China was coping admirably with its population—they all looked so well fed.

On our various train journeys I saw characters painted on the walls of village houses—'In agriculture learn from Dazhai, in industry learn from Daqing', 'Long life to Chairman Mao', and 'Criticize Lin Biao and Confucius'. As I grappled with my first on-location characters, I didn't appreciate that I was looking at the ruins of Mao's call to 'Bombard the headquarters', and that these words on the walls were like spent shells poking out from the rubble after an ideological air raid.

One evening, while posting a letter and looking for treasures in the hotel shop, I noticed that the most experienced 'China hand' among us, a man who spoke Chinese and had spent two years in China during the most intense part of the Cultural Revolution, was attempting to post a parcel to another city. He seemed to be getting terse with the People's Postwoman, and finally appeared quite angry. 'Look', he said in English, to my disappointment, 'I don't care if you post it or not. It's not mine, I don't care if this person gets it or if you decide to keep it here forever.' I was quite shocked. He saw me watching and gave me a wink.

I wondered why on earth he of all people was behaving in such a churlish manner. Years later I found myself doing the same thing, and remembered the incident.

In Canton, at the old Dongfang Hotel, which at that time was a single dilapidated building, I had another memorable experience. I was very fond of the place. China had begun to seep into my senses, and the smell of charcoal, cooking oils, rotting vegetation, and human ordure (and ardour too, perhaps) had begun to have quite a narcotic effect on me. Somehow it all reminded me of talcum powder, I suppose because underneath the whole pungent and slightly sweet formula there was still the smell of soiled humanity. Adding to it all was the incessant cacophony of traffic outside, and it is a strange demonstration of the power of the sense of smell that, even today, I am sometimes reminded of that smell when I hear car horns. The rooms in the Dongfang Hotel had little balconies and the beds had mosquito nets coiled above them like genies wafting out of their lamps. Sandalwood and mould made their contribution to the bouquet. After a day at the Canton Trade Fair, looking at tractors, textiles and models of the Daqing Oil Field, I sat down wearily on the end of my bed. It was one of those beds with a detachable wooden frame on which the mattress rests. The force of my descent detached not only the frame, but myself, and I landed with a great clatter on the floor.

A girl of about seventeen or eighteen appeared in the room. She, like many others, was doing her stint of productive labour at the end of high school. 'Ah', she said, glad of a chance to practise her English, 'you have not yet grasped the principle of the bed'. Obviously, by applying the Thought of Mao Zedong, and applying a logical schema based on dialectical materialism, in particular the resolution of contradictions and the unity of opposites, I could avoid making a fool of myself again. Having broken the ice in this novel fashion, I later went down the corridor to the service desk. I had a copy of the constitution of the People's Republic of China, in Chinese, and I thought the girl might be able to explain a few points to me. 'Beat that', I thought, as I imagined telling the others at breakfast next morning how I managed to sneak into the heart and mind of China by means of this excellent ruse. I needed a victory after the Shanghai Museum, where I had stood earnestly taking notes in front of a sign which I later realized had said 'Do not touch the exhibits'.

The girl was reading Charles Dickens—*Hard Times*. We talked about her difficulties as an 'educated youth' and of course she solicited my advice on 'the best way to study English', a phrase which was to haunt me some years later. In the course of our conversation I asked her if there were any parts of the book which she found difficult or interesting. This line did not elicit much of a response but I persisted.

I said, 'I suppose Charles Dickens is a very popular author in China because his works portray the exploitation of the working class under capitalism?'

'Yes you are right.'

'But do you find it interesting?'

'No, not at all.'

I was absolutely thrilled. I thought we were in for a vigorous discussion of bourgeois liberal literary theory versus the Marxist–Leninist interpretation. I thought I might have a dissenter on my hands. I thought of Wu Han and Yao Wenyuan and the fierce debate about academic freedom and literary merit and the Yan'an Forum on Literature and Art. I thought I might get some insight into how a normal, intelligent person, about the same age as my students, reacted to the kind of censorship and control practised in China. Maybe she resented being confined to politically respectable writers. Trembling on the brink of my discovery, I asked,

'Why don't you like *Hard Times?*'

'Because I have read it five times and there are no more new words in it.'

We went back through the New Territories and retraced our ideological steps. Not all of us had been infatuated. One of the delegation had resolutely maintained, in the face of many struggle meetings, that 'Confucius was right and Mao is wrong'. On leaving the China side of the border post he heaved a sigh of relief and said, 'Thank God we are out of that oppressive atmosphere at last'. He had his pocket picked somewhere between the passport check-point and the train.

Home again, many of us began a round of engagements as guest speakers. I patiently explained to a sceptical member of our school council that China was not the only place where there was brainwashing. 'What about the effects of advertising?' I said, 'Is political advertising any worse than our emphasis on sex and violence and general materialism in the media?' At another function, in which I had presented a talk that I thought was a model of disinterested observation, one of the audience said to me peevishly, 'But you've only told us about the good things. What about all the bad things?' 'So, if I'm going to be objective I can only tell you about the bad things, is that it?' I said, enormously pleased with this opportunity to point out how bias and prejudice work, and conveniently forgetting that even a biased questioner can ask a fair question.

I began to realize just how difficult it is to talk to people about anything in which deep-seated prejudices are involved. It was difficult to move on to a new level of understanding while there were still people who asked, 'But you wouldn't want to live there would you?' When I replied, 'No, but . . . ', they stopped listening, secure in the knowledge that they had found me out. After a while I began worrying about what was *behind* people's questions instead of the questions themselves, and I got myself into a terrible muddle trying to find and manipulate prejudices into the open, like some educational chiropractor. I also began to feel a thorough hypocrite. Last week, as a guest speaker at a Rotary lunch, I had taken some of the audience to task for their anti-communist attitudes. This week I was sneering at some student Maoists for their 'simplistic' and uncritical support for the Cultural Revolution.

There were other, less political, manifestations of this problem. Once, after reluctantly agreeing to show some slides of China at a neighbour's Christian Fellowship meeting, I had held forth authoritatively about how physically inhibited we are as a culture, and then lost my composure completely when I turned around to see a baby feeding noisily at a beach-like expanse of breast. On another occasion, when somebody in the pub was talking about Chinese eating dogs, I pooh-poohed the suggestion, not because it wasn't true, but because he had the wrong reasons for saying it.

As I was struggling with this sort of thing, Wang Hsin-ping was preparing to leave China. As I crossed my bridge, she crossed hers, and burnt it behind her. She had secured permission to join her father in Australia, to follow in the footsteps of that branch of the family which had been in Australia since the nineteenth century, around the time of the Taiping Rebellion. Her father's grandfather left his native Taishan when he was eighteen and went to Hong Kong in search of a better life. In those days Hong Kong was as poor and undeveloped as the place he had left, so he and some acquaintances built a boat and set sail for 'Nanyang'—vaguely Singapore or Malaya. After many weeks at sea they made landfall, not in Singapore or Malaya, but in Western Australia. Undeterred, they set out again on foot across a landscape as featureless and inhospitable as any ocean, in search of the Ballarat gold-fields. Of the dozen or so who landed in Australia, only four or five survived the trek. One of these was Hsin-ping's great grandfather, Liu Yichuang. He worked very hard at the tailings and eventually opened a grocery store in Melbourne, a 'mixed business' enhanced by his countrymen's love of gambling. He went back to China and bought land in Canton, on which later stood the Huanan University of Agriculture. He also bought a grand house in Taishan which, after 1949, became known as the Palace of Culture. He married and had a son, who in turn married and had ten children. Four of the sons went to Australia and one of these was Liu Rongzhen, Hsin-ping's father, who left China in 1938, when his daughter was less than a year old.

Once, when she was a small girl, Hsin-ping had had an opportunity to go to Australia to join her father. He had written to her grandmother and asked her to make arrangements to send Hsin-ping out. However, an uncle had been telling the little girl that 'out there', meaning anywhere foreign, people lived in trees and ate their food with pitch-forks. When her grandmother, in an uncharacteristic display of democracy, asked her if she wanted to go, she had said 'No', and that was that. She thought no more about it. Finally, in 1975, she left China to be reunited with her father, who had not seen her since 1938.

In 1976 Zhou Enlai died, Deng Xiaoping was purged for a second time (after a rehabilitation in 1973), Mao Zedong died, and the 'gang of four' was arrested. A little more than a year later, like the Monkey King with whom he is often compared, Deng bounced back, and the Australian press began talking about more 'pragmatic' policies in China. The era of tourism, the 'open door policy' and the 'four modern-izations' had begun.

One afternoon in Melbourne in 1978, at the college where I was studying Chinese, I met my new tutor. She was looking for something in the audio-visual room. I introduced myself, panicked momentarily when she responded enthusiastically in Chinese, and began my first solo flight in the language. From then on I was not just 'studying'. I really wanted to talk to her and, unlike most teachers, she seemed to assume that genuine communication was the point of the exercise. The story that follows is the result of many years of meandering conver-sation in which I came to see what was underneath the 'passing firewood'.

1

満 灌 之 壺

The Pot of Plenty

The sky in Peking was a special kind of blue, as you would expect in the city of the emperors. Its unrelenting gaze often lent a stifling solemnity to affairs below, as if Heaven itself was on the lookout for any hint of frivolous or disrespectful behaviour. On an autumn afternoon in 1944, in the western suburbs of Peking, a small girl knelt in discomfort and confusion inside the Guangji Temple, not daring to seek out mischief as she normally did. From the corner of her eye she glanced in the direction of the 'iron trees' she had heard about, and wondered if any of them were in flower, an event which, according to authorities, happened once every sixty years. Clouds of incense swirled about, choking all the reverence out of her, and rows of monks and nuns kept up a dreadful moaning. She struggled to remind herself of Grandma's strict injunction never to refer to this as 'singing' but she could not refrain from muttering under her breath in unison, 'dog's fart, dog's fart'.

She had been kneeling for five hours after trailing behind the great coffin all the way from the front gate of her house in Toufa Lane up to the temple. She was dressed in white and held a *ruyi*, the jade spoon-like object which symbolizes high office and good fortune in this world and beyond. Old Lady Wang had died, and Hsin-ping bore a disproportionate share of the responsibility for the family's mourning. It would have been very bad luck not to have had descendants of the same family name in the funeral procession, but Lady Wang's family were not easy to find. Her husband had died long ago, her son was in America and, of the four daughters born to her husband's second wife, only two remained. The eldest, Hsin-ping's mother, was dead. The youngest was dead. The third-born was in America, and the second had gone to Hunan after her marriage. Hsin-ping was the only one who bore the name Wang. In a way she was taking part in a ceremony for herself as well as for the old woman who had been so kind to her. Her own new life was about to begin with the tedious departure for Paradise of her 'Big Grandma'.

The old lady had been ill-favoured—large, squat, scarred from small-pox—and wore thick glasses which gave her a lugubrious air. Many wondered how she had come to be married to Wang Jinfang, Finance Minister to the Guang Xu Emperor and a wonderful catch for any beauty, let alone for her. For that she could thank her father, a well-heeled landlord. One day as he sat idly in his carriage, outside the Western Market, he saw two very fetching young lads, beggars up from the Hebei countryside in the wake of famine. He had always wanted sons himself and very quickly saw the possibilities in these two hand-some and lithe youths squabbling like monkeys on the fringe of the market in search of the tidbits that would sustain life for another day. So it happened that Wang Jinfang and Wang Kunfang were brought up in a grand house in Peking, went to Japan to study, and returned to professional and bureaucratic careers which brought honour upon the family. In return for his adoption by the landlord, Wang Jinfang married his talented but unlovely daughter. Fifteen years younger than his wife, and firmly entrenched in a privileged and powerful position, it was only a matter of time before his mind turned to thoughts of 'flowers and willows', and he began to frequent the streets outside Qianmen, and to be seen rather too often at the Cassia and Lotus Flower Garden, dallying with Moon Sprite or Snow Peach.

He was also a regular patron of the playhouses, and cut quite a dashing figure at the Guanghelou Theatre, spending some of the money he had helped to create as head of China's first paper mint. Every after-noon at three or four o'clock, after he closed the doors of the Yamen, he set out eagerly for the tea-house and the sing-song girls. What a contrast to the heavy burden of imperial office! Bowl after bowl of yellow wine, thick and sweet and numbing. Cool courtyards and charming pavilions, the air redolent with the lascivious magnolia, and beautiful girls plucking at the dulcimer, their faces echoing the subtle beauty of the music like the effect of clouds on the mood of the sea. Often he stayed out all night, moving from one place to another, enjoying girls who sold their art or their bodies, depending on his fancy. His wife often scolded him, not for infidelity but for bringing discredit on the family and being seen with riff-raff actors and harlots and faggots: 'Can't you see the damage you are doing to the family, don't you hear the neighbours laughing?' Somehow the fact that he knew himself to be in the wrong made him even angrier with his wife. Why did Yin Lian always seem like a crabby old aunt rather than a wife to do his bidding? Why did she think so much of herself and her piss-farting foreign oil painting? What worse fate could befall a man than to have an educated wife?

After some time Wang Jinfang adopted a different approach to his problem. 'I can soon put a stop to your worries about the family reputation', he announced one day after a confrontation with his wife. 'Just send that new maid, Xiao Yang, in to me and maybe I wouldn't need to go out quite so much.' The terms of the bargain were not lost on Lady Wang, and, in fact it may well have been an ideal solution to the problem, were it not for the fact that the girl was only a wretched servant and the family would obviously lose face over that. So, the lady of the house went to see the cook, whom she knew to have relatives all over the place. One of these might have the answer. In fact the cook had an immediate suggestion. She had a niece out in the Haidian district, a beautiful sixteen-year-old virgin, utterly unsophisticated and uneducated, a real prize. Such a girl would make an ideal second wife. She would keep Wang Jinfang home at nights and would never pose a threat to Lady Wang's authority.

At first her husband was reluctant to co-operate with this arrangement, and refused to give up his hopes for Xiao Yang, but she persuaded him to go with her and see for himself what he was getting. A trip to the village, a look at the innocent and blank young thing, a toothsome wench with a mind which would never be susceptible to the blandishments of learning, and the deal was done for two hundred yuan. Li Fengzhi was the daughter of a poor and landless farm labourer who simply could not afford to feed all of his five children after a barren year, and had no choice but to sell a daughter. Money well spent, thought Lady Wang, and took the added precaution of dismissing Xiao Yang.

The village girl and the Treasurer to the Emperor married in 1908, in the last days of the Qing dynasty. Despite the arrangement, Wang Jinfang died in his late thirties in 1925, leaving the two widows to live on together for nearly twenty years. Fengzhi, the secondary wife, was still quite young and extremely attractive. But according to Confucian morality, the younger woman could never re-marry without bringing shame upon the family, so she remained a widow and a member of the household, dominated by the older woman and her son. Had her husband not died it is probable that he would have taken a third wife, because Fengzhi had not given him a son, only four daughters, including Hsin-ping's mother, Wang Wanming, and her Third Aunt, Wang Yingming.

Hsin-ping was born in December 1937, in Canton. In the autumn of 1938 her father went to Melbourne to study. Wanming, herself a graduate of Yanjing University in Peking, was ambitious for him and wanted him to take up a scholarship to study mathematics in Germany, but war threatened and so he decided instead to go to the University of Melbourne to study architecture. Six months after his departure, Wang Wanming, now pregnant again, went to a dentist. As a result of having one or two teeth extracted under unhygienic conditions, she developed septicaemia. There was no penicillin, and she died. Letters bearing news of this did not reach her husband for some time because of the Japanese invasion of China. Hsin-ping lived with Third Aunt in Shanghai for a short time, but she was a difficult child and was severely disturbed by the sudden loss of her mother.

Finally, with the Japanese in Shanghai, life became too complicated for Wang Yingming and her husband. They left for Hong Kong and took the little girl with them. They stayed for two years, and then prepared to flee to America. The plan involved a complicated route through South-East Asia and on to America by boat. They did not realize that they could have gone to America via Australia, and so did not consider taking Hsin-ping to her father. Yingming wrote to Lady Wang in Peking asking her what to do, and she wrote back inviting Hsin-ping to come and live with her. She had always adored Wanming, so much so that no-one had dared tell her that her favourite had died in Canton. She thought she had gone with her husband to Australia. Wanming's own mother resented the way she always paid more attention to Lady Wang, 'patting the horse's arse', and always calling out for her first when she returned from school—'Niangzi, Niangzi, guess what I did today'. Lady Wang's only child, a son, had been a disappointment to her and she took great pleasure in this clever and charming girl. She was delighted to have Wanming's own daughter join the household, and spoiled her right up to her death.

After the funeral Hsin-ping's life changed dramatically. 'Poor motherless little demon, accursed little hell-child', her natural grandmother would say, after she had beaten her for some crime or other, cuddling her and weeping over her in the aftermath of rage. Hsin-ping never really understood what this was all about but it usually ended in some form of compensation, like a shopping expedition and a new pair of shoes.

Grandma knew the full extent of the tragedy, although she never saw the young man in the streets of Melbourne, pacing wildly about, clutching a photograph of a young woman holding a baby beside a wreath-laden coffin. This was the first news he had had of his wife's death because the sequence of letters from China had been interrupted by the Japanese occupation. For some years he sent letters and poetry back to the house in Toufa Lane, the paper literally stained with the tears of his sleepless nights and demented days. Grandma's first daughter was dead and her son-in-law mad with grief, and it seemed to her village mind that the child now living under her very own roof might well be the cause of it all. Hadn't her mother had a miscarriage in her first pregnancy?—and hadn't she died while pregnant with the third? In between was this jealous demon who had kicked out the first tenant of the Baby's Palace to make room for herself, and then shut the gates behind her when she was ready to leave, so that no-one else could get in. But what could be done with the child?

Hsin-ping was now a Wang, although her family name was Liu. This was a subterfuge intended to thwart the Japanese, who would not allow people of different surnames to live in the one household because it complicated their records. Despite her acquisition of the family name, Hsin-ping's life was quite wretched. Grandma loved her well enough but was a little afraid of her, and since the family had fallen from its former exalted position, even the servants took liberties. They frequently beat her quite severely, especially when Grandma was out playing mah-jong with the neighbours.

The worst problem for Hsin-ping was food. This had been a problem even while Lady Wang was around. Third Aunt had also studied at Yanjing University and knew all about the new-fangled Westen 'domestic science' and 'nutrition'. As a result, she knew not only what people ought to eat but how much. She had passed on Hsin-ping's dietary regimen to Grandma, who regarded it as a sacred and immutable text, like the Sutras. But she had failed to point out to Grandma that the inevitable consequence of even this diet was growth, and that the ritual was supposed to be modified accordingly. So, Hsin-ping was subjected to an impeccably balanced diet—for a four year old—for most of her early childhood, and was forced to supplement her rations with theft. In one of those cruel ironies which she came to expect of life, this usually led to her being deprived of food as a punishment.

In the twelfth month of the lunar year, 1945, Hsin-ping watched in awe as the ingredients for *labazhou* were piled one on top of the other into a prodigious cauldron. This was the Chinese cornucopia, a hint to the gods to see the family right for another year. The inspired concoction contained every imaginable treasure—rice, sorghum, wheat, beans of every hue, peanuts, chestnuts, walnuts, melon seeds, lotus seeds, dates, hazel nuts—all boiled up together on the evening of the seventh day, ready to be reheated on the morning of the eighth and every morning thereafter until New Year. That night after she went to bed she lay awake for hours thinking the usual excited thoughts of an eight-year-old, but also strangely troubled by a quickening sense of urgency about that great symbol of the passing year, the pot of plenty out in the kitchen. It seemed to demand a gesture.

As her mind wandered over the events of the dying year, the spectre of her frequent wrongdoings and her even more frequent punishments began to haunt her. The pot seemed a damnable provocation when she considered how much of her year had been spent in hunger, but it wasn't just a matter of food. Somehow she always seemed to suffer as a result of Grandma's attempts to shield the house from the unpredictable malice of evil spirits.

The most recent example of this had occurred about a week ago when she and her best friend, Tang Ling, were waiting for Grandma to take them shopping. As usual, the most benign event had contained the seeds of disaster. Grandma and her younger sister had been discussing Hsin-ping's shoe size. Last year it had been thirty-four, this year it was thirty-five. With her child's passion for following numbers into some obscure corner of their meaning, she began babbling numbers in search of a pun or a rhyme. Suddenly she had it. She remembered that doctors used the classification '3, 7' to signify the most advanced stages of tuberculosis. 'Thirty-four is a good number', she chanted, 'and thirty-five and even thirty-six, but what will happen when you buy me New Year shoes the year after next?' Grandma and her sister looked up from their deliberations, mildly puzzled by the child's prattle.

'What are you talking about, child?'

'Well, I'll tell you then if you don't know. Thirty-four is a good number, and thirty-five and thirty-six, but thirty-seven is different—*because* . . . thirty-seven is good for shoes but *very*, very bad for people. That number means you are going to die!'

Almost before the inauspicious word had escaped her lips, Grandma attempted to strike the child dumb with the first thing she could lay her hands on—a broom as it happened. Like a bemused little duck suddenly caught in the path of a water wheel, she found herself menaced on all sides by a mighty engine, flailing noise and destruction. Grandma's frenzy was activated by an urgent necessity to drive the malevolent syllable right back into Hsin-ping's skull before it could get loose and wreak havoc. How many times had this little hobgoblin been warned that you should not use bad words at this time of year? 'Poor' or 'sick' were not bad enough . . . *she* had to go screeching about death, and all the time pretending to be babbling innocently about shoes! How was a pious woman to guard against the surprise attacks of this miscreant waif?

Hsin-ping was able to reflect on the events which had led to her downfall while kneeling behind the doors of the reception room in the north wing. Grandma always followed up a spanking by making her kneel for some hours in this fashion. She even left a cushion there for the purpose. When Tang Ling called back at three o'clock that afternoon Grandma directed her to the place of atonement. As usual, Tang Ling was sympathy itself—'*Aiyou*, Hsin-ping, you are getting shorter every day'. Anyway, the two of them went out to play and the matter was forgotten. It was always that way with Grandma, but not with those other turtle's eggs who hung around the house. Grandma's sister didn't like her at all and, although she didn't beat her herself, she allowed her daughter, who was only fourteen, to indulge herself in all kinds of bullying—at least when Grandma was not around.

Even the servants joined in these games: 'So you like to eat do you? A real little rice bucket, aren't you? We'll fix it so you don't need to eat for a long time.' On these occasions her mouth was stuffed with toothpaste until her gums bled and her mouth was too swollen and sore for her to eat properly for some days. Sometimes they made her kneel on the washing board outside in the courtyard in the hot sun, until her knees were scratched and bleeding and her head swam.

How she hated that bunch of toadying servants and hangers-on, clinging like parasites to the house and feeling free to bully and maltreat her whenever Grandma or Great Grandfather were not around to keep an eye on things. As she lay in bed remembering all this and thinking of the pot of *labazhou*, she grew angrier and angrier. She thought of them all getting up next day and helping themselves to the treasure-laden congee and her resentment swelled and swelled, as did her discomfort as she became conscious of a pressing need to pass water. With the perfect clarity of childish logic, she suddenly saw a means of relief for both sensations. She got up and went into the kitchen, climbed up onto the table, squatted over the pot and pissed wantonly into it. The pleasure was indescribable. Every day for twenty-odd days the flunkeys out in the kitchen prattled on obsequiously about the congee having something a little extra this year, while Hsin-ping sat around with a strange look on her face, apparently not hungry for once.

If the Kitchen God knew any of this, he kept his mouth shut—perhaps as a result of being plied with votive offerings of sticky toffee—and came back from his New Year report to the King of Heaven with all the usual ceremony of fireworks and food offerings, apparently not having informed on Hsin-ping and content to let the matter drop. This encouraged her to steal the sweets Grandma kept for visitors, in a large box with a glass lid. Grandma certainly knew who the culprit was, but you couldn't punish a child during New Year. If you beat her during this time you would have to beat her for a whole year, and she simply wasn't up to that. So, New Year was a wonderful time for the little girl. Old people gave her money in red packets, which Grandma undertook to 'protect' for her, food was abundant, and many of the strict rules of the household were relaxed. Everybody ate together, whereas for the rest of the year she sat in solitude at her own table eating her own miserable scientific

Western rations. Much as she hated some of the servants, this at least produced a more lively atmosphere.

Grandma's younger brother came to stay with them at this time of year. He sold mules and horses in the nearby horse and camel markets and had plenty of money to spend on gambling. Even Hsin-ping was allowed to take part in the gambling which sometimes went on all night, especially on New Year's Eve.

And the circus came to her neighbourhood. Performing bears and dogs dressed in clothes did their tricks in the streets for crowds of excited children, and others whom Grandma considered undesirable. When a mob had gathered around the one-man troupe and his bear or dog, and a bargain had been struck as to price, the show would go on, accompanied by shrieks of glee and amazement from the onlookers. Unfortunately, Grandma was so snobbish about the urchins and ne'er-do-wells who patronized these shows that she decided to stage a command performance in her own courtyard. Hsin-ping was bitterly disappointed to be sitting with a bunch of prune-faced servants and her grandmother in the isolation of her own courtyard, watching the spirit of man and beast extinguished by the polite responses of these lofty eminences who could afford to pay as much as a whole street full of noisy ragamuffins.

On the fifteenth of the first month, the day of the Lantern Festival, Grandma rejoiced in the opportunity to show off her skill at making *yuanxiao*, sweet dumplings made of glutinous rice flour. She really put her heart into this, with days of preparations—making the fillings, arranging the noodles, moulding together the concoction of walnuts and sesame, and bean paste boiled in oil. Finally, there it all was, laid out and ready, testimony to Grandma's art and dedication. Rows and rows, about twenty in each, like the splendid cohorts of the Imperial Army. Hsin-ping had already stumbled upon the treasure and her mouth was watering, but theft was out of the question. She knew only too well what the consequences would be. On the other hand, if she just happened to be running past and sort of scooped one up, that would really be nothing to do with her at all—and the ranks would still be more or less intact even if one or two little soldiers had fallen. This happy deception went on for some time, the need for thought agreeably swallowed up in the activity of running back and forth. After a while however, it became all too obvious that the regiment had been decimated. The mind of the juvenile criminal may not be subtle but it is resilient. Depleted numbers would certainly be noticeable, but what was there to notice if they were *all* gone? Before the advantages of this solution were threatened by nagging doubts, Hsin-ping swooped on the remaining dumplings and wolfed them all down. This was not easy and, in fact, left her feeling utterly sick.

Just then she heard the first of the guests arriving. Grandma's voice was dripping with the smug satisfaction of the artist trying to sound objective about her masterpiece. 'This year I'm sure you'll find that the dumplings are up to scratch, perhaps ... no, well, yes ... perhaps even a little better than last year's. But just give me a minute to arrange things.'

Grandma was making strenuous efforts to sound casual. Her moment of triumph was imminent. The toadying servants went on and on—'Oh take no notice of Madam, she is too modest, everybody knows that her dumplings are easily the best in Peking'. As the guests made their way into the garden to let off fireworks and light flower lanterns, Grandma made the sickening discovery. Heads began to poke around the kitchen door, curious at the delay.

'Oh come on Wang Taitai, you are too cruel, don't torment us any longer. Where are the best *yuanxiao* in Peking?'

Grandma's eyes fixed balefully on Hsin-ping, by now preoccupied with preventing the violent reappearance of the dumplings, which seemed hell-bent on making their fate known to their creator. 'So that's why you've been darting back and forth to the toilet, you've been sick haven't you, you little guts? You've eaten every last one and now you want to die. Come here.' She glanced ominously over towards the altar room where she kept her supply of bamboo canes.

'Don't worry, don't worry, its nothing at all', chimed the guests, with infuriating insincerity. Grandma, reeling from this devastating loss of face, could only manage to mumble pathetically, 'Next year I swear I'll make the best *yuanxiao* you have ever had'. Naturally, Hsin-ping got her beating as soon as Grandma was rid of her guests, in spite of New Year protocol, and she was also prohibited from eating. This was like the key that kept winding her motor of mischief back to the starting point and an inevitable repeat performance. Life appeared to be a vicious circle in which you got hungry, stole food and were forbidden to eat as a consequence. At times, in the winter, Hsin-ping was so hungry she sucked on the ice of Beihai Lake, pretending she had found an inexhaustible supply of some rare delicacy.

About this time, the old manservant, Lao Zhou, left the house and went back home. Great Grandfather came to live rather than to visit as he had in the past. He was a poor old peasant who had never been to school and could not recognize a single character but he was a treasury of wonderful stories. He had an extraordinary memory and had learnt by heart the stories he had heard from wandering story-tellers, who acted out operas, and tales from the classics, for 10 or 20 fen, which included the price of a cup of tea.

He told Hsin-ping a story almost every night, imitating voices and gestures in the most expert fashion. When he did 'The Cricket', he would go into wonderful detail about the kinds of fighting crickets one could get and the kinds of things they had to be fed and where to get the best cricket cages in the city. He described every detail of the 'crab-shell green' cricket and 'old rice-jaws' and the merits and demerits of each.

He was about seventy when he came to live in Toufa Lane with the daughter he had sold. His own life had been bitter and hard but he had never been sick for a day of it and flatly condemned the use of all medicines. He was absolutely fixed in his habits. He rose at five o'clock, drank a little water, walked for about an hour, ate a few dates, found some small jobs to do, ate a bowl of rice for his lunch, pottered away the afternoon, ate a further half-bowl of rice for his supper, went for another walk and then went to bed so as to be able to get up early the next morning and start all over again. He didn't smoke, or drink—not alcohol, not even tea. He didn't use toothpaste, but even at his death at eighty-eight he hadn't lost a single tooth.

Apart from his teeth, he treasured only a few possessions, chief among which was a fur-lined sheepskin coat, bought for him by two generations of the family. They of course intended that such an item should be worn, but they hadn't reckoned on his reverence for it, or on his reluctance to treat it as a piece of clothing. Grandma used to say, 'Baba, your sons and grandsons have bought this beautiful coat for you, why won't you wear it?' Finally, he took some of his old clothing, cut it up into pieces and sewed them into a cover so that the coat would always remain perfect. Even then he only wore it a few times. A pair of shoes, also a present, was similarly entombed. His grandsons bought them, a winter pair with hide soles and uppers, and fleece on top. He was so anxious to preserve them that he made a cover for them out of his old shoes. He even went so far as to paint over the entire cover with ink because he feared that the white thread would get dirty. By the time he had finished, the shoes were as enduring a monument to peasant frugality as the fields themselves.

He used to take a dim view of waste. No one could accuse Hsin-ping of squandering food, but even she was on occasions subjected to his homilies about the evils of waste. Sometimes, in her eagerness to down her miserable ration, she overlooked a few grains of rice in the bottom of the bowl. Great Grandfather would begin to quote from a Tang poem about a drop of sweat from the brow of a peasant bringing forth each grain of rice. Sometimes, if he was of a mind to be less poetic and more terrible, he would remind Hsin-ping that for every grain of rice neglected an extra maggot would come to gnaw at her corpse when she died. This seemed to succeed where the portrait of peasant suffering had failed. She squirmed like a maggot herself at this loathsome thought and went at it as if she intended to devour the bowl.

Hsin-ping's paternal grandfather and family, c. 1916; her father, Liu Rongzhen, sits cross-legged

Hsin-ping's maternal family, 1930
Left to right: *Grandma (Li Fengzhi), Third Aunt (Yingming), Mother (Wanming), Big Grandma (Yin Lian), Uncle (Shenming), Cousin Fan Yuzhong's mother (Jieming) and* (front) *Fourth Aunt (Yuanming)*

Mother (right) and (from left) Fan's mother and Third Aunt, 1921

Grandma in 1934, aged forty-two

Mother (left) and a school friend, Jiang Cunqun, 1933

Hsin-ping's parents and their wedding party outside the altar room of the Toufa Lane house, 1935
Left to right in front: *their 'go between', Yin Lian (Lady Wang or Big Grandma), Liu Rongzhen and Wang Wanming, Li Fengzhi (Grandma) and Jiang Cunqun (Wanming's friend)*

Hsin-ping at her mother's funeral in 1939, being held by Third Aunt

Hsin-ping, aged about six, in the altar room at Grandma's house in Toufa Lane, 1944

Hsin-ping with her cousin Fan Yuzhong, 1948

Great Grandfather lived in the old rickshaw shed by the front gate in Toufa Lane. One day, when it was snowing, Tang Ling and Hsin-ping were heavily engaged in a snow fight. As the old man came out of his den to see what was going on, Hsin-ping said archly, 'Great Grandpa, what's that you've got on your neck?' As he bent and twisted to have a look, she thrust a large snowball down his neck and ran off squealing with delight. Grandma came out to see what fresh outrage had been perpetrated and, after an expert appraisal of the problem and its source, advised her poor bewildered father to take off some of his clothing in order to rid himself of the problem. Unfortunately, like most peasants, he was wearing so much clothing that the snowball had completely melted long before there was any possibility of removing it.

Hsin-ping was often punished for the pranks she played on her Great Grandfather but it did not discourage her and, despite his scoldings and appalling threats about what would become of a child like her, he was quite devoted to his tormentor. But eventually the time came for him to go back to his village to live with the other members of the family. This time his relatives bought him a coffin, not, as one might think, as a rather pointed hint that he was wearing out his welcome, but in celebration of his impressive age. This gesture tapped a well of gratitude deep in the old man's heart. Poor people cannot expect their deaths to be any more significant than their lives, but at least they have a lifetime to save up for a coffin, if they are lucky. The old man had long cherished a wish for an expensive wooden coffin. Now he had one, and his joy was boundless. It was a great, thick, wooden coffin, a voluptuous affair to which he added an annual coat of paint in acknowledgement of his mounting age and good fortune. When visitors came to the house they were inevitably shown his coffin and could not leave without a suitable panegyric on it and the filial piety of his descendants. The coats of paint stopped in 1958.

In the meantime, Hsin-ping and Tang Ling became blood-sisters and partners in crime. There was an established tradition of this in Tang Ling's family. Her father, a general of the warlord armies, had a blood-brother who came to live with them in Peking. His name was Pan Zhuyun and he was also a general, former commander of a Shandong army. While he was living with his new family, he established a church, called Yiguandao, devoted to Fu Ye, the 'laughing Buddha'. The Buddha was actually located upstairs in Tang Ling's house, surrounded by huge mirrors. A great many people came to pray there in that solemn place and, of course, left mountains of food offerings to an apparently unresponsive and certainly overfed deity.

One Saturday afternoon, Tang Ling and Hsin-ping crept, silent and shoeless, up the stairs. Despite these sensible precautions, they were not too anxious about discovery because Tang Ling's mother lay downstairs on her special couch dreaming the afternoon away in a cloud of opium. Like many women of her kind, who could expect to have long careers as widows, she had been introduced to the genteel joys of opium by her own relatives, lest the foolish passions of youth diverted her from a life-time of chastity and decorous mourning. As a result, her most enthusi-astic contribution to the supervision of the girls was to sigh languidly and say, 'Yes children, do go out and play, there's good girls'.

The indoor playground seemed infinitely preferable as they surveyed the piles of food, but the only obstacle to a satisfying piece of desecration was the remote possibility that it was true . . . that if you touched the food put out for Fu Ye, your fingers would drop off, and if you actually ate it, heaven help you, your stomach would burst. Hsin-ping was used to the idle threats of corpulent gods and their syco-phantic mortal househelp, so she tasted the food and . . . survived. Nevertheless, the gods weren't the only ones whose wrath was to be avoided, so they sat under the altar table, gingerly reaching up every now and then to pluck some treasure from the mounds of food above their heads.

So began a ritual, a series of illicit gorgings seasoned with the incom-parable sauce of prohibition and sacrilege. Somehow, down there under the table, they enjoyed the protection of a magic spell of their own and they were invisible, unreachable, immortal. The best time was the fifteenth of the eighth month, the Mid-Autumn Festival, when the table was piled high with mountains of mooncakes and laid out reverently, with a great candle set in the middle. The second floor was on the same level as the neighbour's roof, and it was extremely convenient to get rid of the evidence by tossing scraps on to it. Under the magic table they got on with their feast and their card games. When importunate nature called, as it frequently did in response to their gluttony, they devised the simple expedient of climbing out on to the neighbour's roof and depositing both 'big numbers' and 'small numbers' on his tiles. If there had been a fourth wise monkey, he might well have been holding his nose, because for a very long time no one saw, or smelt, any evil.

Many glorious Saturday afternoons in 1946 passed like this, moments of wonder in a paradise for eight-year-olds, when everything seemed perfect and delight hung like a perfume in the very air they breathed. But the halcyon days had to end, as they did abruptly, when Tang Ling's mother put a stop to it all by locking the door of the 'temple'. This was in winter; maybe she had discovered that the intricate arrangement of *migong*, the sticky honey cakes which were a special treat at that time of year, had been disturbed by mortal hands. It may also have had something to do with the bannisters. The girls had to remove the large wooden knob at the end of the bannisters so that after their feasting they could make their getaway by sliding backwards down the bannisters. They may have forgotten to replace it one day and so left a clue for Tang Ling's mother during one of her rare moments of lucidity.

The temple itself prospered until 1949, after which it was banned, not because of its dubious spirituality, but because it represented a potential source of counter-revolutionary thought. Until that time, many a foolish melon was taken in by this extremely responsive Buddha which, instead of lounging about looking transcendental, used to light up when you prayed hard enough. Hsin-ping and Tang Ling did not take long to discover the power switch beside the statue, or the black and red button under the table on the floor, especially since this was precisely the spot where they performed their own devotions.

In 1950, during the first counter-revolutionary movement, Pan was arrested and sent to prison, where he eventually died. A host of people descended on the house, squabbling and shouting and carting away armfuls of housebricks. One might have been forgiven for assuming that enraged believers were intent on dismantling the fraudulent church brick by brick, but the truth of the matter was that they were actually bars of gold rather thinly veneered with a brick-like surface. Soon, government officials took over the onerous responsibility of removing the bricks, no doubt in the same generous spirit that Grandma undertook to look after Hsin-ping's packets of New Year money.

After they were locked out of the temple, the children, oblivious to the impending threat of civil war and revolution, were forced back on to the streets in search of diversions. One favourite sport was readily available in the smaller streets around the Xidan Market. There were trams in Peking in those days, but the most popular form of transport around the narrow lanes and alleys were the rickshaws, which used to flit about the streets like swallows diving after insects at dusk, narrowly missing each other as they swooped on some juicy morsel. Although these vehicles were the very image of China in the West, they were actually called 'foreign carriages' by the Chinese themselves because they had been introduced from Japan by a Frenchman. The girls were fascinated by them, and usually sought out the most wretched, broken-down rickshaw simply because it was unloved and unwanted. They usually wanted to go from the market to Beihai Park, which was a very short distance north through the Western Arches and east past the Peking Library to the main entrance near the back of the Forbidden City. Such a journey cost only one or two yuan and it didn't matter to them whether they got there sooner or later.

The girls adopted the unusual practice of not sitting in the chair of the rickshaw because the old puller was so old and feeble he looked as if he might expire under their weight. They also felt incipient twinges of guilt about their relative affluence—Tang Ling in a white fox-fur coat, Hsin-

ping in a long woollen overcoat sent from America by Third Aunt. As a
result, sticky-beak friends of Grandma often recounted a strange
sighting. 'You'll never believe this but I could swear I saw your grand-
daughter today, and another little girl, pulling a rickshaw down the
street. The Wangs certainly have come down in the world!' Despite the
hilarity which greeted the suggestion, the old busybodies had in fact
seen the old man and the two girls running together, with him in the
middle like a moth-eaten old mule between two fresh little donkeys,
pulling an empty carriage. Who was he to wonder at the eccentricities
of two rich little madams? It made no more sense than to wonder why
they were rich and he was poor. When they arrived at the entrance to
the park, Tang Ling would say, 'Wait here please, if no one wants you
we would like you to take us back'. His services not being in great
demand, he was always there waiting when they came out. 'Thank you
young ladies, thank you', he would say, bowing and clasping his hands
together in front of him as he took his leave of them after the journey
home to Xidan.

They often sought out the company of the poor, not from any high-
minded egalitarianism or philanthropy, but because they enjoyed their
company more than that of many people of their own class. Poor
families seemed more generous, more welcoming. Even their language
was more comfortable, more fun. They seemed more interested in the
girls than were their own families, who were too busy or preoccupied to
be concerned about their activities unless there was mayhem and a loss
of face involved. The poor, on the other hand, seemed to *want* to know
what they were doing, whether they wanted something to eat, where
they were going and so on. The feelings of vague unease experienced by
Tang Ling and Hsin-ping, not only about obvious differences of wealth,
but differences of attitude and outlook, would remain with them
always, in spite of events which might have hardened their hearts.

Often when the two reached Beihai Park they found they had no
money left to buy a ticket, unless they were to forgo paying the old man
for the ride home. Crime can be a kind of diversion for those who have
no reason to fear authority, and it was a sort of gesture to get into the
park without paying and then give the money they had saved to the old
man. They often waited until a dense crowd had gathered near the
entrance gate and then darted inside, like little carp seeking protection
in a school of bigger fish. Naturally no one would suspect such an
affluent little pair of swindlers—why would they *need* to cheat? As if to
test the system to the limit, Tang Ling would often march in brazenly
after Hsin-ping had been swallowed up in the crowd, discover osten-
tatiously that she had no ticket and, after one or two vexed and puzzled
faces had been pulled, and a pocket or two searched, she would declare
in her best exasperated tone, 'Where *can* that ticket have gone to? It

must be here somewhere. I just *know* I had it a minute ago.' 'All right, all right, go on, in you go', the obliging gatekeeper would say.

Hu Shuilin became a regular playmate in the latter years of primary school. She had joined them after the Japanese left in 1945. Her father was Military Chief of Staff in Peking. Li Axin also came, from the North-East. The gang was complete. Hu Shuilin was particularly impressive because, among other attributes, she had a bodyguard—a Nationalist village conscript of about eighteen or nineteen. He carried a gun, which certainly made him interesting, but the girls didn't like him following them about. They often lured him into the crowd in Beihai Park and managed to shake him off in the twists and turns of the Five Dragon Pavilion. He would wait at the exit from the park near the white-barked pine on the terrace of the 'Round City', thinking that they had to come that way sooner or later. Unfortunately for him, the young ladies had perfected the simplest of strategies for slipping through the cordon—they left by the entrance rather than the exit. This may well have been a valuable lesson to the young man if he had military aspirations, but in the meantime it just got him into hot water with his boss. When they arrived, minus bodyguard, back at Hu Shuilin's place, the grizzled old warrior would say, 'Good afternoon, kids. I see you have managed to escape right from under the enemy's nose again?' He usually looked straight at Hsin-ping.

'Good afternoon Uncle', she would reply, offering him honorary relative status, like a perfect little lady.

'Wang Hsin-ping eh? Wang Hsin-ping. A bit of a devil, eh? Well, run along with you.'

School and homework were beginning to encroach upon their lives now, and there was barely enough of Saturday afternoons left to taunt Hu Shuilin's Muslim neighbour. The girls lived in the south-west corner of the 'Tartar City', and a little farther south, in the western districts of the 'Southern', or 'Chinese', city was the heart of the Muslim quarter. For some centuries, these foreigners from the 'West' had been the butt of Chinese jokes about their appearance and customs. Niujie, or Cow Street, was a focus for all sorts of stories about the way Chinese and Muslims baited each other over dietary habits—especially to do with pork and beef and lamb, of course.

On Saturday afternoons Hsin-ping often went to Hu Shuilin's house and the pair of them would climb out on to her neighbour's roof carrying a pig's tail, which they had liberated from the kitchen, and a piece of string. From this vantage point, they would tie the tail securely to the string and lower it into the neighbour's courtyard. Then they would call out 'Zhu yiba, zhu yiba' ('Pig's tail, pig's tail'). The neighbour's dog, a German Shepherd, soon to be rounded up by the police in a city-wide drive to exterminate rabies, would tear round the corner and go into a frenzy of barking and snapping at the pig's tail. The neighbour, venturing out to see who was breaking into his house, would find nothing but an unaccountably excited dog. It always seemed self-evident that the bait for a Muslim German Shepherd just had to be pork.

While China was in the grip of an appalling struggle between Communists and Nationalists, the four friends simply got on with being children. A Nationalist officer was billeted in the east wing of Hsin-ping's house, but that didn't make a great deal of difference to her. It did mean, however, that a lot of furniture and books had to be moved out of the study. There was one bookshelf in particular which interested Hsin-ping. If you swung the shelf back on its hinges you found another hidden shelf which contained all sorts of interesting things. Grandma knew that Hsin-ping often went to the outer shelf and pored over copies of *Life* magazines of the 1920s and 1930s. Of course she couldn't read them, but she loved the pictures. It seemed to keep her quiet and Grandma was quite happy to let her take these magazines to her own room. She didn't know that her resourceful granddaughter had also discovered the secret shelf.

One day Hsin-ping came out of the study carrying a very large book made of silk. She had been studying it carefully for some time after finding it among the books of the inner shelf. On the cover was a picture, woven in silk, of an old man carrying a lamp. When you opened the book you could see more silken pictures, beautiful, intricate and strange. There were two women with no clothes on, and you could look through a silk curtain to see them lying on their bed. A little cat sat in the corner watching. There were other pictures of a man and a woman, also without clothes, apparently engaged in some strange school of Kung Fu. This was the family copy of *Spring Pictures*, which for two hundred years had been given to members of the family, both male and female, on the eve of their weddings. It had been passed on to Grandma on the occasion of her marriage to Wang Jinfang. Hsin-ping found Grandma in the kitchen and said, 'Haopo, look what I found with all those Japanese books that Grandfather had. Isn't it beautiful? But what are these ladies doing? They look like demons wrestling.' Grandma let out a strangled cry, seized the book and, as she tore out each page, she fed it into the kitchen stove. This incident added to the store of mysteries which included some of Great Grandfather's stories, occasional *hun gushi* (carnal stories, or dirty jokes) and Grandma's baffling assertion that babies were found outside Fuchengmen Gate.

One day Tang Ling invented a new game. Since girls were not allowed to swear, what could be more fun than to lock themselves in a room, close all the windows, draw the curtains and curse themselves into an ecstasy? So, one Saturday afternoon after school, they sat in a darkened room in Hu Shuilin's house and swore and swore and swore. Their repertoire relied pretty heavily on some fairly universal things, like body parts, bastards and mother-fuckers. Unfortunately for the girls, their vocabularies were limited by a lack of contact with peasants, or the costermongers of the southern suburbs, so they ran out of steam rather early. The only one who actually seemed to be good at it was Hu Shuilin. This seemed utterly incongruous because she was adorably pretty and ladylike in manner, but she could use language that would make a Cantonese blush. The explanation lay in the fact that she received an excellent, unwitting education from her father, a rough uneducated old army officer who, among other stimuli to colourful speech, had four wives.

Li Axin's family were from Dongbei, in the North-East, a not entirely respectable place to come from—in fact most Peking residents looked down upon the denizens of this region as wild, uncultivated and unwashed. Nevertheless it was wonderful fun playing hide-and-seek in the Li's house, because some of the rooms had secret doors, behind the mirrors. They also had a telephone, which was always a source of delicious tricks to play on Li Axin. 'Fire Brigade? This is the Li household. Send a truck immediately, the house is on fire.' This actually worked twice, but after that the fireman asked for their telephone number so that he could confirm the call with another member of the household. The call was intercepted by Tang Ling, but somehow the statement 'Yes, this is my mother speaking' did not seem to satisfy the officer.

They tried another little game. In their neighborhood was a cake shop, justly famous for its regional delicacies. They also stocked fashionable Western goodies. Shuilin or Hsin-ping would ring the shop and say, 'Tomorrow being Sunday, we Li's are having a picnic at Fragrant Mountain. Please be so good as to deliver us lots and lots of sandwiches, butter, jam, cheese and cakes.' At school on Mondays Li Axin would often come laden with sandwiches for her lunch and Tang Ling would say, barely suppressing a giggle, 'You must really like Western food'. 'Oh, I don't know', the puzzled Axin would say, 'the stuff just keeps turning up and we can't eat it all. Have a sandwich.'

There was just a touch of spite in these pranks, because Shuilin and Hsin-ping were affected by their families' prejudices against people from Dongbei. There were unpleasant memories in Peking of the rampaging excesses of the North-Eastern warlords and generals in the 1920s, and Li Axin's family were such recent arrivals that their regional speech and manner were obvious. However, all of the girls came from families which had some good and some bad in their pedigree. Hsin-ping's family had of course seen very grand days. They had counted an Imperial Minister among their number and could show you photographs of this eminent personage in full regalia, his sleeves pointing down over his hands in mimicry of a horse's hooves, a symbol of the days when the Man people were fearsome horsemen and their mounted archers struck terror into the hearts of their foes. The Wangs were now a kind of aristocracy gone to seed, the family dispersed all over the globe and an ignorant old peasant woman running the show with a bunch of broken-down servants. Soon the family's former grandeur would make it impossible for the present generation to join the new aristocracy.

To date, notions of class, rank and status had been matters of unconscious curiosity for Hsin-ping, but soon she would be able to make precise calculations of her own 'class' on the abacus of revolutionary ideology. For the moment, however, she was doing well enough. The family was still quite well off, if not rich, and they certainly enjoyed respect in a district noted for its population of scholar–bureaucrat families. She was attending the finest primary school in Peking, and Grandma, despite her own personal contempt for books and learning, never questioned Hsin-ping's right to a good education or tried to take her away from school because she was a girl. Why Grandma was so progressive about this and so feudal about everything else is just a mystery. It may be that educated women were a well-established tradition in the Wang family and she had no wish to break with tradition, or it may be that she thought of Hsin-ping as a kind of grandson to carry on the family name in a career, or it may simply be that, as a lifelong Buddhist, she was capable of containing contradictions in her personal belief system that might have troubled a Christian or Confucian.

Tang Ling's family were also rather high on the social scale, but the picture was complicated by the military connections. Every educated person knew that you could not make a good nail out of bad metal or a good man out of a soldier. There was more than a touch of brigand and rogue about her father, but he had his good side. He was from Henan and had a wife in both Henan and Peking. He was very fat, with a snowy white beard and hair, and had come up through the ranks of the military with no privileges of background but by dint of his exploits. He was an expansive and good-hearted man and had natural sympathy for the poor. Whenever children came to the house he would present them with a straw hat from what appeared to be an inexhaustible supply. In fact this was no illusion—he always felt sorry for the bamboo-hat seller and invariably bought his entire cartload.

Hu Shuilin's family had the most power, if not traditional status, but, with the impending flight of the Nationalists, their position was delicate. Li Axin's family were rich, but they were vulgar 'Manchurians'—and anyway, it was new money. They were in business of some sort, hardly the kind of people one could look up to.

The families were compatible in that they had a good deal in common. They were all well-respected but had a serious blemish or two. They were all comfortable financially but vulnerable politically at a time when China's destiny was in the balance. Perhaps most important of all, there was a little room for each family to feel superior to the other.

Bickering and squabbling among the families often continued long after the children had patched up their differences and gone in search of new trouble. One of the richest sources of tension was the relationship between Tang Ling and Hsin-ping. Grandma didn't much like the association with the Tangs. Strangely enough, although she was never reluctant to detect guilt in her granddaughter on all sorts of occasions where Hsin-ping might have been entitled to the benefit of the doubt, she usually blamed Tang Ling when there was the remotest possibility that she might have contributed to the situation. When others were involved it was a very different story. One such incident concerned Guo Liangde and the bubble-gum.

In 1948, during Qiuye Dianli, the Autumn Evening Festival, Hsin-ping and her classmate, Guo Liangde, were walking home from school, chewing bubble-gum. Bubble-gum disappeared after 1949, but it was readily available in those days. To be fully appreciated, it had to be put to some use other than as a foodstuff. What better thing to do than stick it in your friend's hair—and have hers stuck in yours? Inevitably, later that afternoon, Guo's mother came to the house. She was very large and very fat and wore a preposterous flowery cheongsam which looked as if it would fly apart at any ill-considered movement. Shuddering perilously on the brink of a silken explosion, she confronted Grandma. 'Just look at my daughter's hair! Do you know how much I paid to have it cut? Yes, I said *cut* . . . that is the only way I could get rid of the sticky muck. What have you got to say about that Wang Taitai?'

Grandma listened in silence and humiliation, assuming Hsin-ping's guilt. She did ring their teacher at the school to seek more detail, but she had gone home. There was nothing for it but to give Hsin-ping a belting in Madam Fatty's presence, since she demanded satisfaction. The matter was serious because the school was extremely strict about hairstyle. It couldn't be too long and it couldn't be too short—and it would take months for Guo Liangde's hair to recover its orthodoxy. So, with great ceremony, Grandma selected one of the least vicious of her arsenal of bamboo canes from behind the altar-room door and prepared to give Hsin-ping a few whacks on the palm.

The spirit of Ah Q came to Hsin-ping's rescue. Lu Xun's archetypal character from 'The True Story of Ah Q' was never defeated, no matter what disaster befell him. Even when being carted off to execution, he managed to see himself in a triumphant role, and he certainly had a great deal to offer on techniques for dealing with a beating. For example, when called upon by an adversary to admit that he was nothing but a dumb brute to be beaten, he would claim instead that he was an 'insect', and when released by his satisfied assailant, would immediately console himself with the thought that he was the 'foremost of self-belittlers' and that it was a great thing to be a foremost something. With an ingenuity that would have made Ah Q envious, Hsin-ping reconciled herself to the beating and the humiliation. Traditionally, men sat or walked on the left and women on the right. If she was struck on the left hand it couldn't really be her being struck, because she was a girl! She winced as her substitute received three whacks on the hand. Guo Liangde's mother seemed content, and waddled off in such a manner as to torment every stitch in her dress beyond endurance. Grandma was still hopping mad, and embarrassed 'to death'. 'Of all the people who have ever lived in this house, you are the worst. Your aunts, your uncles, have all lived here, grown up here, but never before have I had people come to the house to complain! Kneel!'

Hsin-ping knelt in obeisance and contrition—but to her astonishment, Grandma burst into a fit of tears. She had found the bubble-gum in Hsin-ping's own hair. Whether she was crying out of pity for the injustice done to the child or a lost opportunity to put Madam Fat-arse back in her box, Hsin-ping could not tell, but she cried and gurgled and cuddled the little girl in her arms.

'Oh why are you so stupid? Who did that to you?'

'Guo Liangde.'

'Why didn't you say so?'

'I didn't remember. We were just playing. Then suddenly her mother came to the house and you started walloping me . . . '

'Ah poor motherless waif, poor unwanted little devil, little seed of the dead, never mind child, we'll get your hair cut too . . . we'll go to the shops . . . I'll buy you a ball.'

Ah Q never had such a complete triumph. As for Hsin-ping, she began to think that this sudden reversal of fortunes was a normal part of life. She grew up thinking, 'You hurt a bit, you kneel a bit but things usually turn out all right in the end'.

In the winter of 1949 the girls frequently heard the roar of Nationalist artillery defending the city from the Communist armies. The war didn't make a lot of difference to the lives of fifth graders, but the sounds of battle were a constant background to their activities, and more and more Nationalist officers were billeted in their houses in the respectable western suburbs of Peking. There were now high-ranking officers in the guest-rooms of the southern wing of Hsin-ping's house as well as in the east wing. Many children didn't go to school at all at this time, and by now Hu Shuilin and Li Axin had left the city with their families, so that the gang was sorely depleted. Nevertheless, Tang Ling and Hsin-ping thought it was an exciting time. They were able to enjoy themselves at the expense of their teachers without a great deal of interference from their preoccupied adult watchdogs. Hsin-ping had already driven her private tutor to the brink, but at least Grandma was able to keep an eye on things at home, and wield a judicious bamboo cane when necessary.

The private tutor was an old family retainer, a former servant who had been present at so many lessons for Hsin-ping's mother and her sisters when they were little girls that she had herself become an expert teacher, at least in the sense that her characters were beautiful and she knew the required texts like the *Three Character Classic* by heart. One day, when Hsin-ping had been set the task of writing out hundreds of characters, following the prescribed forms for mixing the ink, for posture, for holding the brush and so on, she hit upon a fine labour-saving device. Like most children, she was completely impervious to the thought that it may not be original and may not be hard to detect. Her task was to write hundreds of characters in the squares provided on her sheets of paper, paying particular attention to the thickness and proportion of her brush strokes. Hsin-ping decided that it was much easier to fill up the squares on her sheets with a *Three Character Classic* of her own. 'Wang' for 'king', 'Hsin' for 'heart' and 'ping' for 'peace', appeared suddenly and monotonously in the midst of her text. For this she received no more than the usual scolding from the old teacher, who had seen it all before. But there was another occasion which had been much more serious.

Her tutor had nodded off in her chair during the lesson, with only her enormous spectacles maintaining the illusion of vigilance. When Hsin-ping discovered this, in the process of mixing the ink in the regulation fashion, stirring gently in the right direction with the right action while sitting in the right position, she decided the ink could be put to better use than originally intended. Choking back her giggles, she executed a number of broad circular brush strokes over each lens of the old woman's spectacles, until they were both completely blacked out. Then she sat back and waited. It seemed an eternity but eventually she woke up. The reaction was intriguing. First there was a slight movement, indicating consciousness, but little else by which one could judge the process of turmoil that was mounting in the victim's mind. Then there was a shout, and a gasp, as she sprang to her feet in panic, and clawed at the place where her eyes should have been. In the process she banged her head against a wall, and fell down, dislodging her glasses and throwing the light of day on the whole affair. Hsin-ping was given a heavy beating with one of the more lethal of Grandma's canes and spent some considerable time on her knees behind the doors of the altarroom. Despite her propensity for mischief, these lessons were laying the foundation for a skill in calligraphy which all would admire as the hallmark of a cultivated person.

Hsin-ping's chief victim was her sixth-grade class teacher, Jia Ruzhu, a very prim and proper old fellow. He was almost bald, wore glasses and was forever instructing his charges to fasten all the buttons on their tunics. He was also an inexhaustible source of *chengyu* (four-character expressions), which he never tired of writing up on the blackboard. This usually started first thing in the morning. On his arrival in the class-room, there was a ripple of mirth—in anticipation of the day's sport, perhaps. He would respond by drawing a large and rather grotesque face on the blackboard, a face which consisted primarily of teeth. 'Now what does that look like? No good, eh? Well, that's you, laughing. Young ladies should not expose their teeth when smiling. Now, how should we laugh? Like this, you see' (he would purse his lips, demurely, coyly, teasingly, holding the miserable, tentative giggle in behind daintily fanned fingers).

Teacher Jia had opinions about almost everything and was a very strict arbiter of taste. For example, there was the *Niu Yang Ge*, a traditional peasant dance normally only performed by men dressed as women. After the Communist victory, and declaration of the People's Republic in October 1949, schools were encouraged to take a different view of these things, to help free the students from feudal attitudes about relations between men and women and to foster respect for peasant culture. Jia was not amenable to change and certainly not at all sympathetic to forms of culture which he considered low-brow. He much preferred dignified old standards like the recitation of Sun Yat-sen's Will, followed by the prescribed period of silence.

One day, during this solemn occasion, Hsin-ping farted, volubly. It was a tactical error, in that it coincided with the period of silence. Had she been so inclined, she might well have taken advantage of the situation to draw the scholarly Jia's attention to the wealth of metaphors arising from this particular aspect of life. She might have quoted him the one about the hapless fool who could not even fart without breaking his own ankle, or she might have observed that 'If you wish to fart with impunity, you should not first signal your intention by removing your trousers'. As a matter of fact, Hsin-ping had been led astray by this conventional wisdom; because she was wearing shorts under her long skirt that day, she had assumed that she would be well above suspicion. Nothing is funnier to the childish mind than the incon-gruity of a loud fart during an adult occasion, and there are few things which pose a more serious threat to good order in the classroom. Teacher Jia was extremely angry about the ensuing hilarity and tried in vain to counteract it by delivering a chastening speech about the heroic martyrs of the First Revolutionary Civil War.

Corporal punishment was not permitted in the school, but this didn't seem to prevent such things as punching, banging heads on walls, or standing in corners. For serious misdemeanours, students were sent to the principal. Hsin-ping achieved this distinction twice, once involving Teacher Jia. He often used to leave the room on some phoney errand, and then dart back inside, in order to catch the girls doing something they shouldn't. As their moral guardian it was up to him to see how well they resisted the temptation provided by his absence.

One day, a couple of girls balanced a filthy old rag mop above the door to greet him on his dramatic reappearance in the classroom. He was hopping mad and threatened that no one would be allowed to go home for lunch until the culprit owned up.

'Who did it?' . . . Silence.

'Who is going to own up?' . . . Silence.

'Wang Hsin-ping, I am giving you the chance to be honest and own up as the ring-leader of this stupid and dangerous prank.' To Hsin-ping's consternation, since she was genuinely innocent for once, the suggestion seemed to meet with unanimous approval from her classmates.

'Yeah, come on Hsin-ping, own up. We want to go home for lunch. It's getting late.'

'But I didn't do it!' she protested.

'Then how did that mop fall from the door?' demanded Jia, missing a crucial step or two in the process of enquiry.

Hsin-ping, like countless children before her, was trapped between two kinds of doom, like 'a rat in a bellows'. If she were to exonerate herself, she would have to implicate others. So she made the reply favoured by all children everywhere in such circumstances: 'I don't know, teacher'.

And Jia made the reply favoured by all teachers everywhere in such circumstances: 'Oh, you don't know? Well, well, you don't seem to know very much, do you? Perhaps it fell by itself?'

'Yes, it was an accident', said Hsin-ping, pathetically.

Jia pounced on this juicy morsel: 'A mop, unlike certain children in this class, always obeys the rules. It may well respect the laws of gravity and fall to the ground, but' . . . he paused for effect . . . 'it is extremely unlikely that it defied these same natural laws and flew to the top of the door by itself, wouldn't you say, Miss Wang?'

In the face of this scientific *tour de force*, Hsin-ping was reduced to helpless silence, which was accepted as further proof of guilt, and she was sent off to the principal's office. She stood in the corner for several hours. Unlike Grandma's corner, this one contained no cushion and no basket of fruit.

In spite of the mischief and mishaps, Hsin-ping did well in school. It was a queer old place, half Western and half Chinese. In appearance it was certainly Chinese, consisting of several single-storey buildings arranged around a courtyard. The classrooms had grey tiled roofs and red lattice windows and were benignly overlooked by ginkgos and scholartrees (*Sophora Japonica*). The sound of little children squealing and chattering rose over the wall of an adjoining kindergarten, and outside the wall of the school itself there was a narrow lane which permitted only foot traffic or the odd cart or rickshaw. No one seemed to know why this was called Shoupa (Handkerchief) Lane. Perhaps there was a tale of foreigners in the title. At any rate, the school's curriculum had been strongly influenced by the impact of modern Western schooling systems during the Republican period. This was not only an exercise in imitating European and American models, but a recognition of Japan's successful borrowing in the nineteenth century. Much of the philosophical debate about reform in China concerned itself with the need to selectively adopt useful Western ideas and practices, while maintaining a Chinese 'essence', but it was obvious that changes had to be made to an education system which had stagnated under the influence of centuries of Confucian orthodoxy and the civil service examination system.

The school was staffed, in the main, by middle-aged single women who lived on the premises. One such was Yin Quan, the younger sister of Hsin-ping's Big Grandma, Old Lady Wang. She had been at the school for forty years, had taught not only Hsin-ping but her mother before her, and was completely devoted to her vocation. Like her mother, Hsin-ping had proved to be very bright, and had won scholarships year after year. When news of this reached Grandma each year she would shake her head in wonder, unable to reconcile Hsin-ping's academic talents with her constant mischief-making. But then her mother had been the same, according to Old Miss Yin Quan. In fact the mischief and the good results were not unrelated.

For Hsin-ping, homework was a thing to be taken very seriously, to be done thoroughly and without delay in order to clear the decks for action. During the long and enchanted summer vacation, the children were given large doses of homework to be completed in readiness for the new school year. While other kids were out and about exulting in their new found freedom, Hsin-ping was nowhere to be seen for some days. Then the silkworm would emerge from her cocoon and, unlike the others, would be untroubled by thoughts of homework as the autumn semester approached. She was also genuinely proud of her work and loathed having marks deducted.

As a result of her scholastic achievements, Hsin-ping was made a class leader in her final year. Schools were an ideal breeding ground for the contagion of hierarchical relationships and structures, and no class or small group could function without first determining who led it.

Often the very function of the group was forgotten in the process. Factions were as natural to the Chinese classroom as grazed knees or headlice. The manner in which Hsin-ping achieved office was also typical of a related phenomenon—the manipulation of factions from above. She was not an ideal choice from anyone's point of view, in particular the teachers', but what better way to keep her quiet than to use the pretext of her good results to give her some responsibilities? But this was be an elected position and her classmates were not likely to elect her, not because they didn't like her, but because she was too naughty and therefore not a suitable choice for the coveted position. So, the only solution was for Teacher Jia to convince the children that they were being disrespectful and disobedient if they exercised their democratic prerogative and picked someone of their own preference rather than their teacher's. What better introduction to the moral and civic responsibilities of adulthood than to be picked by people who didn't want her for a job she didn't want at the instigation of someone who didn't trust her?

The autumn of 1949 floated by, an idyllic time in spite of the momentous changes going on outside the little school in Shoupa Lane. Hsin-ping was not so inhibited by her new office that she could not capture a splendid fat cicada and coax it into a frenzied, shrill call right in the middle of one of Jia's sententious addresses. And there were cricket fights and games to be organized in the long, long midday breaks. The earth itself seemed to be snoring and somnolent after a heavy lunch, and there was plenty of time for Hsin-ping and her Outlaws of the Marsh to roam the classrooms and corridors in search of forbidden fun. As befitting a progressive modern school, their games sometimes reflected a Western influence—derived in the main from the movies. It seemed inexplicably entertaining to cover the mouth with a handkerchief and tear about the corridors making gun noises. It was never entirely clear why handkerchiefs should be part of the uniform in foreign cowboy films, but Hsin-ping thought it indicated that even the criminals were fastidiously hygienic in Western countries.

On through the winter they roamed and pillaged, like the Taiping rebels, a curious mixture of mythologies. When their kingdom was finally brought to an end by the staff, who noticed a few disturbances here and there in sacred places like the music room or the science laboratory, the question of a ringleader was raised. Once again Hsin-ping was elected.

2

苏都寒流

The Storm from Moscow

In the autumn of 1950 Hsin-ping went to high school. Not just any old high school but Shi Da Nu Fu Zhong—Peking Teachers' University Attached Girls' High—the best in Peking. Since it had been considered the best before Liberation, it now had a head start. After the establishment of the People's Republic on 1 October 1949, it attracted some very famous revolutionary families. Mao Zedong's two daughters, Li Min and Li Na, the former by his third wife, He Zizhen, the latter by his fourth, Jiang Qing, attended the school. There was Mao's daughter-in-law, Liu Songming, married to Mao Anying, the son who would be killed in Korea a year later. Ye Ting, Commander of the New Fourth Army, had a daughter in the school. Liu Shaoqi's daughter and Zhou Enlai's niece were also enrolled. And then there was the staff. The Principal was Su Lingyang, wife of the Cultural Commissar, Zhou Yang, and on the staff there was a Chinese teacher who was the daughter of Li Dazhao, one of the founders of the Chinese Communist Party, and a politics teacher who had taken part in the arrest of Chiang Kai-shek during the celebrated Xi'an Incident in 1936.

With this kind of political pedigree, it was inevitable that the change from American to Soviet teaching method and curriculum took place very rapidly and very thoroughly after Liberation. Soviet style history and politics, Soviet style examinations, Soviet style extra-curricular activities and youth organizations, even Soviet style uniforms—white blouse, black skirt—were the order of the day. Everyone referred to the Soviet Union as Big Brother, unconscious of the connotations this would acquire as a result of George Orwell's works. 'Da Ge', 'Big Brother', and 'Xiao Didi', 'Little Brother', were the symbols of international proletarian unity in this all-girls' school in Peking after 1949.

The influx of high-ranking cadres' daughters did not pose any real problem at first. They were highly respected and admired. They were modestly dressed and had an austere air, suggestive of the Eighth Route Army, the Long March and Yan'an. In age they were a motley group, varying from thirteen or fourteen right up to a marriageable seventeen or eighteen. As a result they did not form an obvious clique. However, they were government sponsored and, as such, enjoyed a different status from that of the private, fee-paying students like Hsin-ping. Gradually the differences between the two groups became more pronounced. The austere look gave way to the privileged look. They were given a dining hall of their own, to which other ranks were not admitted. Their clothing changed markedly in quality and, on Saturday afternoons, black limousines with curtains (Soviet style) and a chicken feather-duster in the back (Chinese style) used to pull up outside the school gates, to take the young ladies for a spin.

While their blood may have been redder than others', it quickly became obvious that their was little 'ink' in it, and their scholastic attainments were even more proletarian than their lineage. After a while it became necessary to put them in a special group in order to shield them from invidious comparison with the children of 'bourgeois academic' families. It also became necessary to give them 'special' exams. In spite of their modest academic results, thirty or forty were selected every year for the next few years to go to Moscow for further study. This was as much a pilgrimage as an opportunity for study, and ideological considerations were foremost in the selection criteria, but the girls needed assistance nevertheless. With the advent of the dual exam system, there was no obstacle to their selection. Other schools were occasionally distinguished by the success of one or two candidates, but Shi Da always had a very large contingent for the Soviet Union. This also helped to avoid the difficulties and all-round embarrassment which would have been inevitable had these students sat for the regular university entrance exams. Shi Da was anxious to maintain its record of 100 per cent success in these exams, and 'Big Brother' was doing his bit.

In order to prepare the cadres' daughters for the Soviet Union, Russian was taught in the school. Liu Aiqing, daughter of Liu Shaoqi, Mao's designated successor from 1961 to 1966, taught this subject. She had in fact married a Russian and had a son by him during her own sojourn in the Soviet Union, but once she went back to China she was prevented from returning to her family, and was eventually persuaded to marry a Chinese. Some of the students had themselves already been to the Soviet Union. Li Min, Mao's daughter by He Zizhen, and a classmate of Hsin-ping, had spent some time there. During showers after sport, Hsin-ping often assailed her with a bucket of cold water—'Aha, the Princess has no clothes on. Look out. I am a storm from Moscow'. So saying, she would empty the contents over the unfortunate princess.

Oral examinations, a five-point system of assessment, and small 'circles', or interest groups based on career aspirations, were other features of the Soviet influence evident in the school. Hsin-ping began to develop a taste for aeronautics, and thoroughly enjoyed her normal academic work and the opportunities for extra-curricular activities. However, the preferential treatment enjoyed by the political nobility began to get on her nerves. Things seemed to get a great deal worse after the formal amalgamation of Yu Cai, a Yan'an school, with Shi Da. Predictably, the issue which provoked her most bitter criticism concerned food: 'How come they eat so well? Four dishes and a soup! What do we get? Scraps, that's all. There's no meat in our dishes at all. And look at their clothes—they even dress much better than us, and we have to pay for everything ourselves! They get to sit in their own dining room at nice clean tables, and even get fruit afterwards! We have to sit wherever we can around the school eating bad rice with weevils in it.'

Many students adopted the practice of bringing their own food from home and cooking it in the school's steamers, which were made available to them. Even this turned out to be a dubious privilege when the rumour went round that the Yu Cai girls boiled their sanitary napkins in the steamers. The fact that so many of these girls were physically mature did not help their cause with the Peking girls, who considered all evidence of sexual development to be symptoms of a disgusting disease. There was some satisfaction to be found in cutting up tennis balls and placing the makeshift 'falsies' under their tunics in mockery of the older girls.

The grievances and the frictions soon reached the ears of the principal, Su Lingyang, wife of Zhou Yang, Minister for Culture and all-powerful arbiter of public taste and opinion in the years to come. She called an assembly to tackle the problem. 'You think you are so badly done by, you private students? Absolute rubbish. Just look at Li Meiqi, for instance.' She pointed at the fattest girl in the school, renowned for her vast lunchboxes brought from home, each resembling a butcher's stall. She did not, of course, mention that Meiqi's father was a wealthy industrialist from the North-East.

'Now as to the matter of clothing', she said resolutely, having routed all opposition on the food question, 'just look at Wang Hsin-ping, of Year One, Class Four. Just look at her fine brown woollen overcoat, brand new and very expensive. Now how can you possibly say there is any difference between you and the government students?' The coat was, of course, Third Aunt's present, sent from America, but this did not detract from its value as a rebuttal of the fee-paying students' case.

Academic inequalities were the most important grievance. The government students had such easy exams and only needed 50 per cent to be promoted. Su Lingyang was not prepared to discuss this, under any circumstances, with anybody. Hsin-ping took out her frustrations on the 'princesses'. Liu Songming, Mao's daughter-in-law, was one of her most frequent targets: 'Ah, there goes Second Daughter-in-Law! Hey, Second Daughter-in-Law, how are things with you today?'

Teachers who joined the staff with the amalgamation of Yu Cai and Shi Da were also a favourite target, since they had not been to a teachers' college and had no formal qualifications. One such teacher, Shi Wei, displayed her lack of expertise rather too prominently: 'Today we will write an essay. The topic is "my partner". One bemused girl wrote about her brother.

'No, no', was the response, 'You cannot say your brother is your partner. Your partner is your boyfriend or fiancee or husband, and I want you to list the kind of qualities you expect in that person.' Like many inexperienced teachers, she was more concerned for the sanctity of her chosen topic than for its relevance. The fact that their school would not permit girls to have boyfriends even if they had wanted them did not deter her from her pedagogical purpose. As for her students, they were totally mystified. Maybe princesses had boyfriends but *they* certainly didn't. Perhaps they should ask their principal if this was another case of discrimination.

Shi Wei was not the only teacher from the Yu Cai school to suffer torment from the disdainful natives, and being heroes of the Revolution could not save them. Teacher Zhang had participated in the arrest of Chiang Kai-shek. The Generalissimo returned the favour and had her arrested and imprisoned after 1945. Since she was extremely tall, what could be wittier than to ask:

'Teacher Zhang, when you heroically suffered imprisonment at the hands of the reactionaries and traitors, did they hang you upside down from the ceiling?'

'Don't mention such things child. Why do you ask?'

'Because your legs are so long they look like they've been stretched.'

In the second semester of her first year in high school, Hsin-ping began to take a keen interest in politics, and naturally much of her emerging sense of right and wrong in world affairs focused on the Soviet Union. She began to ask indelicate questions about the relationships between the socialist siblings: 'Teacher Gui, you say the Soviet Union is Big Brother and we are Little Brother in the family of socialist nations. Well then, why don't they return our land north of Heilongjiang River and east of Wusuli River? You know that land was taken from us by the Tsarist regime in Qing times. Why can't we have it back now that we are brothers?'

She began to accumulate a string of poor marks in politics: 'Teacher Gui, why does the Soviet Union keep half of the oil we find in Lanzhou, just for helping us to find it? If you told me you knew where there was a buried chest of coins and I helped you dig for it, should I be able to claim half of it? That's really unfair . . . of course you have to thank me, because I helped you, maybe you should even offer me some—but not half, that's not fair at all. How can you call that correct socialist thinking?'

Worse than that, with her unerring instinct for disaster, she began to ask the teacher why she only ever got three out of five, in view of the fact that she was so well informed about recent Soviet history. She felt absolutely certain that teachers were bound to be honest and above board about this sort of thing, especially politics teachers.

'Teacher Gui, in my last politics test, did I answer well, or badly?'

'You answered well.'

'But my marks are not good. How come my marks are not good if my answers are all right?'

'It's not a matter of just answering questions. It's a matter of attitude. Others didn't answer as well as you but their attitude is better. You should think yourself lucky. I decided to save you losing face. If not, I could have given you two rather than three.'

'But how can you call yourself a real communist if you think like that? A true communist should seek the truth from facts.'

'I am seeking truth from facts. The truth is your facts may be correct, and your answers may be good but your results are poor.'

Hsin-ping was too young and earnest to appreciate the value of his lesson.

There was another teacher who frequently engaged Hsin-ping's interest. A middle-aged, unmarried woman, she was responsible for the hygiene and domestic science lessons, which included, among other other things, a smattering of sex education. During these lessons, she would close all the windows and begin whispering the Facts of Life while gesturing vaguely in the direction of some imprecise diagrams of the reproductive organs. She kept these half-hidden behind her desk and called the girls out row by row to take a furtive peek. When the time came for testing the knowledge she had imparted, she informed her charges that, for examination purposes, they need not worry about the male bits.

Hsin-ping's curiosity could not be contained within the bounds of this syllabus and so she took Tang Ling and a new friend, Xun Linglai, down to the bookstores near Xidan in search of 'yellow' books which

might make things a little clearer. There were many libraries, bookshops and 'treasures of the study' shops near Xidan, catering to
scholar—bureaucrat families in the area. It was quite normal for the
girls from the school in nearby Erlong Street to go into the library after
class in search of books their teachers had recommended, such as
Shuihu Zhuan (Water Margin). It was not quite so normal for thirteen-
year-old ladies to be enquiring after *Jin Ping Mei*, the Chinese erotic
masterpiece which had even been translated into English, with its
private parts draped in Latin. The dessicated old library attendant
peered down over his glasses at the girls, quite disturbed at their request
but equally intimidated by their well-bred manner. Finally he handed
over ten volumes of the complete, unexpurgated, unabridged *Jin Ping
Mei*.

They hurried away to devour all its secrets—but were bitterly disappointed. For all its fascinating preliminaries to the Mystery of What Men
and Women Do, for all its perfuming of beds and lighting of silver
lamps, for all its talk of 'playing the flute', and 'heads and tails', it never
made much sense until you got the basics straight. To make matters
worse, it seemed that Golden Lotus had begun by consulting a book
of pictures just like the one Grandma had thrown into the stove.
According to the story, she found it most absorbing and 'learnt much'.
Once again the trail of clues had ended tantalizingly with *Spring
Pictures*.

In the summer holiday of 1951, just before the commencement of her
second year of high school, Hsin-ping busied herself in her post as
assistant to the cultural activities committee of the school's Young
Pioneer brigade. She was absolutely delighted to have attained this
position, the culmination of a year's efforts to join the organization,
which was modelled on its famous counterpart in the Soviet Union. She
had made three applications, and the third had been successful. In view
of the fact that 95 per cent of the students in this school were members,
acceptance was not so much a signal honour as an escape from the
stigma of exclusion.

Hsin-ping had had a number of problems with her application. She
was considered by her teachers to be unruly, and the Yu Cai teachers in
particular had found her disrespectful and argumentative. On the other
hand, it was widely acknowledged that she was a bright and capable
student with excellent potential for leadership. Withholding approval of
her application seemed an effective means of controlling her behaviour,
for the time being at least. Finally, she had been admitted, and was
sworn in as a member of the Young Pioneers on Children's Day, 1 June
1951, in a great ceremony in the school hall.

Teacher Chen, brigade leader, made a fine speech, and each new
member was presented with her red scarf by an old member. There

were songs and dances of welcome and the names of all the new members were announced one by one. Hsin-ping was inspired by the ceremony and could hardly contain her enthusiasm for her new role as a 'three goods' student—one who was acknowledged to study well, exercise well and labour well. Maintaining these standards in her studies and in sport was not at all difficult for her but she was uncertain as to how to become a model of productive labour and socialist consciousness. The Working People's Cultural Palace, formerly the Imperial Ancestral Temple in the Forbidden City, provided the answer. Why not put on a song and dance performance in the park for Uncle and Auntie Worker? And why not make the theme of the performance the liberation of the brothers and sisters in Taiwan?

So the organizing group cycled all over the city during the summer holidays, gathering props and costumes from this and that work unit in order to put on a splendid display. There were P.L.A. uniforms and Taiwanese Gaoshan minority costumes and red flags to be borrowed, and then they had the difficulty of finding a suitable tune and appropriate dance movements. For weeks Hsin-ping dinked her fellow Pioneers around the city, helping them to organize rehearsals. It all paid off handsomely when the performances were judged and theirs was acclaimed as the best in the school brigade. As a result they performed not only at the Cultural Palace during weekends but in factories and on the streets during the week.

Their routine was given a special mention by Chen Yongzheng, the brigade leader, a man in his early thirties, not very popular among the girls for a variety of reasons, not the least of them his habit of putting his arm around them while imparting advice. Chen had been particularly obstructive and annoying during the time they had been preparing for the performance. For some reason he always scoffed at their project and would not give his permission to go to this place or that, or arrange introductions for them or do any of the things he was supposed to do as their leader. Consequently it came as a rude shock to Hsin-ping when she heard him holding forth at an assembly of Pioneers about the 'sound guidance of the brigade leadership'. During Chen's long-winded preface, she had contented herself with an aside to her classmate that working with Chen was about as efficient a process as wiping your arse with a watermelon skin, but this remark about leadership infuriated her and she made several very loud and sarcastic comments about it. That afternoon, after class, she found herself being interviewed by Chen.

He demanded to know why she thought so much of herself, why she was disrespectful to her teachers and where she got the idea that she could manage great feats without the assistance of others. She could not contain herself: 'At our brigade assembly you took the credit for leading us. But you wouldn't even help us. When we came to you for help you just made difficulties. How can you say you led us? It's not fair'. Chen turned very red, amazed at her impudence: 'Your trouble is you think you can do everything by yourself, nobody helps you, you don't need the support of the masses. Do you really imagine that this performance would have been possible without leadership? You are too conceited and full of false independence'.

'But you *didn't* help us. We had to do it all ourselves!'

'Where you find a successful organization you will find successful leadership!'

'And what if there's a failure? Would you be responsible for that, or only for success?'

'Where there is failure you will find no leader', said the furious Chen, oblivious to any suggestion of irony.

For a month after this exchange, no one in the school was allowed to talk to Hsin-ping, the idea being to demonstrate to her that she could not get along without the support of the masses. This particular lesson was called *gu li*, and was very hard on a gregarious fourteen-year-old girl. One week passed, and two, and three. By the fourth week she had passed through stages of anger, indignation, remorse and desperate loneliness until, finally, she could feel only hatred. Her heart had been hardened, and she seemed to have regained the moral advantage. But there was more to come.

On 10 December 1951, Chen called another brigade meeting. On this occasion, Hsin-ping was called upon to surrender her red scarf, which was folded with great ceremony and taken away by one of her peers to be placed in safekeeping during an indefinite period of suspension from the Young Pioneers. Her political family had disowned her. The terrible ceremony was concluded with a speech from Chen, quoting the inspirational words of Madame Krupskaya, wife of Lenin and founder of the movement. Then came the final blow.

'Comrades, you all know the story of Vasily, a member of the Young Pioneers in the Soviet Union. You have all seen the film, 'The Red Scarf,' in which Vasily commits mistakes in his dealings with the masses. He is quite conceited, thinks that every achievement is the result of his own original ideas and that he can get along without the help of others. It is true that he is clever but he is also arrogant and self-centered and does not understand the principle of mass-line leadership. You have seen how he is taught a valuable lesson by his classmates. They show him very effectively that he cannot manage alone and, after one month of this lesson, he realizes that he is one of a collective. His membership of the Young Pioneers is suspended indefinitely but, during this suspension, his comrades all help him to see the error of his ways until, finally, he rejoins the Communist Youth League. Comrades! We have among us

our very own Vasily. She is none other than Year Two, Class Four's
Wang Hsin-ping. You have already shown her over this last month how
foolish it is to reject the masses; now you must help her to correct her
attitude.'

Hsin-ping almost fainted away under the stress of humiliation and
injustice. She found her way home somehow after school that day and
cried for hours and hours in her room. She thought of the red scarf
which she had lovingly selected and paid for herself and which had
been officially received in triumph in June only to be removed in
disgrace six months later. She thought of the way she had thrown
herself into the work of the cultural committee, and of the precious
summer holiday she had sacrificed in the quest for 'three goods' status.
She choked and sobbed with rage and disbelief at the hypocrisy of
Chen's speech. A day or two later, in a moment of despair, she pleaded
with him to reconsider his course of action, promising to work hard on
her attitude. Chen would not hear of it, and so Hsin-ping was doomed
to relentless 'help' from brigade members answering their leader's call.
'Let's talk about your attitude', said one of the older ones, who would
in time go to East Germany, get married and never come back; 'Why
don't you just tell me everything you can think of, as it comes? If it's
good, that's fine, if it's not, just let it come out freely and maybe I can
help you'. 'No, no', said Hsin-ping, beginning to get the hang of the
game; 'It's no use worrying yourself about me. I'm not politically
advanced. I'm the most politically backward student in the whole
school. There's just nothing I can do about it. I'm a hopeless case. I'm
stubborn and stupid'. In the privacy of her own thoughts she repeated
to herself, 'Hit me once and I will retreat. Hit me twice and I will retreat
again. But never hit me three times, or I will fight back with all my
strength'. The Young Pioneers had indeed taught her a valuable lesson.

Many people, including the principal, Su Lingyang, explained to her
that she could re-apply to join the movement. They seemed quite
anxious that she should do so, as if the ending were not quite right
unless she did. On these occasions Hsin-ping would say, 'I'm so
backward that by the time I have changed my attitude I will be too old
to join anyway'. 'That's all right', was the usual reply, 'You can prepare
to join the Communist Youth League instead. After all that's what
Vasily did'.

Hsin-ping took no interest at all in this prospect, but the episode of
the red scarf was not finished. She had acquired a political kharma,
with debts to be paid in another life, and there would be times when
her child's candour and idealism would be thrown back in her face like
the buckets of cold water she had emptied over the 'princess'.

3

倒悬之心

A Heart Upside-down

On 9 March 1953, when Hsin-ping was in the final year of junior high school, Stalin died. The whole country went into extravagant mourning for a month, in a manner reminiscent of the days of the emperors. No coloured clothing could be worn, no songs could be sung, no celebrations or festivities could be held and no one could get married—including one of Hsin-ping's cousins, who had planned to be married in March. The more irreverent types wondered if the Soviets themselves made such a fuss, but devotees like Su Lingyang worked themselves into a frenzy of grief over the death of Comrade Stalin. At one of the assemblies called to announce the news, she strained and strained at her misery, until she actually managed to produce tears which could be seen in the back row. At another funeral ceremony for Stalin in Moscow some eight years later, his embalmed body would be removed from Lenin's mausoleum and relocated in a very much plainer grave beside the Kremlin Wall, but he remained at Lenin's side in Chinese iconography.

For Hsin-ping it was becoming increasingly important to decide on a vocation. Since her primary school days she had been interested in aircraft, and in her first year of senior high school she chose as her extra-curricular 'circle' the aviation group. She had set her sights on going to the Peking Aviation College, but she began to hear a number of discouraging things about this. One of her friends wanted to apply for the college and had achieved outstanding results in maths and physics, but her principal had not allowed it because she had an uncle in Taiwan and was therefore a security risk in a strategically sensitive area. Hsin-ping also knew a man of about twenty-five whom she often saw at the swimming pool where they both trained as members of the Peking Municipal Swimming Team. One day, towards the end of 1953, he told her that he had passed the exams for Nanking Aviation College. She congratulated him and wished him well for his future. Two years later, shopping in the street, she saw him again and greeted him in some surprise. 'What are you doing here? I thought you were in Nanking, studying Aviation?' 'My father has a problem', he said morosely.

Suddenly Hsin-ping recalled all those recent caricatures in the *People's Daily* featuring a vicious-looking fox menacing the progressive elements in society. The fox was a pun on the family name 'Hu', which is a homophone with the word for fox. This man's father had been associated with Hu Feng, one of the first targets of the Su Fan movement (the movement to eliminate counter-revolutionaries, 1955). Hu Feng was an author who had written to the Party Central Committee in 1954, protesting against literary restrictions. Su Lingyang's husband, Zhou Yang, later to be denounced himself as a 'literary tsar', led the attack on Hu Feng, which widened into a general hunt for 'counter-revolutionaries'. As a result, Hsin-ping's friend had suffered the penalty of summary expulsion from an institution with no possibility of discussion or negotiation. In order to punish him for the transgressions of his father, he was condemned to that most terrible of penalties in a workers' state—to be made a worker in a factory.

Hsin-ping decided that a career in aviation was not for her; with all her relatives in America, Australia and Hong Kong, she might be investigated at any moment. She began to think of other careers which might involve her favourite subjects, maths, physics and chemistry. She thought of Tianjin University, which had a precision instruments department, but then she met a senior high graduate who had been refused enrolment. Since many students from this department went to East Germany or Switzerland for further study, no one with relatives abroad was considered reliable enough to be entrusted with the opportunity. By the time she was preparing for her own graduation, Hsin-ping was becoming almost desperate.

She had to choose, and whatever decision she made she would be stuck with for good and all. Her teachers suggested that family members should be consulted, but Hsin-ping's only source of wisdom and experience was Grandma. She could not help wondering why her privileged background always seemed to be such a disadvantage. 'Grandma', she asked, 'What should I do about my future?' 'The railways!' said Grandma, without a moment's hesitation.

Hsin-ping wondered why she was so emphatic. It was certainly true that Peking Railway College was an excellent institution and had a fine reputation in engineering, maths and physics, but it seemed highly unlikely that this played a prominent part in the old lady's thinking. The Railways Department was also an independent body, and wages and conditions were said to be excellent, but employees were likely to be sent almost anywhere in the country. Surely Grandma would not want Hsin-ping to go off to some remote place and leave her alone and uncared for in the city? That the railways constituted an 'iron rice bowl', an indestructible source of livelihood that could not disappear even with a change of government, was certain to loom large in Grandma's thinking, but even so it was hard to understand her unwavering conviction that this was the career for Hsin-ping. That is, it *was* hard until she recalled that a neighbour had been telling Grandma about the twelve free tickets to any destination in China which were allocated to each employee annually. This had obviously fired the old woman's imagination and she had begun dreaming of travel. Hsin-ping decided against the compelling case for the railways and turned her attention to architecture.

It was around this time that she was summoned to see Su Lingyang and the student affairs officer, Hu Zhitang.

'Wang Hsin-ping, have you decided on a career yet?' asked the earnest Principal Su. 'Time's getting on, you're nearing graduation and you still don't seem to have made up your mind.'

'But I can't seem to decide what's best for me.'

'You should have no problems. You're a good student.'

'My results are not bad but I do have some other problems.'

'Ah yes', said Su, knowingly, 'There has been some difficulty hasn't there? You know Hsin-ping, we also have made some mistakes in our work. That matter of your suspension from the Young Pioneers was perhaps a little unfair. Comrade Hu and I are aware of that.' Hsin-ping wondered if that was why Chen had been relieved of his duties with the brigade. 'In fact', continued Su in her sibilant southern tones, 'We should apologize to you on behalf of the school for this mistake.'

'It doesn't matter', said Hsin-ping, a little flustered by this unexpected turn of events.

'Wang Hsin-ping, why don't you rejoin the organization? You could join the Communist Youth League.'

'No I couldn't do that. Even if you were to invite me to join, I couldn't do it unless the brigade leader himself invited me.'

'Oh very well', said Su, obviously nettled, but reluctant to pursue the matter for the time being. 'We'll discuss it some more another time. Now what about your choice of a vocation? You seem to have changed your mind several times.'

Hsin-ping realized that every move she had made or considered, whether serious or a false start, had been closely monitored. She didn't bother explaining to them the process of elimination by which she had arrived at her present choice because she knew full well that they were as well acquainted with it as she was herself. In fact she had often remarked sarcastically to her classmates that the unfortunate school administration seemed to get headaches over her difficulties even before she knew she had them.

'At the moment I am thinking of applying to Qinghua University to study architecture.'

'You should go to Teachers' College. Why don't you go to Teachers' College?'

'A lifetime of chalk?' exclaimed the tactless Hsin-ping.

'And just what is so terrible about that?' asked Hu, coldly.

'But I couldn't possibly handle such demanding work', said Hsin-ping, beating a hasty retreat.

'Don't worry', said Su, 'Comrade Hu and I will help you to make your application.' Since the school was attached to Peking Teachers' University, it was highly desirable that there should be a strong contingent of students applying for teacher training. Unfortunately, however, most were strongly influenced by the old saying, 'If you've still got a few sacks of rice to your name, you don't have to become king of the kids'. As a result, quite a few needed help with their applications.

Hsin-ping responded to their offer characteristically. Overlooking the fact that the teachers' college was supposed to *be* a university, she suggested that it would be a waste of her good marks to go to a teachers' college when she could get into a university.

'We think you would make an excellent teacher', retorted Su, her tone becoming increasingly ominous.

'Why?' persisted Hsin-ping.

'During these last six years we have paid close attention to the development of your character. You're an individual. During junior and senior high school you've always retained a distinctive personality. We need your kind to understand others like yourself in the schools. You have invaluable experience to offer us. You know, we have more trouble with this than anything—how to deal with children with their own distinctive personalities. But *you* understand the problem perfectly, so it's obvious that you will make an excellent teacher. You can specialize in maths and physics if you like and you needn't even sit for the entrance exam. We'll recommend your direct enrolment.'

'But why a teacher? Why can't I study engineering or architecture?'

The conversation came to an abrupt end. 'No, no, this will not do at all', said Su, 'We're not getting anywhere like this. You go away and think about what we have said and Comrade Hu and I will give the matter some further thought.'

Hsin-ping went away and thought about it. When the time came to fill in her application for enrolment she wrote:

1. Architecture. Qinghua University.
2. Geology and Geography. Peking University.

After that she alternated in her preferences between Qinghua and Peking universities, specifying any department in which maths and science were prominent, until she had used up her quota of six choices. Unfortunately, she forgot that at the bottom of the application form was the most important 'choice' of all—the school's suggested course of study. After all the agonizing and deliberation, conferring with classmates, seeking the opinions of relatives, testing one possibility and then another against practical realities, studying and sitting for exams . . . it all came down to this, the school's 'suggestion'. And the school's assessment of Hsin-ping's potential contribution boiled down to two characters at the bottom of her application form—*shi fan*, teacher training.

To make matters worse, Hsin-ping had negotiated her way around the application form with her usual disastrous candour. Since she had not listed teaching among her choices, and since the school was determined that she should become a teacher, it was quite clear that she could not expect to be granted any one of her six 'choices'. The application form made provision for this contingency by asking, 'If you do not qualify for entry to the course of your choice, will you accept your country's calling?' Hsin-ping, oblivious to the fact that this was more a threat than a question, had written 'No' without a moment's hesitation. Even Tang Ling might have told her that your ability to say 'No' to a bully depends entirely on the size of your big brother. Hsin-ping thought her results would be good enough and that would be that—and if not she would simply wait until next year and try again, rather than accepting any old rubbish.

In fact her results were good enough for any of her choices, but once again Hsin-ping had set herself on a collision course with her school authorities. They could not even save a little face by offering the third choice, because, out of cunning or perversity, she had put Peking University Maths Department last—and this required the best results of all, that is, around 550 out of 600. How could such a bourgeois-minded student be rewarded with admission to such a prestigious department? Finally she received a letter from the college explaining that, while her marks were excellent in some respects, she did not have the prerequisites in the areas of cultural knowledge, political ideology and health and hygiene. As a result, she did not qualify for entrance to the universities of her choice. Another letter followed: 'If you were unsuccessful in obtaining your own preference in your last application, are you prepared to accept your country's calling?' At last she understood, and wrote 'Yes' in the space provided. In due course she received a letter of congratulations, advising her that she had been recommended for teacher training.

In September 1956 Hsin-ping went to Hebei Teachers' College, which was many rungs below Peking Teachers' University on the ladder of status. She had not handled the situation at all well, but she consoled herself with the notion that she would be able to get out on medical grounds and re-apply for admission to a decent university the following year. In the first two months of her course she was a regular visitor at the clinic. On one such occasion she told a balding, bored old physician that she could not sleep at night. He looked as if he was thoroughly familiar with the problem. When she told him that she had difficulty keeping her eyes open during study, he asked whether she tended to doze off during her basketball matches or swimming competitions. After this rather unpromising exchange, she waited a decent interval before returning to the clinic. During the next consultation she told the wily old character that she had a fever. He took her temperature and found it extremely high—but there were no other signs of the ague. Then he noticed some kind of foodstuff sticking to the roof of her mouth. Yes, he had seen this one before too—eating sweet potatoes just before a consultation, in order to raise the score on the thermometer. With the indefatigable spirit of the foolish old man who moved the mountain, Hsin-ping went back once more. This time the temperature under her armpits was very high. The cause was certainly not sweet potatoes, but it didn't take the canny old doctor long to realize that some very warm object, quite possibly a hot water bottle, was responsible.

She gave up her attempts at medical discharge, half in chagrin and half in admiration of the old campaigner's forensic skills. She settled into her work, deciding that she would become a first-rate student. In the exams she did superbly well, even during the nerve-racking orals put by a board of examiners, comprised of professors, associate professors and all kinds of eminent authorities. This was a very stressful business at times, especially in maths, when students were required not only to perform a calculation but also to explain their method. In her Russian language exam, Hsin-ping was so nervous that her teeth would not stop chattering and clacking, and for some seconds she could not emit an intelligible sound in any language. However, she eventually passed with flying colours, as she did even in the dreaded political study. Her first year of college passed quietly and successfully, with Hsin-ping resigned to her 'lifetime of chalk' and once more emerging as a model, if unpredictable, student. Then came 1957.

On 27 April 1957, the Central Committee of the Chinese Communist Party issued a crucial directive on the 'work style' of Party cadres. The directive followed Mao's 'On the Problem of the Correct Handling of Contradictions Among the People', a speech made to the Supreme State Conference in February 1957, and followed up in a similar speech to the National Propaganda Work Conference on 12 March. In his February speech, Mao had used the immortal words, 'Let a hundred flowers bloom, let a hundred schools of thought contend', and had gone on to explain that this was the path to progress and development for China's arts and sciences. Prohibition of the free play of opposing styles and methods would stunt China's intellectual growth. Difficult problems and controversies should be resolved through discussion and argument, rather than through the adoption of simplistic methods and solutions. These speeches touched a raw nerve, and a torrent of criticism descended upon the Party.

One of those who took Mao at his word was Chu Anping, who had studied at London University in 1935 and, on his return to China, had become editor of *Guancha*, (the *Observer*) a weekly which had attacked the Nationalists from 1946 to 1950. This magazine became the *New Observer* in 1950, and from this Chu went on to become editor-in-chief of *Guangming Ribao* (*Illumination Daily*), official organ of the China Democratic League. He took up this post on 11 April 1957, an absolutely critical time for an intellectual who had deep suspicions about the links between the feudal past and the emergence of one-party rule. He coined the phrase *dang tianxia* (the Party kingdom), to describe the system of rule in China under the communists. The phrase nettled the Party because its implication was so pointed—being a satirical allusion to *jia tianxia*, an old and familiar expression which characterized the Emperor as head of the nation/family. The new Emperor was clearly the Party. Chu, and his fellow newspaper editors, Zhang Bozhun and Luo Longji, miscalculated the Party's capacity to tolerate such criticism and became the chief targets of the anti-rightist movement.

On 2 June 1957, Chu's article 'This Problem of the Party Kingdom Attitude is the Ultimate Source of Factionalism', was published in *Peking Daily* and then circulated to the *People's Daily*. It was a moderate and reasonable article, in which he argued that it was natural for the Party to exercise strong leadership, but that in maintaining control and supervision over every level of work it had simply gone too far. When published in the *People's Daily*, there was little to suggest that it had exceeded the legitimate bounds of argument as encouraged in the 'Hundred Flowers' speech. Suddenly all work units, including those in colleges, were urged to express their attitudes to it, to use it as a vehicle for the dialectical process. When the issues raised by the article were put to Hsin-ping's class, in the form of the question, 'Is Chu right or wrong?', there was very little doubt about the correct response. After all, if Chu was on the right track there would be no debate—only applause. In any event, there were days and days of political discussion.

Normal classes ceased while this went on. Hsin-ping avoided expressing an opinion, resorting to her old stance that she was too politically backward to make a contribution. There came a day, however, when it was painfully obvious that the session would not be terminated until *everybody* had come clean. Hsin-ping put her view as ambiguously as possible, conscious that joining in the criticism of Chu too enthusiastically might rebound on her in times to come: 'There is some merit in what Chu Anping has said, because there are times when Party cadres may lack technical expertise, such as in economics. These cadres should make an effort to familiarize themselves with relevant subject areas before they are appointed to leadership positions in those fields.'

Shortly after this, Hsin-ping became the subject of several 'big-character posters', or slogan banners, which were draped around the college dormitories—'Wang Hsin-ping Agrees with Chu Anping!' In order to emphasize the point, the middle character of her name, 'Hsin', meaning 'heart', was not written as a character, but drawn as a heart, turned upside-down, painted black and, just in case there was any ambiguity about the symbol, struck through with an enormous cross. This was only the beginning of her troubles.

Towards the end of April, Hsin-ping and some classmates prepared to celebrate May 1st, International Labour Day, and May 4th, the anniversary of the student-led movement which broke out in Peking in 1919 in protest at China's humiliation by foreign powers during the Versailles Peace Conference following World War I. Hsin-ping and her classmates laboured for some weeks over the design and construction of a special decorated archway, which would adorn the entrance to the college and commemorate the two great days. Attention was paid to every minute detail, and as usual Hsin-ping was the busiest of all, hoping perhaps to erase the memory of those inverted black hearts which had sprung up like mushrooms around the dormitories. She had taken special responsibility for the banner, which was to be draped across the archway. The text for the banner was to be 'Celebrate May 4th, Celebrate May 1st'. Simple enough, and to the point—hardly the sort of thing to generate controversy, one would think. The work went on and on. There was fetching and carrying of paint and paper and glue and wood. There were endless discussions about the most suitable design. The characters for the banner were lovingly fashioned and paper lanterns were made to be hung from the archway.

Finally, on 30 April, in the late afternoon, they took a break and gazed with pride upon the finished work, their pride and pleasure in

Hsin-ping and her high school swimming friends; she was Peking municipal under-15 champion in 1953

Hsin-ping (second from left, front row) *at Hebei Teachers' College, Peking, 1957*

Hsin-ping's 'Peach Blossom Spring' at Xiamen, 1966

At the Summer Palace, Peking, 1973
Left to right: Lulu (Hsin-ping's daughter), Fan Yilu (Fan Yuzhong's son), Third Aunt, Grandma and Hsin-ping

Hsin-ping and Grandma at Peking airport after Third Aunt's departure for the United States, 1973

Fan Yuzhong, Hsin-ping's cousin, at the Summer Palace, Peking, 1973

Father and daughter in Peking Opera costume: Xun Huisheng (top) in the 1930s and Xun Linglai c. 1980

their achievement considerably enhanced by anticipation of the national holidays which would follow. At precisely this moment the principal pulled up at the gateway, in the college car, and peered out at the archway. After a little while he alighted in order to venture the opinion that it was a mistake to put the two dates side by side on the banner, because they were not really of equal importance.

'May 1st is an international celebration, May 4th is only celebrated in China', he announced, with unassailable authority. 'May 4th is not as important as May 1st. The archway is fine but the banner is a problem. Who designed the archway?' Everybody had a hand in the archway, it seemed. 'Who designed the banner?' Hsin-ping was freely acknowledged to have been the sole inspiration.

After the principal had left, one of the students, who was particularly anxious to be seen as an 'activist', rushed over to the disgruntled Hsin-ping. 'Comrade Wang, Comrade Wang, there is a matter I must discuss with you', she said breathlessly.

'What matter? What is there to discuss?' snarled Comrade Wang, particularly annoyed at having to put up with the notorious little sycophant Ge Zhanyin on top of everything else.

'It's about the banner. Our principal says the banner has an error in it. It implies that May 1st and May 4th are of equal importance because the two days are mentioned side by side—and of course it is clear that May 1st is the more important date because it is International Labour Day.'

'Yes, yes, I can see what he means', said Hsin-ping, grudgingly, 'I can accept that his argument has some merit, but his timing has none at all. You know very well that we've all worked for weeks on this project and he has never been near us. Why is he taking such an interest now that we are all finished and getting ready to go on holiday? Doesn't he realize we've been up all night putting the finishing touches to this archway? Why doesn't he get down from his horse if he wants to look at the flowers?'

'Comrade Wang, you shouldn't speak that way', said Ge, recoiling from this blasphemy. 'It is our principal you are speaking of—and, what's more, the Party branch secretary agrees with him.'

'I don't care who he is—and as for you, you're like a cork in the boss's arse, popping out every time he farts. I don't care who he is—if he's wrong, he's wrong.'

The conversation was duly reported to the principal and Party branch secretary, and Hsin-ping was warned by friends that she had been informed on. Next time she saw Ge Zhanyin she bent double in front of her and, pointing over her shoulder, said, 'Come on, climb up on my back, I'll give you a ride.'

Not content with this, Hsin-ping went about for some time asking the other students, 'Do you know that our Party secretary Liu doesn't use

toilet paper?' In response to the puzzled looks that greeted her cryptic
remark, Hsin-ping would brandish a finger in the air. 'Ge Zhanyin
picks his arse for him', she would add by way of explanation, and then,
when her audience looked a little worried, she would protest in mock
innocence, 'What's the matter? I haven't said anything against our
leaders. I haven't used any dirty language. I have simply told you that
Party secretary Liu Daogong doesn't use toilet paper. What's wrong
with that?'

In due course, a fresh crop of big-character posters appeared around
the college—'Wang Hsin-ping opposes the Party's leadership! Wang
Hsin-ping opposes the report system!' She had not only criticized the
school's leaders, she had attacked the system by which they were kept
informed of recidivists in their midst. It was every conscientious
person's duty to report errors of speech and thought to the leaders and
Ge Zhanyin had simply been doing her duty.

As a result of these incidents, Hsin-ping was in serious trouble during
the 'Hundred Flowers' period, but she was saved from even greater
difficulty by a judicious voluntary application for a stint of manual
labour, which she did on the outskirts of the city for one month. Her
soul was cleansed in this way and her mind purged of impurities by the
uplifting experience of honest toil in the fields. More importantly, she
was out of harm's way for a while. She wrote ten thousand characters of
self-criticism and confession. This consisted of five hundred characters
written twenty times, stating that she had made mistakes in her
thinking. Among other things, she wrote, 'If only one or two of you
consider me to be in the wrong, then maybe I'm not in the wrong at all.
But obviously, if twenty or thirty of my classmates think I'm wrong,
then I must be'. She just had to allow herself this little piece of irony,
because, like Mao himself, she was not entirely convinced that right lay
with the majority. Unlike Mao, however, she was not in a position to
say so.

Hsin-ping's period of labour reform passed without serious mishaps,
and her fulsome admissions and confessions saved her from being
branded a rightist in the winter of 1958. Great Grandfather, on the other
hand, became an unlikely casualty of the political and economic
reforms of the period. A steel production drive had sent cadres scurrying about in search of combustible materials for small furnaces. When
the village bigshot heard that Old Li was planning to waste valuable
firewood by being buried in his precious coffin, he lost no time in
paying him a visit. He explained that the coffin was combustible
material, and that the old man would be demonstrating a much more
proletarian spirit if he were to be cremated, leaving his coffin to
industry. Great Grandfather himself was indeed combustible. A terrible

struggle ensued between the young man's ambitions for his life and the old man's for his death.

'You can't take my coffin', pleaded Great Grandfather, 'That is to be my final resting place.'

'Oh come on', said the cadre, 'You only need a coffin if you are dead. You're not dead are you? I'll tell you what . . . if you die you can have it. That's reasonable. Marxism-Leninism teaches us, "From each according to his ability, to each according to his need". Well, if you need it you can have it!'

No doubt the cadre thought he had blinded Great Grandfather with political science, but he had underestimated the old man's determination. He locked himself in his room, refused all food and drink and died after a week. He was buried in his coffin, aged eighty-eight. Everyone said he could have gone on for years.

The time was fast approaching for Hsin-ping's graduation, and its coincidence with the Party's thirty-seventh birthday, on 1 July 1958. It was also time for students to consider the problem of choosing a work assignment. Remote villages in poverty-stricken backwaters would not normally be expected among the stated preferences of young college graduates, but the heady atmosphere of revolutionary fervour and self-sacrifice led to whole departments competing against each other for mass demonstrations of commitment to 'the national assignment' —which meant, of course, the countryside. Every department wanted to be able to declare that 100 per cent of its students had voluntarily heeded the great call to go out into the countryside and help to build socialism.

Several meetings of the maths department were convened, and the need for a commitment to this sacred cause, no matter how bitter the prospects, was fervently stressed by Party representatives and academic staff members. At one such meeting late in June, the maths department secretary called out, 'Stand up all those who pledge to heed their motherland's call! Stand and swear an oath on it!' Not everyone stood up. That is, everyone except Hsin-ping stood up. As usual, she was not simply being defiant, or perverse, but was anxiously searching her soul. How *could* she swear to go anywhere she was sent? There were only her and Grandma at home. Who would look after the old lady if she was ill? Others had relations at home. It was all very well for them to take the oath, she would like to do it herself, but what kind of person would she be to swear to a commitment she might not be able to keep? And what kind of an oath would that be anyway? The voice of the department's Party secretary, shrill now as a result of his contemplation of Hsin-ping's seated form, broke in upon her thoughts. 'Stand up all those who disobey their motherland's command!' If he expected this manouevre to force Hsin-ping to her feet, he had miscalculated again. She did not stand, because, in her view, it was not her intention to disobey anything—she simply needed to clarify matters before she could make promises. The meeting dispersed and met again in the afternoon.

This time each student was armed with a page of criticism of Hsin-ping. For four hours she endured criticisms and denunciations from her fellow students. Ge Zhanyin was loudest in her condemnation: 'Your country has nurtured you and fostered you, and now you refuse to declare your allegiance. Stand up and answer for your actions!' Even the Party secretary thought this was getting a little hysterical, and he motioned impatiently to Ge to sit down. The meeting dispersed once again. Later that afternoon she was summoned to the secretary's office. Her mind was in turmoil, and her head thumping from the meeting. She was immediately confronted with a question about her refusal to take the oath. 'What's your problem?' he demanded.

'Well, if it was simply a matter of pledging myself to hardship, in order to serve my country, then I would have no hesitation in taking the oath. But my problem is I have to take care of my grandmother, and how can I swear the oath if I am unable to keep it.'

'So you disobey the motherland's command?'

'No, I'm not saying that ... I just can't promise to obey, that's all, because of what I have told you. What kind of person would I be to deliberately make a promise I knew I could not keep? That would make me a cheat and a liar.'

'Oh you don't know what you are or what you want', he snapped angrily. 'Tell me, what *do* you want?'

'I want to work in Peking.'

'So you want to work in Peking, do you?', he retorted sarcastically, 'And supposing I were to tell you that there is no work for you in Peking? The city has filled its quota of teachers.'

'But you told us some time ago that Peking Number Eighty-one Secondary School wants a maths teacher badly.'

He laughed contemptuously. 'You haven't thought much about your situation, have you young Miss? Do you really imagine that you would meet the criteria for that position?'

'But my results are good', she protested, in genuine surprise, 'I got fives in everything'. She left political study out of the argument for the moment.

'And I suppose you are a Party member or a member of the Communist Youth League?' he sneered.

'You know very well I'm not', she said.

'Well', he said triumphantly, 'Number Eighty-one Secondary School insists on Party membership as a prerequisite for their staff. That's to be expected, because the children are the sons and daughters of Party cadres, and why should they have anything less than Party members on their staff? They also want a young, unmarried female', he added, as if this were a casual afterthought.

'Well, I'm young, and female, and unmarried', said Hsin-ping, completely missing the point as usual. People's Liberation Army veterans ran Number Eighty-one and they knew their own minds when it came to selecting new recruits. 'Look, I don't want to disobey anything, that's not my intention at all, but if you don't find me a job in Peking, what's to become of my grandmother?'

'Tomorrow morning there will be another oath-taking ceremony', he announced abruptly, absolutely determined to bring the matter to an end. 'You will have another opportunity to redeem yourself.'

'But what if I can't?'

'Oh for . . . you just will not understand will you?' He thumped the table and shouted. 'Your family background is hopeless. Almost all your damned relatives are overseas. Your father is in Australia. Your father's elder brother is in America. Your mother's sister is in America. You may have difficulty leaving your family, but your family has no difficulty leaving you! You are a very suspect type. You have dangerous connections with foreigners and your background is full of class enemies. Do you know what would be done with your kind in the Soviet Union?'

'No', she said, crying now as she remembered what had happened to her last time Big Brother had entered her life. 'Your carcass would be chopped up and thrown to the dogs! You'd disappear from the face of the earth!' 'Do they kill people with bad class backgrounds?' she sobbed.

'Not necessarily . . . maybe if you were lucky, you'd be sent to Siberia, to a labour camp. But here, you ungrateful wretch, the Party looks after you, educates you, gives you an honoured career as a teacher. And how do you repay the Party, which has been like father and mother to you? You want to pick and choose where you would like to work!' His tone was menacing now. 'It's not up to you, madam, to pick and choose. You'll go where you're damn well sent, and think yourself lucky! You, of all people, cannot afford to be laying down conditions.'

She looked up defiantly, the tears streaming down her cheeks. 'All right, all right. I'll go where I'm sent. Why didn't you just order me to go in the first place? Why order me to pretend that it's my idea to go to some remote place? An oath should not be compulsory. It should be from the heart, otherwise it's a lie and a fraud.'

The secretary began to shout at the top of his voice. 'Wang Hsin-ping, I have wasted enough time on arguing the point with you. Why are you so stupid? I thought you were intelligent, a good student, and

here you are just a wooden-headed dummy! Like some village
bumpkin. Don't you see? The maths department wants to show the
college administration that we all unhesitatingly, 100 per cent, every
one of us, pledge our hearts to the service of the Party, and we want to
make the pledge on the occasion of our Party's birthday, on 1 July. All
we are asking is that you take the oath, and don't spoil it for the rest of
us. Whether you keep your promise or change your blasted mind is
another matter entirely. Worry about that later.'

'Then just tell me what you want me to do', she said miserably. 'Just
tell me and get it over with.'

'Make the pledge. That's all you have to do. Make your pledge, and
worry about everything else later.'

At the 1 July celebration, the maths department assembled in the hall,
preceded by a large heart-shaped box, carried on poles like the Ark of
the Covenant. Inside the box, which was made of silk, were the pages of
a book containing the names of all those who had pledged their hearts
to the Party, and would accept the national work assignment. Some had
cut themselves and signed their names in blood in the book. When
everyone was seated in the hall, a solemn call went up from the school's
Party branch secretary, 'All those who heed our motherland's call,
stand up!' This time everyone stood up.

4

粉笔生涯

A Career in Chalk

In the summer of 1958 Hsin-ping set out for Zhangjiakou, a large prefecture outside Peking. She reported first of all to the County Education Bureau in the township of Zhangjiakou. The Bureau chief, a P.L.A. veteran, informed her that she was to be sent to a place called Qiongli, which was in a county two days by rail and bus from Peking. He asked her if she had any comments or requests. 'Well, yes', she said, returning to a troubled theme, 'my family consists only of me and my grandmother. It's not easy for her living on her own, and I really need to look after her and to see her frequently. This is a very big prefecture, and most places need maths teachers badly. I was wondering if you could assign me to a place within the prefecture that is closer to Peking. You know, from the place I am assigned to it is very difficult to get home. I have to spend a day on the bus and then take a train. Sometimes, if it's been raining or snowing, there's no bus.'

The Bureau chief began looking through Hsin-ping's personal file, a thick dossier containing records of her life from primary school to secondary, details of her family members, secret reports made on her by others, and commentary on particular incidents like the matter of the Young Pioneers and the Chu Anping article.

'Let's see', he mumbled as he browsed through the file, 'None of your relatives has been sentenced to death . . . None are in gaol . . . You did have some trouble last year, but, yes . . . your self-criticism is pretty thorough

... Your main problem seems to be your class and family background. You have a good many relatives abroad, haven't you?' Suddenly he looked up from the file, 'You know your position is very precarious don't you? I'm looking at the final assessment of your class status, made after the anti-rightist movement last year. Your position is to the right of middle.'

In keeping with the Chinese love of numbers and categories, society had been divided into three groups—right, middle and left. Each group in turn had its own three sub-divisions of right, middle and left. Not surprisingly, most people were in the middle category of the middle group. At opposite extremes were the *hongqi*, or 'red flags', who were revolutionary activists, and the *jiyoufenzi*, or active counter-revolutionaries, who were either in gaol or doing manual labour. Hsin-ping was a *zhong-you*, a member of the right-of-middle category, and as such, her soul was always in mortal danger.

'Your position is extremely dangerous', warned the chief. 'During Party movements you are inclined to resonate with counter-revolutionaries. Have you noticed that? You are like a tuning fork, which cannot help but send out the same old note when it strikes a counter-revolutionary influence. When rightists start to warble their opinions, you are inclined to sing along, as you did with Chu Anping. The only reason you have not been coloured in as a counter-revolutionary is because of your thorough self-criticism. Nevertheless, I am quite satisfied myself that you are indeed a rightist. That is your nature.'

Hsin-ping was stunned. 'Look, I only meant to ask, since Zhangjiakou is such a big place, and you must really want teachers everywhere so badly in this prefecture ... '

'Yes, yes, but how badly do you want the *revolution*', he asked, gazing intently at her.

'Well I came *here* didn't I?' she replied tactlessly, and then added, rather hastily, 'I obeyed the command of the Party and my motherland and came here to help in the work of socialist reconstruction'.

'Oh yes, picking over your bowl, finding the fat and leaving the lean. That is hardly what I would call being a revolutionary.'

'But I'm not picking and choosing', she argued, panic mounting as she recognized that she was up against a familiar type of authority, which felt no need to make any kind of sense at all to a subordinate. 'I obeyed my country's call. It's just that you asked me if I have any request, and I have one, which I explained to you, openly and honestly. Zhangjiakou is a big place. If you could possibly find me a posting a little closer to Peking, somewhere where they need a maths teacher, why not send me there? That's all I'm saying. I just want to take care of my grandmother, who is alone and cannot ... '

'Do you want the revolution or your grandmother?' he snapped. 'If you do not want the revolution you must be a counter-revolutionary.'

Swept along in the inexorable march of military logic, and relishing the prospect of mopping up pockets of resistance, he rounded fiercely on her. 'And if you are a counter-revolutionary you are in great danger. You are very young, only twenty, still unmarried, yet to set up home and career. What will become of you in the future if you start out like this?'

Hsin-ping began to think she might well be sentenced to death before she managed to extricate herself from his thought processes. She tried to justify herself. 'Look, I admit I haven't thought much about the future. I didn't really intend to discuss the future at all. I thought you might be able to help me with the present. You asked me if I had any request. I told you. Now you tell me I am a counter-revolutionary.'

'Yes, yes, well, you just go away and think about it some more', he said abruptly, irritated that her protestations were interrupting his faultless situation report.

Hsin-ping went back into the town, to the temporary guesthouse accommodation she had to take because there was no dormitory. The next day she was ill. Her leg swelled up in a painful allergic reaction of some sort. For once her symptoms were genuine. The climate and conditions were quite different from Peking and it often took people years to adapt. She had been in the area for only a matter of days. She went to see a doctor in the local hospital.

'Oh, you have a very bad allergic swelling, I'm afraid. I suggest you need a good rest.'

'But I'm not from around here. I'm from Peking. If I'm to take time off from work I'll have to go back home. There's no accommodation here.'

'All right', said the doctor obligingly, 'You can go back to Peking, that's no problem at all. I can give you a certificate for a month off work.'

She went back to the Bureau chief, who had by now forgotten that she was a class enemy and seemed much more reasonable. 'All right, fine, no problem, have a month off. Go back to Peking. I'll give you a certificate for registration as a temporary Peking city resident.'

'But', said Hsin-ping, presuming upon his change of mood, 'supposing I'm not cured after a month, and I need to extend my sick leave? What would I do then? I can't get grain coupons without my residential registration book.'

'I can fix that', said the chief, as if nothing were too much trouble when it came to demonstrating his powers. 'I'll give you a certificate authorising you to take your book back to Peking with you. Take whatever leave is necessary, and when your time is up, simply bring it back here and we'll transfer it to our files again.'

Neither Hsin-ping nor, presumably, the Bureau chief had any idea of the implications of this arrangement, but the convalescent wasted no time packing her bags for Peking.

One day, soon after she arrived home, she went shopping. As she stood in a queue, she noticed a man in front of her clutching a folder, on which was written the name of a friend—Gong Rizhen. It had to be the girl she had known at college, because it was a most unusual name.

'Excuse me', she said, 'But that folder you're holding has the name of a former classmate of mine written on it. Was that person who owns the folder once at Hebei Teachers' College?' As she asked, she recalled the girl's personality, her burning ardour for the Party and her solemn oaths that she would follow the motherland's call to the ends of the earth. She had been a Party member and an activist.

'Yes', the man replied, 'that's her. Do you know her? She's in Peking now you know.'

'But I thought she was sent to some really remote place', said Hsin-ping, thoroughly puzzled.

'Oh yes', he explained, 'she was sent all right. And she went. But naturally you couldn't expect her to *stay* in a place like that. No, no, she got some friends to help her to get back to Peking.'

Some days later she bumped into Du, another former classmate, a very pretty girl who had vied with the keenest activists in her devotion to the Party.

'How come you're in Peking', asked Hsin-ping, 'I thought you'd gone to Xinjiang or something?'

'Oh no', said Du, quite surprised at the question. 'I'm married to an overseas Chinese and we live together here in Peking.'

Another day, while shopping in the streets around Xuanwumen, she met Cui Weimin. Hsin-ping had introduced him to her good friend Xun Linglai, and they had married. He was always an artful type, old Cui, and, although he was not a Party member, he had still contrived to have himself considered something of an activist. Hsin-ping remembered the tears in his eyes as he let his own blood to swear his oath. Once again she asked her question.

'What are you doing here in Peking? I thought you'd gone to Baoding?'

'Yes, well I had a friend who helped me get back to Peking. I'm at Number Twenty-seven Secondary.'

'But you swore an oath.'

'Wang Hsin-ping', said Cui, shaking his head in disbelief, and reaching into his endless store of aphorisms and proverbs, 'One who considers a thousand things may still miss the obvious!' Anyway, forget it. The point is, I'm now at Number Twenty-seven and doing nicely. My only problem is that I don't have my household registration book.'

'What are you talking about? How come you didn't bring the book with you when you came back to Peking?' demanded Hsin-ping.

Cui looked at her in exasperation, wondering whether it was worth his while even to attempt an explanation.

'Listen, melon head, they don't give you your book back when you leave a place. If only they did!'

'But the Bureau chief at Zhangjiakou gave me mine. I can keep it till my sick leave is up and then hand it in when I go back.'

Cui gave her shoulder a mighty thump. 'What!? You're joking. Do you mean to tell me ... do you know what this means? I'd give anything for my book. I have to stay here illegally with my parents and live off their rations, because I can't get food coupons without my registration book. But you ... you can stay as long as you like, get your coupons, get a job ... you don't have to go back to Zhangjiakou ever again, if you don't want to! You lucky little shit!!'

Hsin-ping was dumbfounded. She had considered looking around for work in Peking, but had resigned herself to the likelihood of failure and inevitable return to the land of swollen limbs. She never dreamt that the crackpot old P.L.A. officer in the Education Bureau had handed her the key to Peking. Unlike Cui, she would not be declared 'black', and could apply openly for work, and even in times of hardship she would not starve. With new-found confidence as a result of her stroke of immense good luck, she went along to the Education Bureau in Peking, in search of a job.

'Oh no, not another one', said the Bureau chief, 'It's always the same around here. Everyone swears to accept the national work assignment. Next thing you know, they're back on our doorstep wanting to know if we have work for them in the city. Nobody wants to obey orders.'

'But', protested Hsin-ping, 'I'm not trying to disobey any orders. I'm sick.'

'Oh, so you're sick, are you? Well, that's different, isn't it? If you're sick, you can't work. If you can't work, you need rest. If you need rest, why are you hanging around pestering me for work? Go home!'

Hsin-ping forgot about teaching for a while. She saw quite a bit of Tang Ling and Cui Weimin and Xun Linglai during this time. Since two of her best friends were now married, her own thoughts turned to finding a partner and, as usual, there was no shortage of friends willing to act as introduction agency and go-between. Hsin-ping had a clear list of demands. Her partner should be tall, well-built, preferably of southern origin, somewhere in Jiangsu or Zhejiang—because they were more elegant and refined than northeners—and he should be some sort of scientist. She also rather hoped, for reasons which she did not state publicly, that he would have a shapely bottom.

Tang Ling took her shopping list, and in due course came up with a possibility. Her own husband, Lao Zhuang, was a doctor at the Children's Hospital, and a pianist in the hospital's band. Occasionally, the Architects' Trade Union invited Lao Zhuang to play at the dances held on Saturday nights in the architects' dormitory. At Tang Ling's suggestion, Lao Zhuang invited Hsin-ping and introduced her to a friend—who happened to be tall, well-built, a southerner and an architectural engineer.

Towards the end of 1958, after a few months of courtship, Hsin-ping married her southerner. In March 1959, she became pregnant, and in December gave birth to a girl, whose given name—Lulu—was a fortuitous combination of east and west. After a short period at home looking after the new baby, Hsin-ping returned to a job which Tang Ling had found for her.

Tang Ling was working as a draftsman in a commercial arts company in the Xuanwu District, just a little south of Grandma's house, and of the architects' dormitory where Hsin-ping now lived with her husband and child. Hsin-ping was given the same sort of work. It was not exactly in her line, but her fastidious attention to detail and her love of measurement and calculation made her a more than satisfactory worker. She quite enjoyed the task of designing maps, charts and tables and drawing things to scale. After a year and a half, the company amalgamated with another a long way from her home, and she had to start looking for work in the Western District. She could easily have found something in a similar line, but she really wanted to find her niche.

After nearly a year out of work, she went back to the Education Bureau, on the recommendation of the Xuanwu District Unemployment Office. It was now 1963 and the situation had changed dramatically. There was a shortage of teachers and they had no trouble finding a job for her. Hsin-ping began her preparations for teaching. This would be a new experience. Although trained as a teacher, she had never actually taught, and was quite apprehensive about the experience. She went along to the school, near You'anmen, a little west of Taoranting Park, during the summer holiday period, and pestered any teachers she could find about teaching methods and textbooks. On the first day of the new school year, like the Yellow River breaking its banks, a great roaring wave of children burst through the school gates and into Hsin-ping's life. From now on she would be Teacher Wang.

Her first crisis was not long coming. It was brought on by a film— *Feidao Hua*—about a young boy who was a knife-thrower in a circus, before Liberation. Ironically, the film was supposed to demonstrate the terrible suffering of children before the Revolution and to impress upon the present generation that throwing sharp objects about the place was extremely dangerous. In fact, interest in sharp-object-throwing was at an all-time high after the film promoted its message, and one day a boy in Hsin-ping's class was perfecting his technique as she explained the mysteries of square-roots. Suddenly a series of loud sobs interrupted her lesson.

'What's up now?' she barked.

The unfortunate girl whose leg had come between the master knife-thrower and his target could barely manage to gurgle out her accusation, 'He ... he ... he cut my leg'.

'Stand up!' commanded Teacher Wang, 'Give me all your knives and bits of metal! I am confiscating them!'

Unfortunately for Hsin-ping's attempt at law and order, 'The Flying Knife' was not at all overawed by her impressive display of authority, did not stand up, did not surrender his arsenal, but instead began calling out at the top of his voice, 'Donkey fart! Donkey fart!' His witty riposte struck such a chord with the other children that, for the rest of the lesson, whenever she opened her mouth to speak she provoked a chorus of 'donkey farts'. The walls were still resounding with this when she fled in tears to the sanctuary of the staffroom.

Hsin-ping explained her difficulties to a colleague, an old and experienced teacher who was noted for his command of the techniques of discipline. She had noticed that, whenever he entered his classroom, all noise ceased immediately. It made her think of the expression 'a lone bird flies into the forest and all others fall silent'. The effect of her own entry was rather more like the sudden eruption of cicadas on a summer day. And yet this old teacher achieved his remarkable control without raising his voice or becoming the least bit excited. Most of the time you were hard pressed to determine if he was even awake. On the rare occasions when some foolhardy creature ventured to speak out of turn during his lessons, he would pause from whatever he was saying, wait several seconds as a terrible anticipation spread through the room, and then say very deliberately, 'What? What's that you say? Oh, please, *please* say it again! Let's have it published in the *People's Daily*! Everyone must learn from you.'

If his charges were disinclined to labour diligently at their tasks, or to listen attentively to his every word, he would say, 'You don't feel like working? Well, neither do I. Let's all have a rest. I get paid the same whatever you do, so why should *I* work?' These methods were apparently very successful, as was his habit of asking to 'see' a student in the staffroom after school. He would smoke a cigarette, drink a cup of tea, smoke another cigarette, mark some homework exercises, drink another cup of tea—all while the hapless wrongdoer stood by his desk, shifting his weight from one foot to the other in discomfort and embarrassment, tormented by the cries of unrestrained glee from freer souls in the playground. He rarely had to deal with second offenders.

Hsin-ping sought his advice and he gave it freely enough, but she could not really imitate his style. She was too preoccupied with being sincere to make a decent fist of sarcasm, but she developed a technique of her own that was every bit as tiresome from the students' point of view. 'Aha, what's this?' she would suddenly exclaim, on discovering an item she would once have confiscated. 'How interesting! Please stay behind after class for a while and we'll look at it together.' Hsin-ping was not simply finding a pretext for detention—she actually intended to demonstrate to students that she was capable of sharing their interest in some strange bauble or gadget, and did not wish to deprive them of it. She considered that she was being a friend, an equal, demolishing artificial barriers between herself and her students and, above all, avoiding the terrible pitfalls of making an enemy of the children by seizing their property. 'After all', she thought, drawing inspiration from the history of the Revolution, 'Look at the Eighth Route Army and the Rules for Discipline in liberated areas when dealing with the peasants. You must not misappropriate the property of those you are supposed to be liberating!'

It never occurred to her that the students might not *want* to share their treasures with her, or that the major deterrent was the shame and irritation of having the confounded teacher participate earnestly in an activity which was specifically designed to *annoy* her. Some of her methods were genuinely appreciated by her students, in particular her refreshing, and rare, habit of admitting the gaps in her knowledge. Most teachers resorted to a very different tactic: 'What? You don't know *that*? It's hardly worth bothering, if you don't even know a thing like *that*!'

Eventually Hsin-ping became a class teacher and took on overall responsibility for a group of children, including the organization of extra-curricular activities. In this capacity she was often to be seen in Taoranting Park on Saturday afternoons, organizing a clean-up, and helping her charges to 'learn from Lei Feng'. Lei Feng was a young hero of the P.L.A. who had kept a diary in which he noted down all the 'anonymous' good deeds he had done for his comrades. He had been canonized in the Chinese fashion after he had been killed in an accident. Thanks to Lei Feng, whose diary was posthumously published, thousands of young Chinese, especially those anxious to join the Communist Youth League, had begun keeping comprehensive diaries of their own, containing richly detailed accounts of their anonymous good deeds. Many of these fell fortuitously into the hands of those responsible for processing applications to join the C.Y.L. In some P.L.A. units, such was the enthusiasm that the alert philanthropist, before going in search of a comrade's blanket to mend anonymously, had first to hide his own, in case a rival Lei Feng managed to get to it while he was out, thus cancelling out the moral profit margin.

In Hsin-ping's school, things had not quite come to this, and students contented themselves with such things as going down to the railway station and cleaning the windows of passing trains. There were occasional excesses, such as attacking the windows before the train had stopped, or making the passengers close windows that they wanted open. Many of the passengers, unacquainted with the spirit of Lei Feng, took the unhelpful view that it didn't matter if a window was clean or not when it was open.

Life was temporarily pleasant and satisfying for Hsin-ping in her new role as class teacher. If there was one discordant note, it was her relationship with some of the girls in the class. They were tidy and attentive and obedient and, unlike the boys, gave her no trouble when they were left unsupervised, but Hsin-ping felt that she had little rapport with them and that they didn't really like her. Nevertheless, Hsin-ping had, almost without knowing it, become a teacher—and would remain one.

5

牛 鬼 蛇 神

Ox Demons and Snake Spirits

Throughout 1963 and 1964 the Socialist Education Movement ebbed and flowed, reaching high and low tides of radicalism. It had begun in September 1962, coinciding with an open split between China and the Soviet Union over matters of foreign policy, and had been initially associated with the 'four clean-ups', an attempt to eliminate cadre corruption in areas such as the allocation of work points, the administration of granaries, and the keeping of accounts. From this it spread into a general and more radical call for reform of politics, economics, ideology and organization. The People's Liberation Army, under Lin Biao, took a leading role in the movement, and by January 1963 had installed Lei Feng as a model of revolutionary self-sacrifice. It also began to publish selected works of Mao.

Jiang Qing, Mao's wife, took a keen interest in literature and art, areas which had long engaged her husband's attention. In particular, she became interested in Peking Opera and revolutionary opera. However, by the spring of 1965 it appeared that much of the radicalism of this period, which had never entirely escaped the constraints of conservatism, had been well and truly blunted. Then came the beginnings of a new movement, in which 'proletarian culture' was to be the inspiration for a great new revolution, in which all the backward and bourgeois tendencies of the years since Liberation would be swept away.

From the end of 1965 to the beginning of 1966, the newspapers carried a number of crucial articles and editorials. There was, to begin with, an article by an almost unknown author, Yao Wenyuan, who became an immensely important figure overnight as a result of his 'On the New Historical Play, Hai Rui Dismissed From Office'. This was an attack on Wu Han, deputy mayor of Peking and a respected scholar and writer, who had written *Hai Rui Dismissed from Office*, a historical drama commemorating a Ming emperor's dismissal of a loyal official. The allegorical implication was that the Communist Party had unjustly treated many loyal and honest intellectuals, whom it had characterized as 'right opportunists'. Wu Han was himself now characterized as an 'anti-Party, anti-socialist representative of the bourgeoisie', and the stage was set for the Great Proletarian Cultural Revolution. An unknown figure, writing an abstruse criticism of a minor play about an obscure historical figure had sparked off a conflagration that would blaze for a decade.

Yao Wenyuan also wrote 'A Critique of Three Family Village', an attack on three literary figures, including Wu Han, who had written popular articles in two Peking newspapers in the early 1960s. *Three Family Village* was a sort of composite pen-name made up of the names of the contributors, who intended to affect the spirit of rustic simplicity of a tiny Chinese village—a sort of idyllic atmosphere giving rise to homespun philosophy. The three 'villagers'—Wu Han, Deng Tuo, editor of a Party organ called *Frontline*, and Liao Mosha, a Peking Party committee member—were suddenly involved in an ominous controversy about whether their opinions should be tolerated in the interests of intellectual freedom, or whether they were dangerous counter-revolutionaries. When Yao Wenyuan entered the lists, by means of his article, printed in two Shanghai newspapers on 10 May 1966, the question was settled and the status of these writers as 'rightists' was put beyond doubt. Despite the warning signs, the academic nature of these articles deceived many like Hsin-ping into thinking that they had little bearing on the practicalities of everyday life.

A circular of the Central Committee, dated 16 May 1966, made it clear that leadership in this new Cultural Revolution had passed from the faction surrounding the mayor of Peking, Peng Zhen, to a group led by Jiang Qing, and that discussion on academic and cultural matters had entered a new phase. Increasingly, life in schools and colleges in Peking was dominated by discussion of newspaper editorials and the preparation of political slogans in the form of big-character posters. On 1 June the Party sounded an 'alarm', through an editorial in the *People's Daily*, entitled 'Sweep Away All Ox Demons and Snake Spirits'. In this article the term 'Great Proletarian Cultural Revolution' officially superseded 'Great Socialist Cultural Revolution'.

The 'ox demons and snake spirits' article expounded Mao's theme that the class struggle between bourgeoisie and proletariat had not finished in China. Revolutionaries should be constantly vigilant for the restoration of capitalism, not only by political and economic means, but through the spread of bourgeois ideology in the form of the old culture, customs and habits. Editorial after editorial appeared in the *People's Daily*. On 4 June, revolutionaries were enjoined to 'strip away the fig leaf of bourgeois liberty, equality and fraternity'. These principles were seen as 'black banners', reinstating bourgeois illusions in the place of true revolution—a 'modesty cloth' which disguised the political pudenda of revisionists. Keen but imperfectly trained translators often carried the metaphor a little too far in the later English version and went on to say that the 'fig leaf' concealed the 'tool of the bourgeois revisionists'. At any rate, no amount of clothing could make a revisionist 'decent' it seemed, especially when the *People's Daily* kept stripping him bare.

In the universities, Party 'work teams' were set up to identify and expose bourgeois elements and, under their leadership, the target tended to change from Party cadres to academics. The schools, in imitation, set up leadership groups called 'preparatory committees'.

In Hsin-ping's school, this preparatory committee would consist of five teachers; they were elected by the staff, but eligibility was very restricted. To be considered, one had to be from one of the 'five red' backgrounds—that is, from worker, peasant, P.L.A, revolutionary cadre or revolutionary martyr background. One hot summer day, from ten in the morning and throughout the night until two the following morning, the school held a meeting to determine who would constitute the committee. Every one of the forty-odd staff members recited his or her life story, following closely a text already made public through open access to personal dossiers containing family histories. As someone near Hsin-ping remarked, this wasn't so bad with the younger ones, but the confessions of the more long-lived staff members unwound interminably 'like an old woman's foot-binding', inch by putrid and painful inch.

The prospect of power had already turned former friends against each other in the run-up to the election. Every day, those who were serious contenders had been out gathering 'materials' against rivals. Finally, five names were announced as successful candidates, and control of the school's affairs passed from the Party branch to the preparatory committee. Suddenly, a number of teachers began to suffer 'exposure'. Big-character posters, denouncing various members of staff, began to appear around the school.

Among the first to be named was Teacher Zhang, an old woman who was highly respected throughout the school as she had long occupied an influential position. She had been a school principal in the Nationalist period and, as a result, had also been a nominal Nationalist Party member. She was in fact a principal only in the sense that she had worked in a one-teacher village school, and a Party member only in the sense that the Nationalists had declared all school principals to be Party members. Her name had been listed thus by the local Education Bureau which administered her district. She had never applied for Party membership and was quite unaware that she *was* a member. Even if she had known, she would not have acted any differently. She just did her job.

After 1949, she came to her new school and worked under Comrade Bai, an old Communist Party member who had been a teacher in one of the liberated areas. Bai was an ignorant and incompetent woman whose only real claim to distinction was her husband's exalted position in the Party; she often called on Zhang's experience to help her out of difficulties. They got on well together and formed an effective team, but Bai relied more and more on Zhang as a sort of unofficial secretary.

The one impediment to the arrangement was Zhang's restricted access to Communist Party documents. Since she was not a Party member she was often forbidden access to the very policy documents which Bai had to interpret and implement in the school. Bai could not manage without Zhang's advice, so she urged her to apply for Party membership. Zhang protested that she was not interested, would probably not meet the stringent criteria for membership and so on, but Bai would not hear of it. Finally, to settle the argument, she filled in the application form on Zhang's behalf, and in due course Zhang was accepted. She was now a member of both the Nationalist and the Communist parties, having applied to neither.

Unfortunately, this kind of duplicity made her an ideal target for the newly formed preparatory committee, which was keen to cut its teeth on a class enemy. She was interrogated by members of the committee in her room in the school's dormitory. After some hours they emerged, leaving her with blood flowing freely from her temples, muttering pathetically, 'I don't know, I don't know'. It was announced that Zhang had made a full and frank confession of her crimes. It didn't matter in the least that she didn't know what the members of the preparatory committee were talking about—after all, *they* did.

All in all, eight teachers were exposed, including Liu, a young woman who was unmarried but had attracted the interest of a number of suitors over a period of time. She was simply in no hurry to marry, but her circumspection led her to be branded a 'delinquent.' Then the preparatory committee announced that there were sixteen others in the school who remained to be denounced. Hsin-ping felt certain she would be one of them.

August came, and with it the Eleventh Plenum of the Chinese Communist Party, held in Peking from 1 to 12 August. In essence, the plenum
emphasized Mao's theories about the continual nature of the ideological
struggle between the proletariat and bourgeoisie, and urged the proletarian forces to expose 'capitalist roaders' in positions of authority and
influence. Revolutionaries were enjoined to root out bourgeois
academics in the process of transforming education, art and literature.
On 8 August the Central Committee published the document which
would be known as the 'sixteen points'. The masses were exhorted to
'transform the old educational system and the old principles and
methods of teaching', and to change the 'phenomenon of . . . schools
being dominated by bourgeois intellectuals'.

In many ways it was convenient for the Party 'capitalist roaders' that
'bourgeois intellectuals' were singled out for attention. The Party
branch secretary in Hsin-ping's school, for example, may well have had
his own troubles but for the timely expedient of *gongbu dang'an* (public
exposure of dossiers on all teaching staff). This tended to take the heat
off Party cadres as the preparatory committee peered into the files
looking for hidden reactionaries. Lest their enthusiasm should wane,
the Party organs continued to sound frequent alarms about the enemy
in their midst.

In due course Hsin-ping found herself once more in the office of a Party
official, explaining her past misdemeanours. She spoke yet again of the
'attitude problem' she had had in 1957, and how she had undergone a
thorough self-criticism during the anti-rightist movement. He did not
seem satisfied with this offering.

'Where is your father?'

'In Australia.'

'Your father's elder brother?'

'In America.'

'Your mother's younger sister?'

'In America.'

'Do you write to them?'

Hsin-ping had in fact received letters from her father, because he had
begun to resume his interest in having her come to live with him in
Australia. During the 'three hard years' from 1959 to 1961, when economic disaster followed the 'Great Leap Forward', he had also sent
tinned foodstuffs to her and Grandma, through the agency of an uncle
in Hong Kong and an aunt in Canton. The oil, meat, fish and fruit were
very welcome, but Hsin-ping had only replied once to his letters and
that was to ask him not to write again because it was too dangerous. 'I
have written to my father once', she said, well aware that this might
have been once too often.

'So', he bellowed, triumphantly, '*litong waiguo!*' He was quoting from the twelfth of the sixteen points which had said that scientists and technical personnel who did not have 'illicit' dealings with foreign countries should be treated according to the policy of 'criticism which preserves unity'. They could be helped to reform their 'work-style' in spite of bourgeois expert mentality. Unfortunately, the full text of the twelfth point did not make it at all clear just what kinds of dealings with foreign countries were 'illicit'. It simply used the phrase '*litong waiguo*', and this came to denote a kind of political promiscuity which covered the whole range of relationships from pen-pal to prostitute.

Hsin-ping left the secretary's office in distress and alarm. Her crime had been given a name. It was no longer simply a matter of her bad background which, theoretically at least, did not prevent her from being accepted as a useful member of society. Now she was a potential class enemy. Maintaining that her 'connections' were open and above board and none of her doing was of no more use than her earlier protestations that she had not 'disobeyed the call of the motherland'. Things were very serious, but there was nothing for it but to get back to work and keep her head down as much as possible.

On 18 August 1966, Mao received a million young revolutionaries in Tian'anmen Square as hordes of ardent students poured out of schools and universities, burning to smash the 'four olds' and raise up the 'four news' in their place. Old ideology, customs, habits and culture had to make way for the new. Mao spoke to one of the million and changed her life forever—and her name, as befitted one who was reborn. When, in a moment which conferred immortality upon her, Mao had asked her name, she had replied 'Song Binbin' (elegant, refined Song). Mao exhorted her to revolutionary action with the words '*Yao wu*' (To arms). From that moment on she styled herself Song Yaowu, and excelled in feats of blood, if not of arms. The young revolutionaries also had a new name, 'Red Guards', and, with their ardour blessed and consecrated by Mao himself, they went forth to 'wash the city clean with blood'.

In order to be close to her school, Hsin-ping had moved back in with Grandma and had left Lulu with her husband in the architects' dormitory. There was no reason yet to fear for their safety, since the trouble had not spread to the Yuetan District, but the campaign to 'smash the four olds' posed a terrible threat to Hsin-ping herself, and to Grandma. Although Grandma was of respectable poor peasant background, she lived in a former gentry household, surrounded by bric-a-brac and memorabilia of imperial times, any one item of which might lead to their doom. Red Guards were visiting police stations and examining the personal files of local people, in order to get some idea of which families would be likely to reward their quest for specimens of the 'four olds'. Grandfather's photographs of his student days in Japan, and of himself in full ministerial regalia, were just the kind of thing that might destroy his surviving family. There were also the boxes of jewellery which Grandma kept all over the house, and clothing sent from overseas by solicitous relatives. There was even a mirror, sent from Europe, and many priceless Chinese antiques, including mahogany and satinwood furniture.

Hsin-ping set about coaching Grandma for the inevitable confrontation with the Red Guards.

'If you are asked, "What is your background?" what will you say?'

'I come from a poor peasant family.'

'Good, but what kind of poor peasant family?'

'Dirt poor peasants.'

'No, no, you'll get us all killed. You have to show respect for the poor and lower-middle peasants and use polite words when you refer to them. Don't say "dirt poor", say "destitute".'

'What does destitute mean?'

'It means poverty-stricken, no money, no land, nothing.'

'Well, that's what I said isn't it, child? Why do you never listen to your grandmother?'

'What about your father?'

'What about him?'

'You know, you should say what kind of peasant he was.'

'He was a farm worker.'

'Yes, yes, of course Grandma, but tell me, what *kind* of farm worker?'

'A poor one.'

'Not just poor, but destitute. A hired, propertyless, slave of the exploiting landowning class . . . '

'But *we* own land now.'

'Grandma, please . . . you can get into serious trouble . . . don't talk about how many houses we own, just talk about being poor in the bitter past . . . and don't forget to say "destitute".'

'Poor is poor', said Grandma, having the last word as usual.

After a number of exchanges of this kind, Hsin-ping turned her attention to the house and furniture. Two chests of photographs were torn up and burnt in the stove, or flushed down the Western-style toilet. Fortunately for her peace of mind, she did not have time to ponder the dilemma of whether the toilet was to be exalted because it was not one of the 'olds' or cast out because it was foreign. The furniture posed the biggest problem. She agonized over it for many hours, knowing it was a prime target, but she just could not bring herself to get rid of the beautiful chairs and tables, or the prized full-length European mirror. Then she had a brainwave. She wrote out sheet after sheet of quotations from Chairman Mao and pasted them all over tables, chairs and the mirror. 'Now let's see who will strike the first blow!' she thought with satisfaction. Already some of the Red Guards had been castigated for inadvertently snipping through quotations from Mao which were printed on the other side of some picture or article they wished to cut out of a newspaper. There were also cases in which some had earned severe criticism for defacing their copies of the Selected Works by making notes in the margin. How could they desecrate furniture which had been redeemed from an unworthy and useless past and converted into instruments of revolution, adorned with sacred texts?

After this, Hsin-ping replaced all the photographs, scrolls and calligraphy in the house with posters of Chairman Mao. Even this was no guarantee of safety, however. A rumour had spread that certain of these posters were considered counter-revolutionary. As panic spread, it became clear what the source of the trouble was. The older posters—photographic reprints—had shown the Chairman in semi-profile, with only one ear visible, namely the right one. It was alleged that the designers were intending to pull off some secret counter-revolutionary propaganda work by suggesting that Mao's true political orientation was to the right. Those who bought or displayed the offending poster were obviously part of a general plot, in which the ear would act as a secret symbol for the maintenance of an underground movement. After August there had been a rush on the shops for two-eared Mao posters, and an inevitable shortage followed.

One old woman, who lived in one of the rooms of a nearby house occupied by several families, was unable to get the approved portrait. One day, Red Guards came stomping into the courtyard, looking for the son of a former landlord, whose background they had discovered from dossiers in the local police station. The old woman didn't realize they were not looking for her, and thought they had come for counter-revolutionaries who displayed one-eared Mao portraits on their walls. She had been unable to replace her old poster and had not yet taken it down. When she heard the Red Guards, she snatched the picture down and began tearing it into strips. Suddenly she was aware of a presence in the room, just as she was hiding fragments of the poster under her bed.

A young man caught her arm, and took the tell-tale pieces of paper from her hand. He abused her savagely for desecrating Mao's image and she was taken back to the school for a 'struggle meeting'—a progression from the earlier 'criticism' meetings, which had been harrowing enough for their victims but usually non-violent. She was hoisted onto a high platform set up on the school's playing fields and, in front of the whole school, students and staff, was denounced for her crime by a teacher in her thirties, the daughter of a high-ranking railway

official. As the leader of the preparatory committee, she had renamed
herself Shan Dong, (one who fanned the flames of the revolutionary
movement). Her sleeves rolled up, she shrieked out at the assembly,
'Our great leader Chairman Mao says, "Counter-revolutionary forces
are no stronger than the instruments which do their bidding! If you do
not smash these instruments, the edifice of counter-revolution will not
fall!" Comrades, what do you say? Do we smash these instruments or
don't we?' 'Smash them, smash them!' screamed the students.

So the old woman, of poor peasant background, whose son was in
the P.L.A., had her hands beaten raw, till frail little bones showed
through the flesh down to her wrists, so that her hands could never
again be used as instruments of counter-revolution. Hsin-ping and
many others stood helplessly by, choking back tears of horror, shock
and rage, at a sight which would never leave them.

Hsin-ping's feelings were numbed by the dread thought that it might
be her turn, or Grandma's, at any moment. The sixteen remaining reactionaries had still to be named, but some who had been identified
earlier were now imprisoned in makeshift cells, called 'cattlepens',
which were set up on the school's premises. These teachers were regularly beaten by Red Guards, in their strenuous attempts to display deep
'class feeling'. If you did not hate counter-revolutionaries, you must be
one yourself—and hadn't Chairman Mao himself explained that there
was no such thing as 'humanity' which transcended class feeling?

The theory of 'blood-line' also began to emerge, notably among
cadres' children, and provided a theoretical justification for the position
that only those who had inherited privilege and power from cadre
parents could be considered above suspicion of self-interest. China's
revolutionary heritage could be defended only by those of impeccable
pedigree. As a result, Mao's call to arms against the 'capitalist roaders'
in the Party was being translated into action, not so much by
commoners, who could not be trusted to guard against the
re-emergence of an entrenched ruling class, but by bluebloods, who
could always be relied upon to represent the masses. By the autumn of
1966, there were signs that Mao was well aware of this, but for some
months the sons and daughters of cadres held sway by means of work
teams and preparatory committees in the schools and colleges.

The city of Peking reverberated to the sounds of 'Smash the four
olds'. This also involved smashing new things as well, if they happened
to be foreign. Girls who had bought Western-style narrow slacks and
high-heeled shoes, selling very well early in 1966 (not so much for their
Western style as for their export quality and low price, due to failure to
penetrate foreign markets) became a target for abuse in the streets.
Bands of Red Guards accosted them and cut open the corners of their
slacks, usually with a good deal more enthusiasm than might be

explained by purely political motivation. Strumpets who had their blouses open at the neck instead of fully buttoned-up had the offending clothing torn open to the waist—as a means of lampooning their slavish addiction to Western bourgeois decadence.

Smashing the 'four olds' did not mean freeing women from the practices of the past. High-heeled shoes were hung up in the nearest tree and the wearer was made to kneel penitently under them for all to see and mock. Those who had succumbed to the permanent wave had half their head shaved—the most feared of punishments, since it marked the victim as a target for further abuse wherever she went. Any girl who had brushed her hair back was likely to be branded 'aeroplane head'. Those who had curls might expect to be tagged 'pearl fur', after the tight, bead-shaped curls.

In restaurants, only peasant food was obtainable. *Wotou* (steamed sorghum or corn dumplings) and *cu liang* (coarse grain) were the only things available, not because of shortages but because they were considered politically nutritious. Red Guards patrolled the restaurants and snack stalls. One afternoon, Hsin-ping and a colleague stood eating *hundun* (wontons) at a street stall. Two Guards came by. 'You there, you two hundun-eating hundan!' yelled one of them, punning on the word for wontons and the stock insult '*hundan*' (rotten egg). 'Stand up! Recite from Chairman Mao's works! Recite a passage before you eat!' After a satisfactory performance, Hsin-ping and her companion were left to finish their wontons, taking care to wash the bowls themselves lest they be accused of exploiting anyone.

Young activists surged through the city, changing the names of streets and restaurants. Almost overnight Peking acquired innumerable 'Fan Di' (oppose imperialism) streets, and 'Zao Fan' (rise in rebellion) restaurants. They say that discussions were held in Shanghai as to whether traffic signals should be converted to the revolutionary system. Red ought to symbolize 'Go', not 'Stop'. 'The Three Isms', feudalism, revisionism and capitalism, were hunted down. There was a simple rule-of-thumb for identifying these evils. 'Feudalism' meant anything before Liberation, 'revisionism' meant anything after Liberation and before the Red Guards, and 'capitalism' meant anything foreign. Everywhere the cry 'chaojia' went up (Search homes, confiscate or destroy the 'four olds').

Red Guards were now looking for concealed weapons in the homes of counter-revolutionaries, and this included such things as kitchen knives and choppers. They also looked for gold, silver and jewels, and sometimes a prompt confession that such things existed seemed to satisfy the investigators that the owners were not beyond rehabilitation, and were not building up a secret cache of arms for an underground cell of the counter-revolutionary forces. The *People's Daily* stirred the blood of the Red Guards with clarion call headlines in support of their activities.

One Saturday afternoon, when Hsin-ping had gone back to the architects' dormitory, as she usually did at weekends, she found Lulu playing with Grandma's beautiful old mah-jong set. This was just the sort of thing that could get them all into trouble if the place was raided by Red Guards. She could not bring herself to destroy the exquisite ivory pieces, which she herself had loved as a child, but she knew that it was asking for trouble to have them in the house. She took Lulu out for the afternoon, and they caught a bus to a favourite park in an adjoining district. The mah-jong pieces went along with them, in a bag which Hsin-ping intended to leave behind somewhere. Unfortunately, there were too many people around, so she decided to take them to the local police station instead and just offer them up as a kind of civic duty, a contribution to the movement, as others of her acquaintance had done with their valuables. Police stations had become veritable warehouses, full of things that people wanted to be rid of in case they were raided.

In the station, Hsin-ping saw a sight neither she nor her daughter could ever forget. A young woman lay on her back in a cell, her clothing soaked with blood, her legs askew, as though boneless. A large, middle-aged man was slumped against a wall. His hands were latticed with deep cuts, and strips of a shirt clung to pulpy, bloody tissue, shot through with veins of yellow. Hsin-ping struggled to comprehend the sight. She thought of an expression she had once glibly explained to a student: *Pi kai rou zhan, ti wu wan fu* (the flesh flayed, the body torn and rotting). Now she really knew what the lines meant. Sick and dazed, she flung the mah-jong set into a corner and pushed Lulu out into the street.

She later came to understand that for many victims of the Red Guards at this time, the police station was the only hope of survival. Sometimes the police would imprison a suspected counter-revolutionary and, in so doing, keep him or her from being tortured and beaten to death. It was not uncommon to hear a sigh of relief when the news came that a loved one had been arrested by the police.

Every day seemed to bring new terrors. One day Hsin-ping ran foul of the students for attempting to correct their bad language. Everybody had to swear—young or old, male or female, you were not a revolutionary unless you swore like a camel-seller. Out of habit she had rebuked one of the boys for saying *gun tamade dan* (Fuck off!)—not realizing that this was revolutionary patois, and that polite speech was one of the 'four olds'. He glared menacingly at her and said, 'Comrade Wang, are you against Comrade Jiang Qing?' 'No, of course not', she said as the dreadful implication began to sink in, 'I wouldn't consider it . . . why do you ask me that?'

'Don't you know', he replied, 'What Comrade Jiang Qing said to a mass rally of students at Peking University? Let me remind you of her words as she concluded her inspirational speech. She said, "Those who are for the revolution, step right up, those who are not can fuck off!" Quickly retrieving an expression of disgust, Hsin-ping blurted out her admiration for Jiang Qing's command of the language, 'Oh well, yes I see . . . well, in that case, by all means, say it, say it as much as you like . . . in fact, let's all say it now, everybody, together . . . '

At this time it also became common for students to address teachers by their given names or, if their background was not good, to call them 'bitch' or 'mongrel'. Staff members who were not in the ruling group were subjected to constant student scrutiny, and were likely to suffer instant punishment for any betrayal of sympathy for class enemies. At a struggle meeting one morning, Hsin-ping drew attention to herself, first for not being vehement enough in her condemnation of a colleague, and then for presuming to do it at all when she was herself 'blown out of the same nostril' as the culprit. The Party branch secretary intervened at this point, and said that while Hsin-ping was herself a dubious type because of her background, the business of the meeting was to deal with the present offender. Comrade Wang could wait. Hsin-ping had seen him do this sort of thing a few times, and often the attentions of the preparatory committee and the students were diverted from their future targets by some more immediate task.

On the afternoon of 23 August the whole school was ordered by the preparatory committee to attend a film. Titled Qiu Mi, *Football-Crazy*, it was reputed to be hilariously funny. The basic plot concerned a doctor Li, who deserted his clinic in order to attend a soccer match. One of his patients was precariously pregnant and needed his attentions, but he was nowhere to be found. Someone thought of the football match, and a boy was despatched around the boundary of the soccer field, carrying a large sign with the message 'Doctor Li, you are needed urgently!' Twenty or thirty panic-stricken doctors Li rushed from the ground, indicating a high degree of absenteeism among the medical profession during football matches. In the past this scene had been greeted with gales of laughter by a population which regarded all professional occupations with a healthy degree of cynicism, but now the film had been branded a 'great poisonous weed' by the managers of the Cultural Revolution, since it clearly encouraged a tolerant attitude to enemies of the proletariat. Only swindlers like Doctor Li himself would laugh at such corrupt and parasitic behaviour. Red Guards patrolled the aisles of the theatre, belts over their shoulders, looking for any sign of mirth on the faces of the audience. Occasionally, someone was dragged outside. Even so, Hsin-ping found it hard to suppress laughter on one or two occasions and pinched her own legs brutally in an attempt to stifle a giggle.

That afternoon, she went back to Grandma's house, wondering how long she could run the gauntlet, how long it would be before she and Grandma suffered a raid on the house in Toufa Lane. So far, even with the threat of exposure in the next round of condemnations of those who had refused the national work assignment, she had not experienced a home raid. This was probably because she was not registered at the police station as a resident of Xidan District, although she lived there with Grandma during term. She had registered as a resident of Yuetan District after she and her husband had moved into the architects' dormitory near Fuchengmen. Since the Red Guards had not yet got round to examining police station files for this district, the residents of Yuetan had enjoyed a temporary respite. However, Grandma was likely to become a target at any time.

On the morning of 24 August, Hsin-ping went off to school in a state of fear and exhaustion. She had been up almost all night, getting rid of anything which might incriminate Grandma, and shifting furniture into storage. Of the fifty-odd rooms in three houses which they had owned in the past, they now occupied four rooms of the house in Toufa Lane. Grandma's bedroom was in the north-east corner next to the special reception room which contained the altar. This was entered by means of the four-leaved wooden door behind which Hsin-ping had spent so much of her childhood kneeling in atonement for her sins. Grandma, now seventy, had begun to hoard things in these rooms. There were things of the past, dangerous things, some of which were hidden under the bed, or *in* the bed, and you could hardly get into her room at all for the treasured bits and pieces she had accumulated.

Hsin-ping's bedroom, in the west wing, adjoined the former servants' bedrooms which were now full of the offending furniture. Grandma had finally been persuaded to part with most of her baubles and trinkets, and these were put in boxes and placed in the spare rooms which the Red Guards could conveniently seal off. They usually reserved these rooms for a more leisurely investigation by pasting banners across the doors in the form of a cross, bearing the terrible curse 'Sealed by Red Guards. Just let any bastard try opening it'.

As Hsin-ping cycled down through Xuanwumen, which used to be the south-west gate of the Tartar City walls, through which criminals passed early in the morning on their way to execution at Caishikou, the Vegetable Market, she shuddered at the thought of those classrooms which had recently been used for interrogation. It was said that they had begun to resemble butchers' yards, the walls and floor stained with blood and littered with skin. She thought of taking flight, but that would only precipitate matters as the students would surely come looking for her. As she approached the walls of the school, she searched for her name among the posters. It was not there, but she trembled as she saw the poster which read, 'Own up all those turtle's eggs who did not obey the national work assignment'. Her old transgression would not go away.

During the morning, two more teachers were named, one being a woman who had stayed in Peking after breaking her wrists in a basketball match. They were made to write out big-character posters condemning themselves for their dereliction of duty, and a struggle meeting was called for the afternoon. Hsin-ping felt certain that her time had come, and that she would be named in this meeting. At lunchtime she went back to Grandma's, wondering what to do for the best. As she turned the corner into Toufa Lane, a mob of children ran alongside, squabbling and screeching like seagulls over scraps as they vied with each other in the urgency of their warnings.

Hsin-ping found the courtyard piled high with furniture, clothing and books, emptied out of the adjoining rooms. A young woman stood, hands on hips, staring balefully at her as she dismounted her bicycle. If she were going to be beaten anyway, she might as well maintain her dignity—and she had already decided that displays of fear and submission by victims enhanced the element of fantasy which arouses bullies. The young woman, her hair severely cropped, was wearing a P.L.A. uniform, and there was a leather belt dangling over her shoulder.

'Background?' she snapped.

'My father is a teacher', replied Hsin-ping, resolutely. So far, so good. Despite their vulnerability over these last few months, teachers were not considered to be incorrigible class enemies, like former landlords. The next question was the real problem.

'Where is he?'

'Overseas. In Australia.'

'Counter-revolutionary, counter-revolutionary!' screeched several of the neigbours, who had gathered in the courtyard, anxious to demonstrate their own revolutionary purity, and keep the Red Guards out of their own homes. 'Foreign devil counter-revolutionary!' they yelled, combining the old and new in political slogans.

'Your father's background?' demanded the woman, menacingly.

'I told you, he is a teacher', said Hsin-ping evasively.

'And what about that old bitch in there?' said the woman, pointing in the direction of Grandma's bedroom.

'That is my grandmother.'

'Today we have not struggled against this old crone. Guess why!'

Sensing some relief from this dreaded confrontation, Hsin-ping replied immediately, 'Yes, I know why you have been so sympathetic. She is an old, former peasant, sold into a scholar gentry family, before the collapse of the feudal system'.

'Correct!' said the woman. 'That is indeed the reason why we have not struggled against her. We have not punished her even though she is a member of a former Qing official family', she added, with the air of one genuinely amazed at her own restraint. 'But do you know what the old witch said to us, how she provoked us?'

Hsin-ping's heart leapt into her mouth as she thought of the many fruity things Grandma might have said to an ill-bred little minx like this who had the sauce to question an old lady of some influence in the district.

'She insulted the poor and lower-middle peasants!'

This came as a huge relief to Hsin-ping as she realized that Grandma had probably used the wrong word for 'poor' again. However, it was going to be quite a tricky business to explain how difficult it was to get a former peasant girl to refrain from language which the children of city cadres might regard as insulting to peasants.

'I asked for her background', continued the young woman. 'She said "I come from a dirt poor peasant family". She is clearly arrogant and contemptuous of the poor!'

Yes, thought Hsin-ping, Grandma knows too much about poverty to hold it in high regard. 'Oh, look, I can see what's happened', she said, 'you have to understand that she has had no formal education, being of poor peasant background. She can't read or write and she doesn't have much of a vocabulary. She just can't remember some of the words she's not used to. She's a real muddle-head at times, and she is getting old, but she doesn't mean any offence at all. She asked me once what 'destitute' means and the only way I could explain it was to say 'dirt-poor.' She certainly didn't mean any offence to the peasants. She is a peasant herself still, in many ways.'

'No, you are incorrect', said the woman, utterly impregnable within the authority of her phoney P.L.A. uniform, 'She *was* a peasant once, but from the time she was sold into this scholar bureaucrat family, she underwent an ideological change. Her attitude and class outlook changed as a result of contamination with the poison of bourgeois life-style and livelihood. There are no feelings which transcend class and the relations of production. The only remedy for her is to reform her thinking through manual labour. She must go to the outskirts of the city to take part in productive labour.'

'But she needs someone to take care of her', protested Hsin-ping, 'I can't get away from the school at present . . . and where will she stay tonight?' The other Guards were busily sealing up the rooms of the house.

'You are a teacher?' said the woman, 'Where do you teach? Which college did you go to? Which high school?'

'I went to Peking University Attached Girls' High and . . . '

'I went there too, and so did many of my teachers. Do you know Zong Tian?'

'Yes, of course, we were classmates.'

'O.K. Where does your Grandmother come from?'

'Hebei Province, Dingxing County.'

'All right, she can go back there to do her labour reform. We'll issue a permit. You can see her off.'

Hsin-ping could not believe her luck. Others had been forcibly relocated under Red Guard escort, which usually meant beatings and maltreatment all along the way. Peking Railway Station was already the scene of uncontrolled, insane violence as those under escort were beaten senseless or killed while waiting for a train. But Hsin-ping and Grandma could virtually organize themselves, just as if they were going on a normal journey. Hsin-ping returned to the school in the afternoon, reasonably confident of escaping further harassment for the time being at least.

The afternoon passed in relatively moderate criticism meetings, and her name was not brought up. In the evening a squad of about twenty Red Guards came to the house and took away all the things piled in the courtyard. They told Hsin-ping that they would not take anything Grandma had earned by dint of her own savings, as opposed to property which her parasite husband's family had gained through exploitation of the workers and peasants. Grandma's gold and silver bracelets and necklaces were not considered to have been earned. The old lady complained bitterly about her jewels, which meant far more to her than any of the rare calligraphies or paintings, but Hsin-ping managed somehow to silence her. Grandma was not at all swayed by arguments that she was lucky to be alive—that seemed to her to be the very least that respectable folk could expect—but she resigned herself to leaving the city. It would take more than an eviction to get the better of her. The Guards sealed up the entrances to the house with the now familiar crossed banners and drove off in their trucks.

The two women first had to find somewhere to spend the night. Old Lady Wang's sister, Yin Quan, had a room nearby. She had taught in Hsin-ping's old primary school in Shoupa Lane for forty years and lived quite close to Grandma's house. It should be a simple enough matter to put up there for the night. However, when they arrived, Hsin-ping wheeling her bike with Grandma perched on it to save her useless little feet, they found the old lady sitting on her couch, shaking uncontrollably. Her head had been half shaved.

How could it have happened? She had been a teacher all her life, she had never exploited anybody, she had supported the revolution and taught her students to respect and observe its ideals.

'They said I came from a big landlord family', she muttered, 'that my brother-in-law was an official in the Qing government'. Hsin-ping tried to soothe and comfort her. At least she was still alive. She explained that they had come to ask for a place to stay for the night, but the old lady's eyes glazed over and she seemed to drift off: 'Where are we? What kind of place is this? Why is every place a courtroom? Why is every place an execution ground? Whatever is said loudest is the law. What kind of place is this?'

Later they discovered that her life-long friend and living companion had been dragged away and beaten to death, because she was of the Man nationality, a distant relative of the Qing ruling family. Hsin-ping kept trying in vain to soothe the one she had called 'Jiu Gong', 'Ninth Grandpa', an honorific male title bestowed on the ninth child in Lady Wang's family because she had never married. She just kept repeating the same speech: 'Why is every place a courtroom? Why is every place an execution ground?'

Hsin-ping tried to convince her that she should leave the house and go with them, because the Red Guards might come back at any time, but she didn't seem to hear. She just couldn't understand what crime she and her friend had committed, after a lifetime of humble and poorly rewarded service as schoolteachers. What did they have to do with big landlords and Qing rulers? Finally, Hsin-ping and Grandma left the old woman alone in the house. They never saw her again.

They decided to try another relative, the daughter of one of Grandma's younger sisters. There should be no family background problem here, because Grandma's niece was married to a P.L.A. man. She responded very generously to their plight, and told Hsin-ping to collect her remaining belongings from the school next day and stay as long as was necessary, and safe. After all, they had not been told exactly *when* they should leave Peking, and they had a certificate which stated that Hsin-ping was permitted to arrange Grandma's departure for the village. However, when she returned from picking up her things the following afternoon, she found a new problem.

Grandma's niece reluctantly explained that they would have to leave, because of her number one and two daughters, who were Red Guards. Previously, they had always addressed Grandma as 'Yi Lao', 'Great Aunt', but now they had changed their tune. 'Get that old bitch out of here!' they had told their mother on discovering Grandma. She could not afford to ignore them, because they might bring other Red Guards around, just to show that not even family loyalties could prevent them from doing their revolutionary duty.

Third daughter took Hsin-ping and Grandma to the station and helped them to get a ticket for Grandma's three-hour journey to Dingxing. Her nephew's son was the only relative left in her old village, but they hoped he might be able to help her. She seemed utterly help-less and frail outside her own house and sphere of influence, but they had no choice but to bundle her on to the train. Things might have been much worse however for, all around them on the platform, groups of youths harassed and beat those who were being accompanied into exile.

6

世外桃源

The Peach Blossom Spring

Hsin-ping returned to her room in the architects' dormitory. Her husband was away in Inner Mongolia working on the Yellow River dam, so she and Lulu, now aged seven, had the place to themselves. Things began to change for the better. From the 'ox demons and snake spirits' phase and the birth of the Red Guards, and through the period of 'smash the four olds', Peking had been almost flattened under a tidal wave of student passions.

In early September 1966, Premier Zhou Enlai, China's most beloved modern figure, issued an order that the Red Guards were not to take the law into their own hands. There was a national government, he said, and there were laws and there were police. Raiding homes, confiscating property and beating people were not legal activities. Wrongdoers should be handed over to the proper authorities for investigation and punishment. This order saved countless lives. The eye of the storm had passed, and among the debris left for bemused citizens to contemplate were the millions of provincial youths who had washed up in the city after the 'high tide' of revolution. In the meantime local youth had left Peking on pilgrimages to the holy places of the Revolution, hoping to be 'tempered' in the process of emulating the legendary feats of the Red Army. Schools, factories and work units in many cities were now preoccupied with billeting the invading armies of youth.

In Hsin-ping's school, the teaching staff spent their days cooking and

caring for their new charges, but at least it appeared that the most
sadistic and violent ones had left the city with the new movement to
establish revolution in the countryside. Mixed with the thugs and
zealots were countless idealistic youths who craved freedom more than
a free hand at violence, and for them the movement provided a unique
opportunity for unrestricted travel, new experiences and experimentation with ideas.

About this time, Hsin-ping realized that Grandma had no winter
clothing, because she had left in such a hurry. She bought some warm
things, with the intention of taking them to Grandma by train, but by
now it was mid-October and Red Guards packed the station again, this
time on their journey into the provinces to spread revolution. She didn't
have a hope of getting a train ticket. Her husband was by now back
from Inner Mongolia. As it was quite common for teachers to set out on
revolutionary journeys of their own, she left Lulu at home with him and
cycled off to Grandma's village, with the winter clothing packed on the
back of the bike. She started out at six in the morning and arrived at six
in the evening. After making a few enquiries, she walked her bike
across the fields to the brigade leader's house, and explained what she
was doing there.

'You've come to see your Old One', said the brigade leader, using the
familiar but respectful term employed by villagers.

'Yes, I've brought her a few things.'

'Look', he said, in a rather confidential tone, 'why don't you just take
her back with you?'

'But the Red Guards said she must do manual labour', said the
puzzled Hsin-ping.

'Yes, yes, I know all about that', he growled, 'I can give you a certificate that will fix that.'

'But they said she had to do labour, to change her ideology.'

'What is the point of sending a woman over seventy to work in the
fields and change her ideology? When she left this village as a girl, she
was young and useless. Now she is back and she is old and useless. She
doesn't belong here. I don't give a fart what her ideology is or whether
she changes it. She has bound feet. These Red Guard brats really know
their stuff about peasants, don't they? It's a pity they don't just stay out
of the way, in their schoolrooms reading books, instead of helping us.
They can march their great highway to revolution and we'll just tread
our own little wooden bridge. What good is another useless mouth to
feed? Why don't you just pay us for the two months' worth of grain she
has eaten and take the poor old lady home? She is only a burden to us.'

Pondering this unexpected turn of events, Hsin-ping trudged her bike
across the fields, following a cluster of lights to Grandma's nephew's

house. The nephew and his wife greeted her hospitably, but it was soon apparent that they were looking for an opportunity to be rid of Grandma, as they already had three children to feed. The Old One had been doing her stint of labour by sorting sweet potatoes into large and small. This she did all day, in company with the village's young children, who were too small to go out into the fields. She had not suffered struggle meetings because the villagers did not care much for that sort of thing. Anyway, it was hard to get too worked up against people because nearly everybody in the village was related in some way or other. Hsin-ping explained to the nephew that the brigade leader was willing to give them a certificate, complete with the official commune stamp, that would enable Grandma to go back to the city. He and his whole family were absolutely delighted to hear this and they all spent a pleasant night in celebration at the house.

Next day the brigade leader came to have lunch with them, and they all had another feast of beancurd. Since his imprimatur was required on the certificate, discussion turned to the formalities. 'Listen', he announced, in an expansive tone, his belly well satisfied for once, 'why don't you just write out the words and I'll stamp it for you?' Not only was this obliging, it also avoided placing a strain on the brigade leader's literacy. Hsin-ping eagerly wrote out a statement to the effect that the commune administration had decided to send the old woman back to Peking, and the brigade leader produced a fine looking seal-stamp from his pocket and plunged it down on the paper, with an air of enormous gravity and solemnity—without attempting to read a word of it.

After lunch, it remained only to get the commune committee chairman to affix his particular seal to the document. Hsin-ping walked across the fields to his 'office' at about three o'clock. The door was wide open and the wind and dust howled around the bare walls. There was a table and chair in the middle of the stone hut—nothing else—so she went off to look in the fields. She found the chairman and he motioned to her to squat down beside him in the position beloved of peasants, on haunches, elbows resting on knees. Peasants seem to be able to maintain this posture for hours at a time, especially when there are cigarettes to be smoked. He too was very pleased to be getting rid of Grandma, who was one of eight useless extras who had been sent down to his village by the Red Guards. As he did not have his stamp with him, he asked her to return to the office and stamp it herself. She paid him thirty yuan for Grandma's victuals, handed over a wad of food coupons which she always kept with her, found the stamp, and applied it vigorously to her own writing on the document. Then she went back to the house to fetch Grandma.

There was no point in trying to get a train at that time of day, and little point in spending another night in the village, so she decided to perch Grandma on the back of her bike and ride back to Peking, following the road next to the railway. In fact she was only able to ride when the road was not clogged with flag-waving, knapsack-bearing Red Guards going to or from Peking. The rest of the time she wheeled her bike. All along the route were 'rest stations' bearing banners of welcome for the Red Guards. These provided water, tea and a little food, in a sort of re-enactment of the co-operation between villagers and the P.L.A. during the Civil War. Hsin-ping knew that she also could call upon their natural hospitality from time to time. However, before it came to this, she spotted a better option.

At the side of the road was a parked truck, and two workmen having a quiet loaf. They exchanged greetings. She told them she was taking her grandmother to see her sick sister in Peking, and asked if she might buy a 'ticket' for the two of them and their bicycle to ride in the truck. The men protested at the suggestion of any payment and insisted that the poor old lady should join them in the cabin because it would be too cold for her in the back. After much see-sawing on this topic, it was abruptly settled when Hsin-ping bundled the bike into the back of the truck and unceremoniously lifted Grandma up after it. Grandma let Hsin-ping know that in her opinion she had overdone the self-effacement. All the way back to Peking a fierce wind ripped at their hair. They finally arrived in the south-west of the city at nine o'clock, and the workers dropped them off at Caishikou. From here they managed to get a bus, and were back at the architects' dormitory by nine-thirty. Hsin-ping left Grandma outside, while she checked for any Red Guards in or around the building. There were none. Perhaps things had really changed.

However, life was still enormously complicated and delicately poised between survival and disaster. Unlike Hsin-ping, Grandma had not managed to get her residential passbook thrown in with her repatriation deal. As a result, she could not get food coupons, and had to live on the rations available to Hsin-ping, her husband and daughter. Fortunately, their neighbours were sympathetic, and eager to help as much as they could. The old lady who represented their dormitory on the street committee knew that Grandma was living in the house without official residential registration, but she could not believe that a poor hobbling old lady with bound feet could possibly pose any threat to the revolutionary order. Although many people wished to help, and nobody in the immediate neighborhood appeared likely to give them any trouble, this was a dangerous and tense time for the family. Grandma's network came in handy, however, and she managed to produce, from her inexhaustible supply, a cousin whose doctor husband had died some time ago and who now lived alone in a house in the east of the city.

According to the cousin, she had a policeman neighbour who would keep the residential records out of the wrong hands. After Grandma had moved in, the policeman came to visit her. It was obvious that he knew she was unregistered as a resident of this household, but, as he put it, 'I just do my job and mind my own business. If I must take action, then I must—but I don't go looking for trouble'.

As Red Guards continued to flow out of the city, and provincial youths flowed in to take their place, some sort of order began to take shape. Activist energies were now preoccupied with questions of which key Party figures were the true 'capitalist roaders', and the Red Guards began to divide into factions on questions of organization, administration and 'line'. The rallies, and the huge crushing marches, continued from time to time in Tian'anmen Square. In all, there were eight, involving a total of eleven million students, from 18 August to 26 November. They had all come hoping to see and hear the 'Great Helmsman' at the site of the proclamation of the People's Republic of China.

By late November, the Peking Red Guards were beginning to run into difficulties in the provinces. There were widespread expressions of dissatisfaction from local authorities, who resented their attempts to involve themselves in administration. At times this resentment was perfectly reasonable, but there was also a hidebound conservatism, self-interest and lack of imagination among cadres, which made them suspicious of any initiative. Many idealistic, talented and creative leaders sprang up among the ranks of the Red Guards, along with the ones whose only satisfaction came from the familiar abuses of power. But whatever the case, the workers and peasants were less than enthusiastic about their new helpers.

Confusing reports of unrest filtered into the city from the outlying counties, and then from other cities. Workers were apparently organizing their own groups to counter the influence of the students. After reports of open, violent conflict between the two, Premier Zhou had to assure the Red Guards that *they* were entitled to protection from violence at the hands of local authorities and workers. The Red Guards then seemed to gain the upper hand again, at least in the cities, and by the beginning of December were conducting arrests of Party Central Committee members whom they considered to be reactionaries.

The Qinghua University and Peking University Guards named Mao's designated successor, Liu Shaoqi, and his 'chief collaborator', Deng Xiaoping, Secretary-General of the Party, as numbers one and two 'bourgeois-roaders' respectively, and pressure began to mount for their expulsion from the Party. The varied criticisms of Liu included the assertion that he had been a 'Soviet-style revisionist' all along, but in particular he was attacked for the role of the work teams in universities and colleges during June and July. Had the work teams deflected criticism from true revisionists and prevented the emergence of the 'mass line' at the beginning of the Cultural Revolution, in order to protect Party authorities? The emphasis had changed from hunting out 'bourgeois academics' to exposing Party reactionaries. Mao continued to lend his massive moral support to student revolutionaries, who justified the iconoclastic nature of their activities by quoting Mao's famous comment at a Yan'an rally in 1939, 'rebellion is justifiable'.

Red Guards were encouraged to maintain their attacks on even the most eminent figures, such as Zhou Yang, chief of the Central Committee propaganda department, by means of the 'sixteen points' document, which was interpreted as forbidding harsh counter-measures against the student revolutionary movement. A variety of conflicting statements were issued by the Central Committee about the growing tensions between workers and students. Some decreed that workers and peasants should not oppose the students, and some reminded students that workers and peasants were the most reliable elements of the revolution, and did not need to be stood over.

Meanwhile, the journeys of 'revolutionary exchange of experience' continued. Millions of students—and teachers—set out to travel anywhere they pleased in China. They did not need train or boat tickets, only an authorization from their school or college. An official 'vacation' period of six months lent official endorsement to the simple fact that students were relishing their new-found freedom and the exhilarating experience of having the pressures of their intensely monitored lives lifted for the first time ever. They could not have been persuaded to return to school. In Peking especially, public utilities groaned under the weight of the millions who descended on the capital, in order to be near the centre of the Cultural Revolution.

Since her husband was still at home to look after Lulu, and Grandma was safe for the time being, Hsin-ping decided to take advantage of the opportunity for travel and experience. She set out in the company of two other teachers and six young female students. They had no hard-and-fast notion of where they wanted to go, but in general 'the south' beckoned, not least because of the approach of a Peking winter. There was considerable debate about the most desirable destination, with Canton and Shanghai being the two clear favourites. Hsin-ping had an uncle in Canton whom she particularly wanted to see, but she was content to go to Shanghai if that was what the others wanted. In the end they resolved to leave the matter in the lap of the gods. They would take the first train that came along, as long as it went south. They arranged to meet at the Peking Railway Station.

Early one morning, Hsin-ping set out for the station, carrying two bags. One contained a change of clothes and one a box of candied dates, the only food she could get hold of which was suitable for the journey. She caught a bus near Fuchengmen but it ground to a halt long before the station came into view. There were people everywhere and, even with a Peking bus driver's fine disregard for obstacles of any kind, it was just impossible to make any headway through the throng of would-be pilgrims. She walked to the station, by now well aware that she would never be able to find her companions in the crush. On the basis that their most favoured destination had been Shanghai, she asked the way to the queue for the Shanghai train. There were several queues for trains which may or may not have been going to Shanghai, so she searched up and down them all, with no luck.

All around her were wretched, shivering students from the south who had come up to Peking wearing only light clothing. They lit fires on the platforms and were sitting, hudddled around the flames, looking like the remnants of a defeated army waiting to be taken captive. After some time Hsin-ping spotted two of her companions. They had not seen the others but had decided to remain in the Shanghai queue rather than risk separation. There had been no train for twenty-four hours, so it looked like a long wait. In the meantime, the others, who had seemed very keen to go to Shanghai, might join them.

Suddenly, at about six o'clock in the evening, the station was galvanized into action. The orderly queue, which had served its purpose by keeping the crowd tidy until the train arrived, disintegrated at some invisible signal, and people flew hither and thither in a cloud of limbs and luggage. There was as yet no train in the platform, but a horde of grimly determined passengers launched themselves at the place where it was expected to stop. Within minutes it became apparent that there was actually something solid under the mound of bodies spilling out on to the line. Hsin-ping clawed and gouged and scrabbled along with the best of them, making good use of her considerable athletic talents. She was vaguely aware of something soft which enabled her to get a leg up to one of the windows and finally to tumble down on to a table inside a compartment of the train. Her friends had disappeared in the melee. She perched clumsily in the middle of the table, like a bird with a broken wing, and peered around her.

Luck had not deserted Hsin-ping, in that this train was bound for Canton. However, she had no food, except for the candied dates, and her money was useless because the dining car was at the end of an absolutely un-navigable human channel. There was very little possibility of movement of any sort, a fact which was to become rather painfully obvious to those located directly beneath the luggage racks, from which the tortured occupants were obliged to relieve themselves from time to time. Even for those in the lower berths, there was no point in striking out on the epic journey in search of toilets, because they were occupied—for their space rather than their specialized function. The old lament about unproductive and impassable cadres—that they didn't want a shit themselves but wouldn't let anyone else get near the latrine—took on a new meaning for those passengers who were not fortunate enough to secure a berth in one of the toilets.

The one great consolation in all this discomfort was that the train was really rattling along, and covered the distance from Peking to Hankow and the Yangtse Bridge at Wuhan in about thirteen hours. It had pelted through Hubei Province into Hunan, and it looked as if the usual thirty-six hour journey would be greatly reduced, if only the passengers could stand up to it. However, after Wuhan, as if to tantalize its new-found suitors, the train adopted the cocquettish trick of tearing along at breakneck speed for ten or fifteen minutes, and then stopping unaccountably for hours at a time, causing passengers first to murmur their devotions and then to curse it for a heartless slut. From Hankow to Canton took four more days, and the passengers grew accustomed to the delays, and learnt to take advantage of them by organizing orderly evacuations of the train for the purposes of ablution and excretion.

By accident or design the stops often coincided with a lake or river, and on occasion there were opportunities to get something to eat in a nearby village. The danger was, of course, that if you strayed too far, you might be left behind in some god-forsaken village. There was absolutely no way of knowing just how long each stop would be, and a number of unfortunates were seen fading into the distance as the train rapidly outstripped their attempts to catch up. It seemed as if the train, like the students themselves, was exulting in its first release from rigid controls and had set about driving its former masters mad. Just as the travellers were finding the comfort necessary to make the rest of the journey tolerable, with a splash in the river and a snooze in the grass, the Spirit of Rebellion would lurch off without warning. Heads would pop up out of the fields for some distance around, while those engaged in relieving themselves would utter anguished cries as they left their work unfinished to take off after the train.

Hsin-ping had nothing to eat for these four days except candied dates. She had few opportunities to leave the train and her position was so cramped that by the time they arrived in Canton she could hardly walk. Her feet had swollen terribly—and there was another serious problem she had not anticipated. She could not understand a word of Cantonese. Her first language had been Cantonese, but here she was, at the age of twenty-nine, unable to communicate. Somehow it had never occurred to her that this would be a problem. She left the station and hobbled out into the street, asking a number of passers-by if they knew how to get to Huanan Agricultural College, where her uncle, an entomologist, worked. They understood her Mandarin questions well enough for the most part, but she could not understand their Cantonese replies, so she asked a number of them to write the replies down in the character script common to both languages. However, no linguistic device could compensate for ignorance of Huanan Agricultural College.

There were 'welcome stations' scattered about everywhere in readiness for itinerant Red Guards and, finally, she asked her question of a man standing near one of these. He was a driver. Concerned about her condition, he offered to help her find her uncle, but begged her to rest first. He took her to a small farm at Huangpu. It was afternoon and everything seemed still and silent, but after a while people came running out of their houses carrying buckets of warm water. The villagers insisted that she put her feet into the water, and so she did, plunging them into bucket after bucket until she began to feel some blessed relief and the swelling started to subside. She had a meal and stayed the night with her benefactors, but next morning, after offering her heartfelt thanks for their unreserved kindness, she set out to look for her uncle. The driver insisted on taking her to the college and eventually they found their way to her uncle's place, a small European-style house indicating his status as a professor. Unfortunately, his status as a professor had also led to his house being boarded up by Red Guards.

Hsin-ping said her farewells to the driver and went around to the back door. As she knocked, an old woman sitting nearby called out to her in a pronounced Shanghai accent, 'Who are you after?' Hsin-ping explained. 'Oh, no', said the woman, in some alarm, 'I wouldn't go looking for him, if I were you. That whole family is in big trouble. You know, he was a professor, and his wife was a college principal. They've both been declared black and sent to the countryside for labour reform two or three weeks ago.'

Hsin-ping thought how incongruous it all was. Her uncle had never had the slightest interest in politics, and in fact could never get the hang of anything outside his own beloved world of insects. Even in that area, in which he had already acquired an international reputation for his work on the control of insect pests, he had a number of blind spots. Once, when he had visited her in Peking, Hsin-ping had had to explain to him that mosquitoes entered your room at dusk and left in the early morning, and so to combat them you did not need sophisticated insecticides so much as to close your windows in the evening and open them in the morning.

With no one to stay with, and no one to talk to, Hsin-ping had to think of somewhere else to go. She used her school's travel authority certificate to get another free passage. 'This is what I call real communism', she thought, as she helped herself to a boat ticket to Shantou, where she intended to look up an old friend. After two days on the South China Sea she arrived in Shantou only to find that her friend was not at home either. Her place had been raided and the family property confiscated, because her father had gone to work in Hong Kong some years ago. No doubt she also had been sent into the countryside. Feeling anxious and disappointed, Hsin-ping trudged to a nearby school where a makeshift guest house had been arranged for travellers, and stayed overnight before arranging yet another passage, from Shantou to Xiamen.

Xiamen seemed different from the beginning. There was no atmosphere of strife and fear. There were big-character posters, and a number of people had been identified as reactionaries and capitalists, but there was no sign of persecution or violence. Hsin-ping began to relax and to enjoy the unique scenery. The island on which Xiamen is located is in the mouth of the Nine Dragons River, at the entrance to the Taiwan Straits. Connected to the mainland by means of a causeway and rail service since 1949, it still seemed suspended both in time and space from the affairs of the mainland. It was inhabited by large numbers of overseas Chinese, originally from Fujian Province, who had returned to the motherland to pass a comfortable retirement and to spend their money on patriotic gestures in the way of public buildings and amenities. The hills were dotted with European-style houses in a benign and beautiful landscape. It was a place of tranquility.

Hsin-ping particularly wanted to visit Gulangyu—the Islet of Pounding Waves—half an hour by ferry from Xiamen. She had read about it as a child, about the Ming general, Zhen Chenggong, who had trained his soldiers there before setting out to liberate Taiwan from the Dutch. She had read that Gulangyu was also known as the 'Garden on the Sea', and that there were beautiful forests and a rocky peak called Sunrise Cliff. She took a room in a public bathhouse and, after eagerly sampling some of the hundreds of special dishes for which the area is noted, went to bed quite early. She wanted to be on the island before dawn, so as to position herself on top of the cliff and watch the sunrise. Everyone said that this was an unforgettable sight.

She missed the sunrise, because she did not reach the island until around seven o'clock, but she spent an enchanted day, hopping and singing like one of the crickets in Great Grandfather's stories, and skipping along deserted tracks and paths. It seemed that she had the whole island to herself, so she sang at the top of her voice, and ran and jumped and bellowed, absolutely intoxicated with peace, silence and freedom. She went back to the bathhouse in the evening, had some supper, and again went to bed early in order to make another attempt to see the sunrise from the top of the peak on Gulangyu. Next morning she rose at four, and was on the ferry out to the island well before five. Before sunrise she had climbed the narrow steps leading to the peak, more than 1000 metres above sea level. She found the rock at the top on which were carved the three characters 'Ri Guang Yan', 'Sunrise Cliff'. Again, there was not another soul to be seen anywhere on the island, and she sat down on the rock to wait for the sun to join her.

The horizon was black and grey, just lightening a little here and there with patches of blue. Suddenly, like a playful fiery ball from the legend of Hou Yi, the sun bounced out of the sea. Hsin-ping gasped in wonder at the sight. After some time she went exploring again around the island and found one other person, a fifteen-year-old girl who had also quit school in order to go travelling. They felt like gods and magic beings from the ancient *Book of Mountains and Seas*, mischievously cavorting about in the world of mortals, just for fun. They returned to watch the sunrise the next day, and the next. The student asked no questions, and the teacher offered no explanations.

This interlude came to an end when the central leadership of the Cultural Revolution ordered that all students and teachers return to their schools and wage revolution by resuming classes. Hsin-ping returned via Hangzhou and Shanghai. The contrast between Shanghai and Xiamen could not have been greater. She stayed with relatives in a dirty, poky room in an apartment block. Eleven families shared a kitchen, and the only toilet was a wooden bucket partly concealed by a flimsy curtain erected next to the bed where her cousin and his wife slept. Hsin-ping shared a bed with their three children, and was woken every morning by the sound of the bucket being dragged downstairs to the waiting nightsoil cart. As she flinched at the thought of the brimming bucket, she realized that she had been very spoilt in Peking, since both Grandma's house and the architects' dormitory had modern plumbing. In fact the architects came in for some severe criticism for designing themselves fancy lavatories of a kind that most of the proletariat had never seen. She remembered a relative from a nearby village who came to stay with them and washed his face in the toilet bowl.

Hsin-ping broke her journey with a trip to Hangzhou, where savage fighting had broken out among Red Guard factions. From here she went on to Ningbo, a fourteen-hour journey by boat to the ancient seaport which had been famous for centuries for its fishing and boat-building, and the trading acumen of its inhabitants. She stayed with her husband's parents in the rich and fertile land known as 'the land of fish and rice'. Her father-in-law worked in a winery, making yellow wine, and her mother-in-law raised vegetables in their home garden. In fact the soil was so rich and their plot so large that they were entirely self-sufficient in vegetables. For some days Hsin-ping enjoyed this place, and noted with great interest the differences in culture between southern and northern Chinese.

To her mind, southerners were very clean. She had expected this, because it was one of the things that she had borne in mind in seeking out a southern husband. However, she had to get used to some things which challenged her preconceptions. One day when out walking she saw two sisters from a neighbouring household, washing their things in the river. One sister was washing cooking pots and the other was flushing out the nightsoil pot—in the same water. Of course, the secret was to wash the cooking pots upstream and the nightsoil pot downstream. Hsin-ping began to see just how much cleanliness depended on a plentiful supply of fresh water—and here the water was so sparkling clean that you could see fish flashing about.

She took particular note of the local *mores*, as if she was on a journey in a strange land, peopled by a different race. On one occasion, when waiting at a bus stop with her sister-in-law, she was seized with the urgent necessity to empty her bowels. Her sister-in-law pointed to an open-sided shed, and a dilapidated sign bearing the character 'men'. 'But that says 'men's toilet', protested Hsin-ping. 'Yes, that's right', agreed the sister-in-law. She entered the toilet cautiously, and found that it contained two large wooden benches, one facing the other, and each with a number of holes, at reasonably regular intervals. This was another surprise. Northern public toilets, which Hsin-ping seldom frequented because of the long queues, consisted of holes in the concrete floor, over which you squatted. Obviously, these southern ones were designed for a longer stay.

The disconcerting thing for Hsin-ping was that, despite the sign outside, the southern practice was for both men and women to use the same toilet, and to sit side by side, or facing each other, performing feats of evacuation which, in her view, required at least segregation if not complete privacy. She was by no means a prurient or inhibited person, and had always encouraged her students to take a modern, socialist view of physical functions and sexual relations. On the frequent occasions when there was merriment in her classroom as a result of some unscheduled flatulence, she would gently reprove the gigglers and remind them that the expulsion of gases was vital to good health and nothing to be ashamed of for boys or girls. Nevertheless, this situation tried Hsin-ping's broadmindedness to the limits and, as she sat down, desperate to relieve herself, she prayed that she would not have to socialize.

However, not long after she had committed herself to action, a middle-aged woman waddled in, carrying a basket of vegetables over her arm. Tugging impatiently at her clothing, she wriggled up on to one of the holes and set the basket down at her feet. Then, with a great deal of largely ceremonial heaving and sighing and grunting, which included one very long and drawn out 'ai-yaaaa!' as she reached the climax of her endeavours, she unburdened herself, while Hsin-ping struggled to maintain some semblance of decorum and restraint. She then struck up an animated conversation with a newcomer, another woman, concerning her vegetables—where she had bought them, how much they had cost, how inferior all vegetables were these days, and so on. Hsin-ping was completely unnerved by this. She could not bear the prospect of having to engage in conversation with a man under these conditions, and cut short her business before she was put to the test.

Under the stimulus of these unfamiliar things, Hsin-ping had as happy a time here as in Xiamen. No one took any notice of her, or paid any attention to what she said or thought. She had no record, no background, no one gave a damn about her relatives overseas. She skipped and sang, just as she had done in Xiamen. The place reminded her of an ancient story about a fisherman of the Eastern Jin dynasty, who discovered an enchanted place called the 'Peach Blossom Spring Beyond the World'. Having left it, he was never able to find his way back. Hsin-ping never found it again either. She returned to Shanghai in November, in order to resume her journey to Peking, and found that the troubles had continued in her absence.

Just after New Year 1967, the 'January Storm' hit Shanghai. The clouds had been gathering throughout 1966, and had precipitated the Red Guards. The words of Yao Wenyuan and other key Cultural Revolution leaders struck at the Party's window like hailstones. At first the glass had merely cracked—now it shattered into a thousand fragments. It shattered very easily because of an old fault—the struggle among students in schools and colleges for power and status.

The Revolution was now seventeen years old, and the question of succession to the leadership was very much on the minds of China's youth. Those whose parents had taken a leading role in the Revolution were deemed red by pedigree, and felt that they should inherit their parents' power along with their redness. Those whose parents were members of the old elite had inherited privilege and power in spite of the Revolution, by means of an education system which selected and promoted those who had the advantage of a middle-class, professional or intellectual background. The workers and peasants were reddest of all, by nature and by birthright, and their children also inherited redness—along with low status, lack of educational opportunities, and exclusion from power.

The new elite was anxious to exclude the old from youth organizations which acted as feeders for the Party. Since those who were of middle-class origin could not easily *become* red, no matter how sincere their commitment to the ideals of the revolution, they tended to harbour resentment against 'phoney activists' in the youth organizations. On the other hand, those who argued that it was wrong to discriminate against good people on the basis of bad background were accused of being sympathetic to the old privileged classes.

In June and July, Party cadres and their families had managed to hold ground against radical elements which threatened to take up Mao's challenge to attack the restoration of bureaucratic privilege and self-interest. In the months following, however, suspicion had fallen increasingly on key Party figures, and Liu Shaoqi in particular, for having diverted the Cultural Revolution from its true course during the 'ox demons and snake spirits' phase. Mao endorsed the right and duty of young revolutionaries to rebel against the highest authority, and condemned the 'white terror' of the early months as a form of suppression of the masses. Everyone agreed fervently with him, but disagreed violently about what he meant.

Contention about what constituted genuine revolution, and who was best qualified to wage it, spilled over from Red Guard factions into work units. Schools, factories, shops, all splintered into hundreds of groups based on two major factions—the Scarlet Guards (Chiweidui) and the Rebels (Zaofandui). The Scarlet Guards chose for themselves a title which emphasized their legitimacy, by linking them with armed units of the masses in revolutionary base areas during the Second Revolutionary Civil War (1927–1937). This organization recruited largely from those who had become accustomed to thinking of themselves as natural heirs to power. They claimed Mao's endorsement for strong Party leadership of the Revolution. The Rebels, on the other hand, pointed to Mao's trenchant criticisms of the bureaucratic work style, and to the egalitarian, populist aspect of his various statements. They stressed Mao's allusion to the Paris Commune of 1871 as an embryonic model of genuine, grass-roots democracy.

Rebel students and workers had begun to forge alliances in November 1966. The Shanghai Workers' Revolutionary Rebel Headquarters was formed. This organization stimulated the growth of Revolutionary Rebel groups in factories and work units, which were in turn endorsed by Zhang Chunqiao, who was a member of the central Cultural Revolution leadership group. The Shanghai municipal authorities reacted by appealing to the Scarlet Guards to resist the Rebels, and conflict then broke out in factories, shops and public utilities. The strife in Shanghai, which had previously been known as the January Storm, came to be known as the 'January seize-power'. Scarlet Guards tried to take over the factories in an attempt to preserve the control of the Shanghai municipal authorities, and the Rebels countered by calling strikes. The Rebels seemed to enjoy the support of the central Cultural

Revolution group, but it was not clear how far they would be allowed to go without some form of central leadership intervention.

The official Shanghai newspaper, *Wenhuibao*, was seized by Rebels in January, and became a mouthpiece for condemnation of the municipal authorities and the Scarlet Guards. The conservative forces seemed to have been routed, especially after Mao lent moral support to rebellion, and the P.L.A. appeared to be leaning towards the Rebel side in what had so far been a civilian struggle. However, a number of influential people, including Zhou Enlai, warned that Shanghai's example of power seizure should not necessarily be emulated in other cities. The dividing line between legitimate revolution and unlawful usurpation of authority became more and more blurred. Even the firebrand Jiang Qing warned that cadre leadership would not necessarily be abandoned in the establishment of a new order, but would be subject to greater mass scrutiny.

At the end of January, Zhang Chunqiao and Yao Wenyuan, who, with Jiang Qing and Wang Hongwen, would become known as the 'gang of four', convened a preparatory committee for the Shanghai People's Commune. This was an attempt to bring a variety of organizations of workers and students under the one umbrella—a new, locally based form of proletarian dictatorship, in which members were elected according to the principles of the Paris Commune. Like the original, the Shanghai Commune did not last long. It was proclaimed on 5 February 1967, and later in the same month Mao himself was quibbling and equivocating about it in a way which left many Rebels wondering whether they had been sold out. It looked very much as if Mao was frightened off by the prospect of a genuine withering away of State and Party organization in the formation of a 'People's Commune of China'. Mao's preferred model was a 'revolutionary committee', a 'triple alliance' of Revolutionary Rebels, old cadres and the P.L.A. This would guarantee that, while the Party might be subjected to change, it would not be supplanted by a new source of authority. The short-lived Shanghai People's Commune danced to his tune and began calling themselves a revolutionary committee.

Hsin-ping weathered the January Storm in Shanghai, although she had a few anxious moments. She stayed with her brother-in-law, and in his family she was able to see a microcosm of the faction-fighting. Her husband's brother was a factory technician. As such he had experienced no special privileges, had developed few 'connections' to speak of, and had no influence or power. He was therefore naturally sympathetic to the Rebel position, which had taken hold in his factory, and became a member. His wife, on the other hand, was a Party member. Since she felt that she had some hard-won status to lose if the Rebel position prevailed, she became a member of the Scarlet Guards. The house became a battleground. Outside in the streets loudspeakers competed with each other in the intensity and volume of their respective messages and, inside the house, husband and wife screamed at each other with equal ferocity. At least this domestic strife was still a matter of *wendou* (a war of words) rather than *wudou* (armed conflict), but nevertheless the atmosphere in the house was unbearable. Hsin-ping went back to Peking, and found that the contagion had spread, and that a parallel factionalism was rife.

When Hsin-ping went back to work, she found that one of her colleagues—the one who had been branded a delinquent for having too many suitors—had died. Apparently she had cut a hole in the ice at the Summer Palace and jumped in. No further 'exposures' had occurred, but the pressure was mounting for those who had not chosen sides in the faction-fighting to come clean about their allegiances. Already the group who had not committed themselves, including Hsin-ping, had been dubbed the 'more gutless than mice faction', and it appeared that fence-sitting was the most dangerous tactic of all, since it might provide the factions with a common target for their resentment and hostility. Since Hsin-ping and the other members of the mouse faction considered that they had not done well at the hands of the Royalists, they opted for a Revolutionary Rebel stand. Like dissenters in the English Revolution, however, they knew they were unlikely to prosper, no matter which brand of intolerance prevailed or which Elect came to power.

Work, such as it was after the cataclysmic events of the last seven months, had ground to a halt in the factories, shops, schools and hospitals. Hsin-ping wondered at the confusion. Not even the struggle between socialism and capitalism had split the Chinese people like this, she thought, concerned that the only ones who could benefit from such chaos were the Taiwanese Nationalists. Armed conflict had by now spilled out into the streets, and every work unit was engulfed in a bitter struggle between those who wanted to produce and those who wanted to sabotage production—and each faction took its turn at both. Then she heard the news that the strife had invaded even the Peach Blossom Spring Beyond the World. Fighting had broken out in Xiamen.

清队清人

Purifying the Class Ranks

During February and March 1967, the P.L.A. moved into schools and work units in an attempt to impose order in the form of revolutionary committees—a solution dear to Mao's heart. But an old problem reappeared. Red Guard organizations, which contributed representatives to the committees, were once again to be formed on the basis of red background. In February a Central Committee directive emphasized that Red Guards should be chosen mainly from those of worker, peasant, soldier and revolutionary cadre backgrounds, but in practice this meant that the conditions which had allowed cadres' children to dominate the Communist Youth League, and the early Red Guard movement, would also allow them to hold sway over the revolutionary committees.

The Rebel faction suspected even more strongly now that they were witnessing a re-enactment of June and July 1966, in which a Party-approved structure had supervised the suppression of genuine revolutionary organizations. The revolutionary committees appeared to be another version of the work teams. To make matters worse, the army, which earlier had seemed sympathetic to the Rebels, now seemed to be leaning heavily in the direction of the Scarlet Guard faction.

By the autumn, Mao had made it quite clear that he did not want a continuation of the factionalism within the Red Guards, and that he was concerned at the prospect of radical, anti-authoritarian, 'ultra-left'

elements gaining control. The new revolutionary committees incorporated representatives from both major factions of the Guards, but in
general the Rebels felt that they had been sold out—if not by Mao
himself, then by someone who was manipulating him in the interests of
central Party control and maintenance of the status quo. The army took
charge of the schools between autumn 1967 and summer 1968, but the
factions continued to exist in all levels of organization, including the
army itself. From time to time there were major outbreaks of fighting
between the factions, leading to armed conflict, not only on school
campuses but in shops and factories.

Things were relatively stable in Hsin-ping's school. As in a great
many other organizations throughout Peking, the soldiers seemed
indifferent to their responsibilities as facilitators of the Revolution, and
were bent on living up to a rather older model of military behaviour.
Many had come into the city from the outlying border regions, where
they had been deprived of female companionship for some considerable
time. Rumours began to circulate about a 'work-style problem' among
military cadres. The soldiers themselves were rather less coyly dubbed
the 'big umbrella faction', an allusion to the alleged size and speed of
their erections on encountering an unaccustomed abundance of female
comrades. Around the school it became evident that fashionable
big-character posters no longer consisted of one name but two, male
and female co-stars, sharing equal billing in some vaguely expressed
misdemeanour or 'work-style problem.'

It was common knowledge that the P.L.A. cadre who was running
things these days was seeing rather a lot of one of the young female
teachers. She was of worker background, and perhaps the two had a lot
in common, but none the less it seemed odd that most of their meetings
took place in his room on the fifth floor of the staff dormitory between
the hours of eleven p.m. and five a.m. Unfortunately for them, the area
at the foot of the staircase provided excellent acoustic conditions for
anyone who wanted to listen in on work-style problems. The young
woman obviously benefitted considerably from her contact with the
P.L.A. Shortly after their meetings began, her application for Party
membership was approved, having been rejected on three previous
occasions. A story went round that in another school one of the P.L.A.
swains had been foolish enough to confide his exploits to a colleague
who supported a rival faction. A pair of binoculars was trained on his
room from a building opposite and, when the lovers had incriminated
themselves to the satisfaction of the investigators, they were arrested.

Throughout this period such stories became commonplace, and the
much revered P.L.A. suffered a loss of esteem. In schools, there were no
real lessons or schoolwork to speak of. Military cadres conducted
sessions in reading the works of Mao and these sessions degenerated

into mind-numbing boredom for staff and students alike. Many schools and work units lost all respect for the P.L.A. as leaders and administrators of civilian organizations, and this exacerbated the dissatisfaction already evident in the radical, activist groups. Faction fighting resumed its former intensity, and the messages promulgated by the central Cultural Revolution group oscillated between support for youthful revolutionaries in their attempt to wrest power from conservative and authoritarian P.L.A. influence, and anxiety at the prospect of anarchy, as Red Guards, P.L.A. units and worker groups became embroiled in violent conflict. Sometimes the central Cultural Revolution group—the 'Centre'—supported the army and sometimes it called strongly for its rectification. Counter-revolutionaries were still the common, nominal target of all factions, however, and investigations were launched into even the most unlikely sources of sedition, under the increasingly strident leadership of Jiang Qing.

At the end of 1967, Hsin-ping's childhood friend Tang Ling, visibly pregnant, was investigated. This was because of a poem—'The Immortals'—which Mao had written in memory of his first chosen wife, Yang Kaihui, who had been executed by the Nationalists. Two former workmates at the commercial arts workshop where she and Hsin-ping had worked in the early 1960s had been reported as having praised Yang Kaihui to the skies and having frequently pored over this poem in her memory. This was tantamount to attacking Jiang Qing. As a result, representatives of the Public Security Bureau and the Party secretary visited Tang Ling almost every night for some weeks, seeking confirmation from her that they had engaged in this heresy while she was working with them.

Tang Ling could scarcely remember what happened from day to day, let alone eight or nine years ago, and she was even less inclined to take any notice of anything which did not concern her directly. She had no hope of dealing with their roundabout suggestions and insinuations, and responded to their impatient and hostile questioning first by looking utterly bewildered and then by crying, but she could not provide the 'evidence' they required, even after they had prompted her inadequate memory by providing her with a 'clue'. The clue consisted of telling her exactly what her workmates were supposed to have said and when. They had made it perfectly simple for her. But she just kept saying she could not remember.

As a result she was herself investigated for harbouring counter-revolutionaries, and struggled against in a mass meeting. She was forced to her knees and struck repeatedly, but in the end was saved from a worse fate by her pregnancy and by those quick-witted enough to employ it in her defence. Several people in the crowd called out to the young devotees of Jiang Qing, who had organized the exposure of counter-revolutionaries, that her unborn child was an innocent successor to the Revolution and should be protected. Fortunately, Tang Ling's tormentors were in a rather progressive frame of mind. She might easily have fallen victim to an older custom—that of punishing all those who are connected with the criminal. The feudal practice of rounding up such people to 'accompany' a relative to his fate had survived in revolutionary struggle meetings. In any case, Tang Ling escaped without serious injury to herself, but her child was born prematurely.

At the beginning of 1968 Hsin-ping went to visit her old friend in hospital. Tang Ling had just had a son. As they sat talking, Hsin-ping noticed the appalling filth in the maternity ward. Piles of food brought by well-wishers were left rotting, and mice scuttled to and fro. She even saw a rat making off with an egg. There was no one to carry out hygiene work, and the floor was thick with dust blown in on Peking's notorious spring winds. Tang Ling was telling her of a conversation she had had with a nurse. The nurse had asked her 'What group do you support, what stand do you take?' 'I support the Revolutionary Rebels', said Tang Ling. 'You are discharged' said the nurse, 'Take your baby and go home. You can't stay here'. Tang Ling had given birth only the day before, but she didn't want to argue because the hospital was no place for a sick person and she was anxious to get out. Operations had become a farce. Rebel nurses would not assist Scarlet doctors, and Scarlet nurses would not work with Rebel doctors and so on. People who couldn't move were unable to relieve themselves because hospital staff would not assist a patient who belonged to an opposing faction. Tang Ling had been preparing to leave when Hsin-ping arrived.

As the two sat discussing the situation, there was an uproar outside in the courtyard. Hsin-ping went to the window, brushed away the dust with her sleeve, and looked out on an extraordinary sight. There was a whirl of arms and legs in a scene resembling one of the Monkey King's more dramatic exploits in Heaven, accompanied by all the din of the Peking Opera. Hsin-ping could not see very clearly but she could distinguish doctors, nurses—and patients. She could not believe her eyes. Convalescent patients in wheelchairs could not wait to propel themselves into the fracas. A patient came hobbling into Tang Ling's ward searching frantically for a wheelchair because he could not walk as far as the courtyard. A nurse rushed to get him a chair, but he could not sit down in it anyway. He had just had haemorrhoids removed and was bleeding profusely, but he seemed desperate to take some part in the action. Hsin-ping helped Tang Ling and her baby to leave the hospital as quickly as possible, and took them home safely through the confusion.

After spring the violence escalated. Supply trains carrying arms and ammunition to Vietnam had been seized and employed in factional warfare. Cities and towns were the centre of local wars, and college campuses, railway depots and factories were the scene of fierce pitched battles. The question of the use of violence by Red Guards had been very complicated since the beginning of the Cultural Revolution. At times, Mao appeared to be very disturbed by the violence and disorder generated by the faction fighting, and at times he appeared to be suggesting that this was a prerequisite for revolutionary change. Jiang Qing was also ambivalent. At times she deplored the violence, at other time she stressed that revolutionaries should not allow themselves to be pushed around by reactionary elements.

Among these reactionary elements was the P.L.A. itself, or at least that section of it which had gone too far in suppressing the Rebels in February 1967. This period was referred to as the 'February adverse current' and through the spring and summer of 1967 central Cultural Revolution leaders such as Jiang Qing, Lin Biao and even the moderate Zhou Enlai had exhorted revolutionaries to be vigilant against a revival of the diehard conservative element which would choke the life out of the Cultural Revolution if allowed. The Centre appeared to be steering a hazardous course between 'ultra-right' and 'ultra-left', with the 'great helmsman' at the wheel.

Over the next few months, 'ultra-leftism' and 'anarchy' were the labels used to distinguish between legitimate and illegitimate factionalism. Despite its honoured place among the intellectual antecedents of the Chinese Revolution, the meaning of the word 'anarchy' was very quickly debased from its literal Chinese meaning ('without government') to the universal popular usage, 'without order'—and that, of course, implied 'without the Party'. In order to define and contain factionalism to the point where it encompassed enough revolutionary activity to prevent the re-emergence of the old leadership, without threatening the prospects of the new, the Party organs published an analysis of factionalism in April 1968. It distinguished between 'bourgeois' and 'proletarian' factionalism.

Now it was all perfectly clear to everybody. Proletarian factionalism was the kind supported by the Centre. Bourgeois factionalism was the kind supported by anybody else. The only remaining difficulty lay in determining who it was that the Centre actually supported. There were times when young radicals must have felt like their class mates waging revolution in the villages, many of whom had dared to strike a blow against the yoke of feudal morality by walking arm and arm in public, only to suffer the indignity of having angry peasants, whom they were supposed to be liberating, tip buckets of nightsoil over their heads.

For the Red Guards, of various factions, the bucket came from a tremendous altitude, thrown by Mao himself. In the summer of 1968 Mao dramatically dissociated himself from his 'little generals' and, in a meeting with student leaders on 28 July, he took them to task for the chaos they had unleashed in the name of revolution. According to some, Mao had tears in his eyes as he said, 'You have let me down' and 'You have disappointed the workers, peasants and soldiers of China'. Within a couple of days a new phase of the Cultural Revolution had begun and a new troubleshooter was sent into schools and work units—the 'worker-peasant Mao-thought-propaganda-team'. These organizations had the support of the P.L.A., but were not specifically identified with P.L.A. control as the earlier ones had been. As before, however, their task was to organize the establishment of 'revolutionary committees' which would consist of an alliance of favoured elements who were expected to impose order on the chaos. The teams were composed ostensibly of a majority of workers and peasants, and the wayward student leaders were now required to submit to working-class leadership in the continuing struggle against counter-revolutionaries.

To demonstrate his pleasure at the way one such team had settled the strife in Qinghua University, Mao presented the members with a gift of mangoes. His action, in passing on to the thought propaganda team a 'treasured gift' from a foreign delegation, symbolized the end of the Red Guards as Mao's favourites. The gaols began to fill with younger victims—Red Guards—who were accused of selfish careerism, ambitionism and factionalism. Those who had promoted the ideal of Paris Commune democracy and of a new liberal society were considered no less criminal than those who had indulged themselves in brutality, sadism and the abuse of power. In a wave of Mao fetishism, plastic mangoes appeared above doorways and on tables in homes all over China, symbolizing Mao's blessing of the new propaganda teams.

Also in the summer of 1968, a new call went out to 'purify the class ranks' of bad elements, and the issue of one's background became paramount again. Despite the relatively benign influence of the thought propaganda teams, the pendulum had swung back abruptly in the direction of the established order of the Party. In the new campaign to purify, to sieve out bad elements and to identify the true successors to the Revolution, those who saw themselves as legitimate heirs by dint of birth were in no mood to hand over their inheritance to interlopers. The workers and peasants, like faithful family retainers, might well be left something in the will, but middle-class changelings would be put firmly in their place. The first to be arrested, beaten, or killed were often those of 'bad background' who had dared to take a revolutionary, activist stance between 1966 and 1968. They had clearly forgotten themselves with the dissolution of the Communist Youth League, which had previously served to remind them of their inferior status. In many other cases the issue of background was less important than old rivalries, hatreds and jealousies, which were given a new lease of life with this opportunity to identify bad elements in the class ranks.

Individuals in every school, factory and farm were encouraged to investigate others thoroughly, but this time there was an increased emphasis on evidence, with the result that investigating teams had to be sent out all over the country to look into accusations. Since people had often come from another province to their present work unit, extensive travel and lengthy periods of time were usually involved. Many of the investigating team members were far more interested in the opportun- ities this provided for new experiences than in hunting down counter- revolutionaries. The investigations often ended in exoneration of the accused but, while evidence was being sought, countless numbers spent time in the makeshift prisons and 'cattlepens' of their work units. 'Ox demons and snake spirits' were once again the target of the Cultural Revolution. The movement to purify class ranks gathered in intensity. Simultaneously, in a repeat of events of the Great Leap Forward and the Socialist Education Movement, great stress was laid on the need to 'go down to the countryside' in order to re-discover the roots of revolution.

The process of transfer of millions of youths to the countryside began with the punitive exile of fractious Red Guards; upper secondary school students then poured out of the cities. Many began filtering back almost as soon as they had left, living without their household books on illegal rations and illegal employment, and setting in train a series of social problems that would take years to correct. Others simply stayed out in the villages for years, eking out a meaningless existence and feeling betrayed and forgotten, unwanted by the locals and unable to make any useful contribution to their communities. They felt a lasting distaste for the crudity, poverty and ignorance of peasant life. Yet others, whatever their anxieties about the loss of privileged city residence, found useful and rewarding work in the villages. They would look back on their years in the countryside as a tough but enriching experience, and would always remember their peasant friends with affection. Whether the purpose of this mass movement to the countryside was the re-discovery of revolutionary purity, a cure for unemployment, or a disciplinary action against the unruly youth who had served Mao's purposes but had now become a nuisance, was a matter for private musings.

The study of 'Mao Thought' became more and more religious in quality. The application of Mao Thought to the solution of political problems was like the invocation of a magic spell, and monotonous incantations from his works were a feature of everyday life throughout China. Now in junior primary school, Hsin-ping's daughter Lulu came home one day in 1969 with a request to know what was meant by 'opposing the restoration of capitalism'. She also wanted to know about the cardinal sins of Graft, Embezzlement and Waste. She had been asked to give an example of how Mao Thought might be applied to eradicating these evils. Hsin-ping found it extremely difficult to think of examples for a child whose experience of graft, embezzlement and waste was limited. So, she put it this way: 'Well, for example, you shouldn't waste water. If you wash your hands and you splash the water all over the place, that's waste, or if you don't turn off the tap it's in a way betraying . . . I mean, not caring for your country. Let's see now . . . why don't you say something like this: "Last night I left the tap running. A little later I thought of Chairman Mao. I thought of his words about waste and I remembered the tap. So I got up straight away and rushed into the kitchen and turned it off."'

Next day an unhappy little girl complained to her mother, 'Mama, you got me into trouble! Today we read about graft and waste. When the teacher asked each of us how to use Mao Thought to fix this problem, almost everyone in the class said the same thing—about wasting water, just like you told me last night. The teacher said we had all copied from each other.' Hsin-ping experienced a sense of fraternity with innumerable hapless parents, confronted with a generation whose loyalties were being transferred from their families to the state. They could not afford to appear ignorant of Mao Thought when asked questions by their children, but had to avoid saying anything contentious. Saving water was an obvious way of saving one's skin.

Each morning Lulu got up and, before anything else, pledged her day to Chairman Mao. 'What task do you have for me today Chairman Mao?' she would ask. In the streets, after sunrise, people gathered to sing 'The East is Red', a reference not only to communism, which after all was only an idea, but to Chairman Mao, who was the real red sun in their hearts, the celestial power which gave them all life. Meetings in factories and schools began with a twentieth-century mantra—'Eternal life to Chairman Mao. Good health to Vice-Chairman Lin'. Many experienced a kind of vague curiosity about what sickness had afflicted Vice-Chairman Lin Biao, that he should need such constant encouragement in the matter of his health. Some thought that he did in fact have a terminal illness—ambition—and that perhaps the difference in status between 'eternal life' and 'good health' was enough to make a vice-chairman hanker after promotion.

Every day in Hsin-ping's school there were meetings to study Mao Thought. Each such meeting began with a call to take out the 'Quotations from Chairman Mao'. Everyone stood up and recited the usual prayer for Chairman Mao and Vice-Chairman Lin, after which a selection was read from the *Little Red Book*, as it became known outside

China. The book had its origins in the earlier P.L.A. custom of studying the works of Mao, and in the practice of the *People's Daily* in featuring a Mao Thought-for-the-day in each issue. The words were Mao's but the tongue was increasingly Marshal Lin's, as propaganda organs swung their resources energetically behind the service of the Mao cult. After the reading, the congregation was asked for its opinion on the text. Someone would stand up and cry out, 'First, eternal life to Chairman Mao. Good health to Vice Chairman Lin'. Everyone else would rise and repeat this. Then someone would speak in fervent praise of the selection. Another eternal life to Mao, and then someone else would stand up to offer an 'opinion'. These meetings usually lasted two or three hours.

In the mornings, as she entered the school's courtyard, Hsin-ping would place her bike against a wall, face the portrait of Chairman Mao outside the entrance to the classrooms, and recite a passage from The Book. But she kept thirty yuan in cash in her pocket, and enough coupons for thirty kilograms of grain. As she recited, she glanced around the walls to see if her name appeared anywhere in a big-character poster. She was ready to get back on her bike and race down to the station the moment she saw it.

Denunciation by poster was an ever-present threat. The last time it had seemed imminent was some twelve months before, when drawings of foxes had appeared abruptly around the school. Basically, Hsin-ping had been on the side of the Rebels, if for no other reason than that she was ineligible for any 'good background' faction, but she maintained a low-key commitment in order not to attract attention. However, she had run the danger of being labelled 'a fox that plays dead, a heart that nurtures a demon'. Lukewarm support for her faction soon led to accusations of deviousness, and posters with cartoon foxes on them began to spring up around the school, caricaturing her as a sly creature, hatching some unspeakable plot in a still bosom. She had survived this period, probably because she was not the object of much envy and, by the time the obvious targets had been dealt with, some of the heat had gone out of the situation. But she had used her morning prayers to good effect ever since.

The hunt went on for counter-revolutionaries hiding in the class ranks. Because Mao had placed some emphasis on the idea that investigations should unearth proof against an accused person, without which that person should ultimately be released, there was a great deal of historical research going on into the backgrounds of a variety of people. One day at a meeting in the school, it was announced that one of the staff members had hands that were 'soaked in blood' because he had been involved with a German Catholic orphanage in Shandong Province in the 1920s. Orphanages were places where foreign devils used

Chinese children for all kinds of unnatural practices and unspeakable rites. The very least of the evils perpetrated was a slave trade in children. During the meeting it was announced that the school had a 'historical counter-revolutionary' on the premises, who had assumed a 'false skin' and was masquerading as a teacher. The army representative on the revolutionary committee called upon this miscreant and traitor to own up, but there was no movement from the assembly. 'Very well', said the army representative, 'You know who you are. You have one more day to think about it. If you do not come forward voluntarily and confess your crimes you will be dragged out at our next meeting'.

The next day a man named Huang was exposed as the historical counter-revolutionary. He was struggled against and beaten, but would not confess to his crime, so he was put in the cattlepen and subjected to labour reform on the school premises. He remained imprisoned in the cattlepen for a year. It later transpired that the evidence unearthed by a zealous policeman a year before, the evidence on which he was convicted, had contained one or two errors. Although the suspect fitted the description given in an old file in most respects, including family name (if not given name), details of age had been overlooked in the haste of enquiry. The file indicated that the criminal was born in 1905 and should have been sixty-three at the time of his exposure by the policeman. The suspect was in fact thirty-six. A year later the mistake was discovered and the school authorities released him from his pen with an apology. He was declared a 'good comrade'.

A similar problem befell a primary-school friend of Hsin-ping. This was the fat girl who had always had the big lunch boxes and had been popular with Hsin-ping and the other sports-minded girls because of her size and strength. She could hold two or three opposition basketballers at bay while her team-mates regrouped. She had graduated as an engineer from Qinghua University some years before it became a hotbed of Red Guard activity, and lived quite near Hsin-ping. She was very fond of Lulu and often called by to see her. On one such day, she broke down in tears.

'I can't go on', she sobbed, 'My life is ruined, with all this "purifying the class ranks" business.'

'But why?' asked Hsin-ping, bemused. 'You're O.K. surely? Your husband is a Party member. They always manage to stay on top no matter what happens. What problem could you possibly have?'

'No, no, you don't understand. It's my father who is in real trouble, and it could ruin him and us. He has been struggled against in Tianjin for two days.'

'What for?'

'Well, you know his name is Li Honglin?'

'Yes, so what?'

'They say he's a historical counter-revolutionary—a traitor.'

'What are you talking about?'

'They say he is Li Hongzhang, you know, the one who used the Navy's funds to build the Summer Palace, so we were not ready for the Japanese in 1894.'

'But your father's name is not Li Hongzhang!'

'Yes, but they say he changed his name from Li Hongzhang to Li Honglin.'

'Well, he didn't make a very good job of changing it did he? Why didn't he change it to Sun Yat-sen?' Hsin-ping was tempted to laugh out loud at the absurdity of it all, but understood how grave a problem it was for Li Meiqi and her family.

'He has been struggled against for two days. They say he'll die soon, and then they'll come for us.'

'But Li Meiqi, I'm surprised at you. You of all people, a Qinghua graduate. You know very well that Li Hongzhang lived during Qing times, during the Manchu dynasty. *Your* father is still living! If he were Li Hongzhang he would have to be well over a hundred years old. Is your father a hundred years old?'

'Yes, I know all about that, but unfortunately none of the investigators had your education, Hsin-ping.'

'But there must have been plenty of people in the factory who knew this. Why didn't they speak up?'

Hsin-ping knew the answer to her own question before she had finished uttering it. To speak up would be to defend a criminal. In the early days of the Cultural Revolution, people were often beaten simply because they had been accused. Things had changed now— for the worse. You were beaten only if there was proof against you, but proof could always be found if need be, and how could anyone oppose beating or maltreating a person who was a proven bad element? Not even Li Meiqi's husband could help without betraying the fact that he was harbouring sympathies for a hated class enemy. Hsin-ping did not see Li Meiqi again and never knew what happened to her or her family.

As criticism of those who had 'illicit relations with foreigners' was revived in even greater intensity than before, Hsin-ping kept thinking of the old adage, 'There are thirty-six ways of coping with a problem, but the best way is to disappear'. In the city, public trial meetings were becoming more and more frequent. A million spectators passed through the Peking Workers' Sports Stadium to see the trials during the movement to 'suppress counter-revolutionaries'. Work units throughout the city were required to send representatives to these gatherings. School children were sent, in the spirit of 'killing the chicken in front of the monkey'—frightening the wits out of any potential wrongdoer by demonstrating his punishment. Hsin-ping, in her role as class teacher, often had to decide which monkeys needed this experience.

Normally, those sent to represent the school at the trial were 'red flag' types, teachers of good class background, and Party members. But in every delegation of ten or so, there were one or two students who had been sent as a result of stealing, or quarrelling or unruly behaviour. Once or twice Hsin-ping had little choice but to send children who had stolen books. Her private feeling was that such children must be decent types, to want books so badly, but she could not afford to overlook the crime. They came back from the trial meetings in a state of distress, and were unable to concentrate on their work, or even to speak, for some days.

A typical public trial began with the presentation of dossiers to each work unit in attendance. These contained information on twenty or thirty people, and listed their crimes. Sometimes it was rape, or 'sodomy'—often committed by very old men who seemed unlikely monsters of depravity—but the majority were accused of political crimes associated with their background as alleged landlords or spies.

A story came back from one of the trials about a young woman who was accused of selling State secrets to a foreign embassy. This story enjoyed some currency, because it had the flavour of sexual fantasy and folklore about it, making the politics easier to swallow. It appeared the woman had wanted to escape from China. She tried to contact people in foreign embassies who might help her, but to no avail. For a start, she just could not gain entry to the embassies. Then she hit upon an excellent ruse—she painted her face black and dressed extravagantly to look like a staff member from one of the African embassies. Once inside, she revealed her true identity to one of the staff, threw herself upon his mercy and asked him to help get her out of China in return for sexual favours. In view of the widespread belief among Chinese that black men cannot resist Chinese women, the escape attempt would appear to have been built on a pretty solid foundation. But, according to the story, the brotherhood of socialist nations prevailed, and the woman was reported to the authorities. She and her husband were shot at one of the very first public trial meetings. Hsin-ping enquired of witnessess what crime the husband had committed, but all anybody seemed to know was that he was a teacher at Number Twenty-five Secondary School.

Hsin-ping and many others in her school shuddered as the details of another story unfolded, and they thought of their own records. Yu Luoke was a 22-year-old of bad background, whose father had been branded a rightist in the late 1950s. As a result, Yu had been unable to go to university, and was outspoken in his criticism of the over-emphasis on red background which accompanied the early phase of the Cultural Revolution. He published several articles on this theme, and was particularly critical of the notion of inherited revolutionary characteristics, the idea that 'dragons beget dragons and phoenixes beget phoenixes'. This view was exemplified in a well-worn piece of doggerel:

> If the old man's a revolutionary, the son is all right.
> If the old man's a reactionary, the son is a bastard.
> If the old man's neither, the son is a weakling.

Jiang Qing's famous comment, that anyone who was not a revolutionary could fuck off, was added to the verse, and heredity was raised to the status of an objective law in determining who was or was not a revolutionary.

Yu, like many others, objected to the way this theory was used to exclude people from positions in the Party. Less ambitious critics noted that the background theory was even used to exclude people from positions in the bus. Red Guards employed a version of it to determine seating arrangements: if your parents were workers you could sit, if they were teachers you could stand, and if they were landlords you could walk.

Yu had kept a diary, in which he wrote:

Is background important? Yes, after all, Chairman Mao taught us that we all bear the unmistakable imprint of background on our attitudes. Each of us has a class orientation, derived from differences in our means of livelihood. We all bear the mark of class. But it is wrong to deny people the opportunity to rectify their way of thinking. Those who lag behind the progressive forces can mend their ways. Those who have lived since Liberation, side by side, in harmony and goodwill with workers and peasants, should not be condemned and excluded because their fathers were landlords.

When the Red Guards began raiding homes, Yu asked his sister to hide his diary and this she did—in a public toilet near the museum in Tian'anmen Square. Unfortunately, it was found the very next day. After its discovery, Yu was tried and sentenced to fifteen years' imprisonment for counter-revolutionary activity. He refused to sign a statement of acceptance of his sentence, because he believed he had committed no crime. He argued that he had a right of appeal under the constitution. He was struggled against, but still refused to confess to the crime. He was sentenced to twenty years' imprisonment, then life. Still he would not confess or sign the document. He was finally threatened with the death sentence. Then he was given a public trial, in front of ten thousand people, and shot. His diary was proof that he was a counter-revolutionary.

During the movement to purify the class ranks, the public trials and executions gathered in momentum. The accused were dragged from a car at the stadium, paraded before the masses, accused, denounced and shot, all without a word in their own defence. One woman, it was said, had her vocal chords severed so that she could say nothing against her captors before being executed. There was no defence, no represen-tation—after all there was no need for bourgeois parasite lawyers in a modern, socialist country. In a grotesque blend of feudal and modern cruelty, a 'bullet bill' was often presented to the family of the victim, a reminder of the days when executions were so thorough that even the corpse had to be flogged.

As in 1966, personal files became a matter of life and death. They contained details of every major event in a person's life, including things that happened in primary and secondary school, comments made by others about character and behaviour, details of family and friends, relationships with others and so on. The P.L.A. took a leading role in identifying and investigating those of dubious history and, because the investigation teams went so thoroughly into a person's past, the search often spread to faraway cities where long-forgotten contacts and associations were revived in the quest for evidence.

Hsin-ping experienced several 'external investigations' during this time. Once, she was re-united, in memory at least, with a figure who had ceased to have any significance in her life, and whom she had rarely troubled to recall since she was in high school. In her final years of high school she had been a keen swimmer, and had often represented her school in the city-wide swimming competitions. She often trained with a friend and her boyfriend, who was a physical education teacher. The last she saw of them was in 1955. In 1969 three investigators called her from the classroom to ask what she remembered of the man, and any conver-sations she had had with him. Was there anything he seemed dissatisfied with? Did he make any complaint about the government? She said she could not remember. One of the investigators became extremely angry and thumped the table. 'Of course you remember', he declared.

'Are you investigating him or me?' asked Hsin-ping in response to his hostility.

'You must help us', said a woman, trying to smooth things over. 'We need to know this information.'

'But I can't help you. I just don't remember. We went swimming together, that's all. I don't know what we talked about. Swimming probably. I can't solve this problem for you. Ask my leaders, ask my friends. If you think I'm in the wrong, by all means criticize me, but I just can't say any more.'

'You are not being honest with us', they shouted.

Hsin-ping was by now in danger of the accusation that she was shielding a counter-revolutionary. However, because of the emphasis on proof, the investigating team needed two or three witnesses to inform on her—just as they needed her to inform on her old swimming companion. Once again she was lucky. Because they were unable to get any reports of suspicious behaviour on her part, they went on to other targets in the meantime. In some ways this investigation spared her from the more serious charge that she was a person with illicit foreign connections. While she was being investigated for evidence that she was protecting counter-revolutionaries, she was not being investigated for something else.

A little after this incident, she ran into another problem of a similar nature—again caused by swimming. When Chairman Mao came out of hiding in 1966 and went swimming in the Yangtse, it seemed to boost his political fortunes tremendously. The whole nation was invited to rejoice in the event. Whenever Hsin-ping went swimming, she immersed herself in difficulties. She used to have a boyfriend of sorts in high school, and they often trained together for the swimming events. His name was Zhang Shen, and his family background was extremely interesting. He did not seem clear about it himself, and had sketched out a rather fuzzy picture to Hsin-ping, but he was connected with Zhang Zuolin, the 'Tiger of Manchuria', the most powerful of the Chinese warlords during the 1920s.

Zhang Zuolin had climbed in rank from an enlisted soldier in the Sino–Japanese war of 1894–1895, in which China lost control of Korea and Taiwan, to ruler of Manchuria—also on Japan's shopping list. He had also ruled much of northern China, including Peking, until driven out by an expedition in 1928. On his way back to Manchuria, Japanese soldiers bombed Zhang's train and he was killed, paving the way for a Japanese pretext to seize Manchuria from the Chinese. The pretext, and the invasion, duly took place in 1931, when Zhang's son, Xueliang, was ruler of Manchuria. Hsin-ping's boyfriend had a father and grandfather who were blood-brothers to Zhang Xueliang and Zhang Zuolin respectively. Coincidentally, they had the same family name, a very common Chinese surname, but they were related only in the sense of being close friends and comrades-in-arms. Zhang Shen's father had been a divisional commander in Zhang Xueliang's army, and his grandfather had been a general in Zhang Zuolin's. Zhang Xueliang had another place in Chinese history as one of the officers who arrested Chiang Kai-shek in the Xi'an Incident in 1936. He was later himself imprisoned in Taiwan for his part in the arrest. None of this had ever been of much significance to Zhang Shen, who simply liked swimming.

The first hint that his background, with its full complement of unsavoury warlords or 'bandits', would give him any bother was during the movement to eliminate counter-revolutionaries in 1955. He had been keen to go to Tianjin University, but because of his back-

ground was sent to a college to study mining architecture. This disappointment exacerbated an already troublesome inclination to make
cynical remarks in public places, with the result that he and a small
group of friends developed something of a reputation as a 'counter-
revolutionary clique'. They were suspected of stealing the lecture notes
of would-be Party members, and were inclined to be playful in the
dining hall. When given food they didn't like—such as noodles made
from sweet potato starch—they would toss it into the toilet. They quar-
relled with many people about many things, and among their adver-
saries were people like the departmental Party secretary and the college
Party secretary.

However, their biggest problem came from an entirely unexpected
direction. The circle of friends extended across the 'eight big colleges' in
their vicinity, including the Medical College, the Mining College, the
Geology College, the Foreign Language Institute, Peking University
and Qinghua University, all in the western suburbs of the city. It
included old school friends of the 'counter-revolutionary clique', and
gatherings often took place in one or other of the colleges. One of the
group, who always rode his bike to their meetings rather than taking
the bus, drew up a useful map, linking the colleges by means of short
cuts across the fields and villages. He presented each of his friends with
a copy.

Another storm cloud was gathering over the group. At that time,
whoever was accepted for university or college had his or her name
published in the *People's Daily*—a great distinction. The group used to
mark the names of acquaintances, former classmates, and friends and
relatives whenever they appeared in the paper, and kept copies as a
record. For some reason, they developed the habit of indicating the
closeness of the relationships to themselves by means of a system of
symbols—a triangle for friends, a circle for the friends of friends, a
square for relatives, and so on.

Inevitably, both the short-cut map and the enigmatically inscribed
copies of the *People's Daily* fell into the hands of the Public Security
Bureau. In 1955, all members of this group were arrested and imprisoned
for six months, since the Public Security Bureau could not accept that there
was no sinister code or underground organization involved in all these
complicated goings-on. They were released after an investigation and
allowed to go back to their studies. Every one of them resisted the very
strong temptation to complain about their treatment. In fact, they all
strenuously upheld the right of the authorities to have dealt with them as
they did, and praised the police for conducting such a fair and reasonable
investigation. Obviously they had learnt a great deal in prison. As a result,
in 1957, when the hunt was on for rightists who had complained about the
Party and the State, their records indicated that they had praised the

Public Security Bureau, and had been deeply moved and impressed at being given an apology after their release.

Twelve years later, two investigators came to see Hsin-ping at her flat and asked her to 'hand over' some information. 'You must help us', they said. 'You must tell us what we need to know about a person called Wen. Has this Wen ever ventured any opinion in your presence? What kind of opinion was expressed?' Since the Chinese pronoun '*ta*' can mean either 'he' or 'she', the investigators' further questioning left Hsin-ping without a clue even as to the gender of this person, whose name meant nothing to her. She could think of only one person by the name of Wen, and that was a teacher she had in high school. That didn't seem to be the one, and her replies were regarded as completely unsatisfactory. The first meeting lasted two hours. They came back on the second day and went through the same routine. By this time, they were accusing Hsin-ping of concealing something. On the third day, after a number of these accusations, she said to them in exasperation, 'You keep saying I'm not being honest with you, but I have just never heard of this person. I've thought and thought but I just don't know anyone by that name, and I never have—except for the teacher I told you about. None of my friends, relatives, or workmates is called Wen. Couldn't you just give me a clue?'

The investigating team left the room, argued animatedly outside the door for some minutes, then came back and said, 'Did you ever know a person called Zhang Shen?'

'Of course', she said, recalling her swimming partner and almost-boyfriend of fifteen years ago.

'Yes, I knew him for a year or two when I was in high school. I haven't seen him since he went to college.'

'Did you ever visit his home?'

'Yes, on Saturdays and Sundays—often.'

'Well then', said the chief interrogator menacingly, 'his mother was named Wen. Now do you still insist that you don't know this person?'

Hsin-ping was shocked and frightened. 'But I was only about sixteen then, when I used to go to his place. I didn't know what his mother's name was. How could I, a child, refer to her by name? I always called his parents "aunt" and "uncle". How could I be so rude as to use their names? Anyway, I never saw much of his mother. She lived in another part of the house.'

'What opinions did she express?' asked an investigator, ignoring Hsin-ping's denials.

'About what? I just don't know what you're talking about.'

'About the commodity supply system!'

Hsin-ping felt sick at this revelation. She remembered that in 1953 and 1954 the coupon system had started. She didn't remember Zhang

Shen's parents saying anything in particular about it, but everyone in China had an 'opinion'—and in Chinese, 'opinion' and 'objection' are extremely close, both linguistically and politically. Perhaps she *had* said something about the commodity supply system—about the fact that there was a general lack of commodities to be supplied. At that time everybody had enough coupons for just two or three items of clothing, and this caused quite a lot of 'opinions'.

She struggled through the rest of the investigation, protesting that she knew nothing about her old friend's mother's opinions about the commodity supply system in 1954. She was accused again of harbouring a class enemy. An external investigation led her accusers to Shanghai in search of incriminating evidence from her past, but ultimately produced nothing. In the meantime, many people whom she had regarded as friends gave her a wide berth, out of self-preservation rather than malice, she supposed.

Like others under investigation, Hsin-ping was often required to go to other schools to witness struggle meetings where teachers were made to 'do the aeroplane'—that is, their arms were shoved up high behind their backs, forcing them into a head-down, delta-winged position, in which they could be beaten and humiliated. On one such occasion she saw an old man being harassed as a 'counter-revolutionary'. It was summer and he was sweating profusely, crouched in the 'aeroplane' position. Some of his colleagues were screaming and ranting at him, 'In the past your kind has ridden on the backs of the people'. 'So', thought Hsin-ping, 'Yesterday he rode on the backs of the people. And today you're riding on *his* back. Will there be a tomorrow, when we can all ride on yours?' But she kept her mouth shut.

As the meeting wore on, the violence got worse. Suddenly a young female teacher sprang out from the meeting, screaming that her family were workers who had been oppressed by monsters like this. She flew at him, punched him, and kicked him as he lay on the ground. A middle-aged teacher called Liu, sitting beside Hsin-ping, let out a sharp cry. Hsin-ping grabbed her fingers and squeezed them with all her might to prevent her making another sound. Such an admission of sympathy would lead to Liu's own exposure as a class enemy. Hsin-ping dared not say anything to warn her, she could only squeeze her hand mercilessly—and hope. During this time many people dared only to hate, and not to speak. There were times, when the mob was screaming, that simply not screaming with them was an act of defiance. Teacher Liu understood the significance of Hsin-ping's silent rescue. Some time later when they met in the street, she embraced her benefactor with tears in her eyes. Still they did not speak.

Shortly after this, one of Hsin-ping's colleagues became a target. He was normally responsible for discipline and good order among the students during rallies and assemblies and, as a result, there were times when he had remonstrated with them about their youthful high spirits. Recently he had made the mistake of attending so carefully to his responsibilities, in particular to arranging the students in neat files, that he had neglected to raise his arm and shout 'eternal life' to Chairman Mao. He was observed by other teachers who were present at the sports ground that day. In due course he was reported for his lack of feeling for Chairman Mao and the Revolution. Everybody else had been shouting at the top of his voice, why hadn't he? He was 'dragged out' from the class ranks and investigated for nearly two years, after which he was released.

The schools had by now established a system for collecting reports on various people. There was a kind of reception room, where duty teachers received reports from all those who had information to offer. The parents of students in the school often came, not necessarily because they wanted to cause trouble for others, but because if they did not it would raise doubts about the intensity of their desire to purify the class ranks. One could hardly claim to be a good type unless one exposed some bad types.

One day, Hsin-ping was on duty in the reception room. The mother of one of her fourth-year students came into the room. Both mother and daughter were renowned tell-tales and gossips. The mother announced that she wanted to make a report on a teacher called Wang Huifen, a man Hsin-ping knew quite well.

'Yes, what would you like to tell me?' she asked the woman, wondering what poor old Wang had done this time. He had a reputation for getting himself into scrapes through the most improbable circumstances.

'In 1965 Teacher Wang was teaching my daughter current affairs from the newspaper', said the woman.

This seemed proof enough of his moral turpitude, judging by the look on her great moon face, and the triumphant glint of her massive teeth.

'Yes, yes, what kind of current affairs?' asked Hsin-ping, a little impatiently.

'The newspaper. He gave her a lesson on a newspaper item.'

'And what was the trouble?'

'He said that Albania opposed the revolutionary forces!' she said, as if it were all self-evident.

Hsin-ping blinked, took a deep breath and set about looking for clues with which to crack this cipher. 'Really? I don't quite understand what you mean, could you tell me a little more about it?'

'He insulted our socialist brother country Albania by saying that they suppressed the forces of the people's revolution in 1965.'

Hsin-ping re-visiting her primary school in Shoupa Lane, 1987

Hsin-ping's primary school (top) and secondary school, with 'Metternich' her form history teacher, 1987

'Oh, I see', said Hsin-ping, feeling that the less said, the better.
'Anything else?'
'No.'
'O.K. I'll write all that down.'
'That teacher is a counter-revolutionary', said the insistent woman, apparently not satisfied that justice had been done.

At lunch time, Hsin-ping sought out Wang Huifen. 'Did you say anything indiscreet about Albania in current affairs four years ago? I had a report on you this morning for insulting Albania, and I can't figure out what the stupid woman is prattling on about. You could be in trouble, Lao Wang. You have to think, try to remember, please.'

'I remember quite well', said Wang without hesitating, 'I told you about it once before. I was talking about the September coup in 1965 in Indonesia, and I think I said something about Suharto and the rightists overthrowing Sukarno. You know, Sukarno was our friend and Suharto was not. Sukarno even visited China. Liu Shaoqi and Wang Guangmei visited Indonesia in 1963. Sukarno was very friendly to the Chinese and helpful to the Communist Party, but Suharto persecuted the Communists and stifled the people's revolution, including the People's Army . . .'

'Yes, yes, all right, all right', said Hsin-ping thoroughly bemused, 'But what on earth has any of that got to do with Albania?'

'Nothing at all. You know what I'm like. All these foreign countries sound the same to me, Ethiop*ia*, Alger*ia*, Alban*ia*, Indones*ia*, so I said Albania when I meant Indonesia. I explained all that at the time. It was just a slip of the tongue.'

Hsin-ping wandered away from their lunch together, thinking that this report was bound to make things difficult for old Wang. She reached into her pocket, took out the piece of paper on which she had made her report, tore it up and threw it away. Fortunately for both of them the matter was never raised again.

The song of the Great Helmsman reached a crescendo under the skilful baton of Lin Biao in 1969 and 1970. Children were taught the 'loyalty character dance' and learnt the 'three loyalties', to the Party, to the People, to Mao. Hsin-ping wondered how this could happen. During the height of the adulation of Mao, she kept thinking of those days in high school when she had known his daughters, the 'princesses', and had joked with them about this sort of thing. She remembered one particular occasion in senior high when they had taken part in a rally and march-past in Tian'anmen Square. As the ranks filed past the Forbidden City, saluting Mao with the customary 'Eternal life to Chairman Mao', Hsin-ping had kept her eyes glued on Li Min, Mao's daughter and step-daughter of Jiang Qing. She had carefully manipulated things so as to be next to her in the parade. She desperately wanted to know if Li Min would say 'Eternal life to Chairman Mao', or 'Eternal life to Papa'. Afterwards Li Min asked her, 'What do you think you were staring at back there?' 'I wanted to know if you would say 'Eternal life to Chairman Mao' or 'Eternal life to Papa', said Hsin-ping. 'Oh, cut it out will you! Get lost!' said Li Min. 'Quit pestering me, insect.' From this, Hsin-ping concluded that Chairman Mao was just her father.

These days it was a different story. Even if Mao himself did not believe that he was a god, he didn't seem to mind Lin Biao saying so, and even if Mao's own children did not worship him, everyone else's were obliged to. What's more, children everywhere had to put him above their own parents, if necessary by reporting on them when they were bad. The system of mutual reporting went on everywhere, in streets, neighbourhoods and work units, but most feared of all potential informers were little children who had learnt the loyalty dance.

Every aspect of daily life became a rich source of accusations, as the spying and reporting intensified. People watched how much others ate. If they did not have much money but often invited guests for a meal, it seemed likely that they had acquired money—or friends—dishonestly, and their behaviour was duly reported. In the building where Hsin-ping lived there were thirteen families living in eight flats. Every evening someone was on duty at the front gate to ask visitors which flat they were looking for and which persons they were visiting. They were still on duty when the visitors left, and they always noted the time. This information went to the Public Security Bureau, who reported it to the relevant work unit, who placed it on the relevant personal file. Mao himself had placed the emphasis on the need for thorough investigation, in accordance with the axiom 'Where there are waves, there must also be wind'. But if there was no proof, the suspect had to be released and the file closed.

From Hsin-ping's point of view, Mao always seemed to be obsessed with 'contradictions among the people'. On the one hand, as in 1957, he seemed to think that differences of opinion were healthy and necessary. On the other hand, ten years later, he seemed to think that there ought to be no fundamental contradictions among the truly 'proletarian' elements. But was he interested in resolving contradictions or in eradicating those who contradicted? Was he interested in 'a hundred schools of thought' or was he, like the Qin Emperor, interested in burning books and burying scholars? Were those being investigated really potential class enemies or were they just *his* potential enemies? Despite their silence, Hsin-ping and thousands like her could not help wondering why Mao had stirred up so many waves since the late 1950s.

Hsin-ping noticed that the investigations always seemed to ensnare people whom she regarded as proven and loyal communists, whether she agreed with their policies or not. She was haunted by the knowledge that so many veteran cadres, heroes of the Long March and of the Anti-Japanese and Civil wars, had been denounced and humiliated by fanatical youths who had never struck a blow or fired a shot for the Revolution, who had no idea about the evils of the old society and were not really interested in reform other than as a pretext for smashing things. That many of the victims had been old friends and comrades-in-arms of Mao seemed less important than that they and their wives were old enemies and rivals of Jiang Qing. This gave rise to bitter mutterings among many of Hsin-ping's acquaintance that Mao could not control 'that actress slut of his'. Jiang Qing certainly must have known that after Mao's death she was in some danger, and at times this may have provoked her to deal ruthlessly with her actual and potential enemies. Or was she just carrying out Mao's orders?

Neither Hsin-ping nor any of her friends and colleagues discussed their opinions openly. In any case, the events which befell these great figures seemed beyond their reach and understanding. For Hsin-ping, the most shocking thing was the treatment of people who could not possibly have had anything to do with the intrigues of emperors, concubines and eunuchs.

There was, for example, the case of a cousin of one of her old classmates. She was a doctor and had been a committed communist since her youth, and a devout patriot during the Anti-Japanese War. She became involved with the Americans in the fight against the Japanese, studied English night and day and finally went to Chungking, after the fall of Nanking, where she had worked as an interpreter for American military advisers. After the defeat of the Japanese, she went back to medicine and became a specialist in tumours.

In 1968 she was denounced as a traitor hiding among the masses, struggled against in a meeting, beaten, labelled a spy and forced to do manual labour. She was not allowed to see patients, only to clean toilets and collect nightsoil. Many people who had worked in the underground in enemy-occupied areas such as Shanghai were dealt with in this fashion. When it came to accusations of past misdeeds, they were the ones who had greatest difficulty, because they had been involved in clandestine operations with foreigners and with the enemy.

The doctor spent three years under investigation. She was allowed out of her cattlepen only for labour, except on one occasion when she was allowed to visit her husband—who was dying of cancer. Malignant politics seemed to breed malignant tumours during these years and experts could do no more to save their loved ones than could the simplest peasant. The doctor's husband died and she went back to her cattlepen. Three years later, after a thorough investigation into her background and past, she was declared 'a good comrade', and allowed to resume her work. Unfortunately, her reputation had been so tarnished by the investigation—or rather she was so great an embarrassment to those who had persecuted her—that she could not work in the hospital any more. She was sent to Gansu in the remote north-west of China, where she worked as a one-woman hospital. She still did the cleaning, because there was no one else to do it. Her expertise in cancer and in X-rays was never used. After a while she wrote to Hsin-ping, 'The sun comes up. The sun goes down. Most days I see one or two patients. Other days maybe three or four. Each one pays a tiny registration fee, and I earn about twice the salary of a factory worker. I am a waste of the people's money.' Hsin-ping marvelled at the tenacity of her patriotism, that she should still be concerned about the people's money—the 'people' having been so profligate with her skill.

Those pronounced guiltless after investigation were officially 'liberated' and reinstated as 'good comrades' in public meetings. Nevertheless, they were often despatched to some remote corner of China after their exoneration. Hsin-ping knew an old woman who had been a Nationalist officer, a general in the North-Eastern Army. She had surrendered towards the end of the Civil War and, like many others had received protection from the Communists in return for her co-operation. She was 'liberated' after an investigation and became a teacher. During the campaign to purify the class ranks, she was imprisoned and re-investigated for more than a year. Finally, she was re-liberated, and returned home to her husband.

He was overjoyed to see her and to think that at last their ordeal was over. They sat talking for some hours and then, in order to celebrate the homecoming, he announced that he would cook her favourite dish for supper. She had always loved *jiaozi*—the famous northern delicacy of meat-filled dumplings. He went out to the kitchen and she heard the cheering sounds of his activity and the splash of water as he washed his face and hands in a bowl in preparation for this long-awaited meal. After a curiously long time, the silence broke in upon the multitude of things she was meaning to tell him, and she went to find out what was taking such a long time. He was slumped over his washbowl. Dead. Liberated. Hsin-ping knew many such stories, in which people had clung to life through years of fear and anguish, only to let go when the tension was released. As more and more class enemies were declared innocent, after harassment, intimidation, torture and imprisonment, people became more and more cynical.

China had been plunged into violence and chaos over the search for 'China's Khrushchev'. Who was it? It turned out to be the heir apparent to Mao himself. Liu Shaoqi was officially named and denounced in October 1968. Then there was Deng Xiaoping, the 'number two capitalist roader'—after Liu. It seemed to many unsophisticated minds a re-enactment of a familiar episode in Chinese history, when a peasant leader who became emperor with the help of trusted friends suddenly began to see those very same friends as rivals. After the summer of 1968 it seemed that the Red Guards, too, had served their Emperor's purpose. Those who escaped gaol were likely to be sent out into the countryside to work. Quite apart from these passionate and often crazy youth, Hsin-ping knew many friends, relatives and colleagues who had worked quietly and competently for years and had taken pride in their country's progress, only to be declared counter-revolutionaries, spies or criminals. Many of those who survived their investigations were subsequently offered an apology. A mistake. Sorry. By 1970 people were bitter and sullenly contemptuous of the leadership.

One day, Hsin-ping and a colleague, with whom she rarely spoke, stood together looking at a wall-newspaper about a state reception for a foreign delegation. The positions of the hosts in the accompanying photograph were extremely significant. Zhou Enlai was off to the side, while Jiang Qing was pictured right in the middle. Hsin-ping and old Teacher Wu exchanged glances in an unguarded moment, and each saw the anger in the other's eyes. She had always feared and distrusted Wu, and thought him dangerous.

The next great test of Party credibility came in 1971, with the demise of Lin Biao. Lin Biao was the next heir apparent to Chairman Mao after the disgraced Liu Shaoqi. He was Mao's 'closest comrade in arms', a hero of the Long March, Chief Marshal of the P.L.A., and the driving force behind the Mao cult which had swept China during the Cultural Revolution. Suddenly it was announced that on 13 September 1971 Lin Biao had been killed in a plane crash in the Mongolian People's Republic, after an attempted assassination of Mao. Over the next few months, military personnel who were linked with Lin Biao, especially in the air force, were weeded out, and a new image of the Marshal emerged from the wreckage of his plane. Overnight he was to become a traitor, a renegade, a revisionist, a capitalist roader, a rightist—and a voluptuary.

An investigation of Lin Biao's home 'revealed' a special bed with massage capabilities and a facility for urinating without rising from the bed, high-heel shoes by the score, bundles of American currency, French perfume, opium pipes—and a Confucian scroll. The son, Lin Liguo, was alleged to have employed the services of the air force to scour the country taking pictures of beautiful girls, so that he could choose one to suit his highly refined palate. When photographs failed to indicate the subtleties of feature and movement that he prized, he was said to have organized movie films of the candidates. People expected their political masters to indulge themselves in all manner of bizarre hanky-panky, but widespread cynicism attended these revelations. The only time such details came to light was when some powerful figure 'fell from the stage' and had to be discredited. After this affair, the Party had some difficulty in whipping up the passions of earlier times. Whatever they did looked very much like an attempt to divert people's attention from the real issue—a power struggle at the top.

8

批林批孔

Criticize Lin Biao, Criticize Confucius

While the scandal about Lin Biao was gaining momentum, there was another stunning political change in the wind. China's foreign policy was changing direction—another source of confusion for the hapless Chinese citizen who had been brought up on a strict diet of American imperialism. This diet was entirely inadequate for the demands of *realpolitik* and threatened to stunt the growth of the new United States–China relations. It was said that in the interests of China, and the various national liberation movements, a wedge should be driven between the two superpowers, the Soviet Union and the United States. The moment was ripe for a softening of Chinese opinion of the United States, and vice-versa.

The American journalist Edgar Snow and his wife Lois went to Peking for the twenty-first anniversary celebration of the founding of the People's Republic of China. The *People's Daily* published a photograph of them on the balcony overlooking Tian'anmen Square, standing beside Mao himself. The Mao thought-for-the-day in this issue was 'Peoples of the world, including the American people, are all our friends'. In April 1971 a United States table-tennis team visited China and 'ping-pong diplomacy' was born. In July, Henry Kissinger, President Nixon's Special Advisor on National Security, flew to Peking to begin secret preparations for the President's visit the following spring. As Jiang Qing herself put it, 'the great powers come to our gates'. In the autumn of 1971 China entered the United Nations. In 1971 too, Gough Whitlam commenced overtures on behalf of the Australian Labor Party, which would soon form Australia's next government, and so set the agenda for Australian attitudes to China for the 1970s and 1980s.

The scandal about Lin Biao and his family continued unabated throughout these globally significant moves. It was not reported in detail in official party organs, but the big-character posters which appeared around Zhongnanhai—the area of the Forbidden City where homes and offices of Party and State leaders stood—were much less reticent. These were the real Chinese newspapers, and they were much more adept at the lurid and eye-catching headline than their turgid and repetitive official counterparts. But still no one could be certain what the central leadership was really up to, either domestically or in terms of foreign policy.

A central order was received in all schools in Peking and Shanghai some months before the Nixon visit. The Nixons had expressed a wish to be relatively informal in their visiting schedule—a wish that almost every foreign delegation would repeat with infuriating monotony—and in consequence, the preparations had to be even more intense than had already been envisaged. Preparation for the spontaneous and informal meet-the-people-see-the-real-China type of visit required the greatest organization of all.

The first and most obvious problem had to do with *sixiang* (attitude, mentality). For so many years anti-American propaganda had been so fierce. What if some kid walking down the street was asked his opinion about this or that by some smart-arse American journalist? What if the kid got it wrong and said something 'impolite'? In due course, a new formula was promulgated in the schools, explaining the apparent volte-face in foreign policy—'there are no eternal enemies and there are also no eternal friends'. Obviously this was perfectly in keeping both with the shifting kaleidoscope of world affairs and with the principles of dialectical materialism. Many a Chinese citizen came to the conclusion that all they had been taught about the resolution of contradictions into a new synthesis, and about the 'unity of opposites', meant simply that, even when things seemed absolutely inconsistent and contradictory, they were not really. That was only another one of the contradictions, which the leaders could explain—if you gave them time. In the meantime however, heaven help you if you got it wrong—then you would certainly become 'an eternal enemy', even though there was no such thing.

So it was that teachers in all schools, including Hsin-ping's, were given a strict order that students should not be allowed to leave the classroom unsupervised during the Nixons' visit. Any teacher who failed in this responsibility ran the risk of being branded a class enemy, a spy, a subversive. The kids could play cards all day long if they liked, but teachers had to be able to account for all of them all of the time. Between autumn 1971 and spring 1972, normal classes once more came to a standstill, with the only academic work being the preparation of answers to questions which stray foreigners might put to children after school hours. Questions and answers were learnt by heart and the 'chance' meetings were carefully rehearsed.

Soon a story went round about a model answer given to a foreign journalist by a primary-school child. The journalist spoke excellent Chinese and asked the most topical and contentious question of all: 'What has happened to Vice-Chairman Lin Biao?' The child replied, *ge pi zhao liang*—part of a children's nonsense ryhme in which *ge pi* (literally, to fart), is a reference to the expulsion of air from the body after death. Lin Biao had 'popped off'. The equivalent enigmatic effect might have been obtained had an Australian child told a visiting Chinese journalist that Prime Minister Harold Holt had 'taken a dive'. In any event the Chinese child became something of a legend overnight. He had told the truth and yet revealed nothing—and he had made a monkey out of the foreigner into the bargain.

Elaborate planning went into preparations for a welcome rally in Peking for President Nixon, and only the best looking and most talented were selected to take part in a sporting performance to be given in his honour. The audience, which was supposed to consist of ordinary workers, school children and so on, who had bought their tickets for the show on a first-come first-served basis, were in fact Party members, also of good appearance and impressive physique. There was a majority of young women, because they could wear bright, attractive, coloured clothing. Those of school and college age who were selected for this duty were declared exempt from classes—and examinations—and required to practice as members of the audience every day for six months. The audience was organized into units of five, each with a leader who was responsible for co-ordinating the group's rehearsal and performance. In ancient China, political control had been exercised by a system in which ten households were grouped together under a leader, but modern China, influenced by the Soviet Union, or just twice as thorough perhaps, seemed to prefer the number five.

Regular meetings were held between the group leaders and those responsible for organizing the sports, and among the matters discussed was the question of applause. A good deal of time was devoted to the proportion of acclaim which should greet the speeches of the American guests and the Chinese hosts. Eventually a formula was arrived at. When the Chinese leaders made a speech, everyone would applaud loudly. When the American leader spoke, everyone would go through the motions of clapping his palms together, but only one would make an audible sound. 'Not too hot, not too cold' was the guideline, in order to express politeness but some reserve. This was practised for ten days, but in the meantime the joint talks had gone so well, especially on the question of Taiwan, that Mao himself issued a new instruction—'Turn up the heat!' There was an emergency meeting of the group leaders and on the day of the performance the word was passed around to pep things up a bit, in order to demonstrate enthusiasm for the way things had gone. The new instruction was that when the American leader spoke, four out of five were to complete their claps.

The foreign predilection for spontaneity took a nasty turn during the tour, when Mrs Nixon mentioned visiting a children's hospital. This was fraught with danger. How could you control what a sick child might say? Tang Ling's husband, Lao Zhuang, witnessed the solution to the problem, as did a neighbour's husband, since they were both working in the children's hospital at the time. The neighbour was an engineer who had been engaged to a doctor, but who had been prevented by her work unit from marrying him because of his foreign connections. 'You want a doctor for a husband? Fine. We'll introduce you to one, but you will not be marrying this fellow.' They found her another doctor—a Party member—who was very nice, but very ugly. From him and from Lao Zhuang, Hsin-ping heard the story of the preparations for Mrs Nixon's visit.

First, the place was scrubbed and painted. Standards of cleanliness suddenly underwent a dramatic improvement, to the point where it resembled the exercise of military discipline more than the practice of normal hygiene. According to some sources, half a million Chinese yuan were spent on toys for the wards, and anything that could be replaced or re-decorated was swooped upon. However, the problem of what to do about the children remained. The staff themselves, if unsuitable in some way, could be concealed. Lao Zhuang, for example, had to be removed from the ward because his father's younger brother lived in Hong Kong and a person with those kinds of connections could not possibly be trusted in the presence of a foreign official. He went down into the basement along with many others—and that is where the children ended up too, except for those of impeccable revolutionary background. All those with overseas connections were relegated to the basement and, in their place, former patients whose files indicated that they were not security risks were brought out of retirement to re-enact their former roles as patients. When Mrs Nixon came, and asked the usual questions, the children were to reply that this was a wonderful hospital, that uncle doctors and auntie nurses were so kind, and that acupuncture didn't hurt a bit.

A further problem struck the visit's organizers when Heaven itself became fractious and sent down a snow-storm the night before the

American party was due to visit the Great Wall. If the Americans experienced transport difficulties, or could not actually walk along the wall at Badaling because of the snow, it would raise questions about why China did not have snow-clearing machines like those in America. China would certainly lose face. However, when the tourists rose on the morning of their trip, they marvelled at the roads, free of snow despite obviously heavy precipitation the night before. China obviously had advanced technology. They probably had it long before the West. Perhaps they had invented snow-clearing machines along with gun-powder and silk and bagpipes. After all, this was the world's oldest continuous civilization. When the Americans got to the wall, they saw that the whole section at Badaling had also been cleared. They did not see the hordes of disgruntled peasants who had been up all night sweeping, and cursing about foreign big-shots. Nor did they see the countless truck-loads of salt which had been dumped on Peking's streets during the night. If, as legend has it, the mortar in the Great Wall is made of the blood and tears of the Qin dynasty workers who built it, then salt was still being rubbed into the wounds of common labourers two thousand years later under Mao. Had the tourists been around in the Qin dynasty they would have noticed that the Chinese did indeed have snow-clearing machines even then.

After the Nixon visit, more and more foreigners visited China, including the corps of 'foreign experts', who came either in tourist delegations, or as individuals working in Chinese institutions on one-or two-year contracts. Interest in the Cultural Revolution began to focus on what was going on in education. As it happened, elitism, bureaucracy, examinations, marks, and teacher authoritarianism were all popular targets in Western countries, and it was easy to empathize with this side of the Maoist line. As in any such exercise, however, something was lost in the translation. Interpretations of the Maoist line varied from a literal and quaint-sounding batch of indigenous ideas and practices to the more familiar, but equally misleading, patois of Western reformist educators. Perhaps Mao was, like Ivan Illich, a 'de-schooler?' Certainly a large part of China's recent upheavals had consisted of getting out and about rather than remaining in the classroom—except during the Nixon visit. What had the students learned during their 'long marches', their exercises of physical and ideological tempering? Even as a local, Hsin-ping felt that, for all the hardship and suffering and injustice of these terrible years, there *had* been many good and progressive things. Teachers *had* been too authoritarian, and the exodus from the classroom *had* allowed students to question the difference between what schools could teach and what human beings could learn. Like Hsin-ping, thousands of young people had experienced a Peach Blossom Spring. Mao himself had stated quite clearly in 1964 that the most prominent problem in Chinese education was dogmatism. That the old Confucian dogmatism was replaced by a new Maoist dogmatism seemed to many to be an appalling mis-interpretation of Mao's intention; to others it seemed deliberate, rank, hypocrisy, and to yet others—like Hsin-ping herself—it seemed like the almost inevitable result of attempting to disturb the awesome inertia of Chinese culture and to convert China from feudalism to socialism overnight.

By late 1972, the Cultural Revolution had entered a new phase of radicalism, focusing on debate about Confucius. The Confucian legacy had always been at the heart of intellectual revolution in China, whether the starting point was the May 4th movement of 1919, or the student eruptions in 1966. At the core of China's intellectual traditions was the Confucian Canon—the Five Classics and the Four Books, including the Book of Changes, the Book of History, the Book of Rites, the Spring and Autumn Annals, the Doctrine of the Mean, the Analects and the Mencius. For six hundred years the Four Books had been memorized and recited by countless students and had formed the basis for the civil service examinations which determined China's scholar bureaucracy.

This tradition stressed a hierarchy in which the State and the family were linked by clearly defined relationships, and certain duties and obligations attended each position in the hierarchy. At the heart of it all was the notion of filial piety, which entailed absolute obedience and devotion to one's parents and, by analogy, to the emperor, father of the nation. There were also a series of strictly prescribed duties and rituals associated with family and ancestors. The more powerful a family was, the more likely it was to practise orthodox Confucian ritual, because it was precisely from their conspicuous Confucianism, especially the success of family members in the examinations, that they derived political power and kept it. While this system produced an élite, it was not a hereditary élite as in Europe, but a meritocracy of sorts, in which those who had time and money to prepare for the gruelling examinations could bring honour and power to their families. This distinction was not achieved by a great many who were of peasant origin, although the possibility always existed for a poor boy to make good through the support of some local philanthropical bequest such a clan community chest.

For most of its history, the system produced an unquestioning, uncritical acceptance of rote-learned texts; excluded the vast majority of the poor; made no allowance at all for women, for whom educational attainments were a matter of occasional 'poetical effusions', and, above all, elevated the teacher to a position of almost supernatural authority. The Confucian emphasis on the master–disciple relationship and on the authority of the teacher had survived even the hazards of the twentieth-century European-style classroom, which seemed to many old teachers to be an attempt to confine every conceivable threat to the dignity of the teacher within the space of one room.

What Hsin-ping had hoped for in the Cultural Revolution was not just a denunciation of the old ways, but the adoption of the positive side of Mao's view of education. Threads of this line were discernible throughout the late 1960s and early 1970s, in spite of the impenetrable tangle of power struggles and the massive knots of bureaucratic ignorance and self-interest. The conflict in education was described as a choice between 'two roads' to development, one associated with Mao, the other with Liu Shaoqi. The 'Liuist' line was said to be Soviet-style and revisionist, with emphasis on building a corps of experts and managers who would lead China in Soviet-style urban, industrial development, at the expense of the masses in China's countryside. This corps of experts would be a privileged, bourgeois élite who perpetuated themselves through the system of examinations and grades. That at least was the thumbnail sketch painted by its critics. The Maoist line was based on mass participation in, and management of, the schools, combined with a programme of labour and production-oriented experience for urban youths, who had been cloistered away from the realities of worker–peasant life. The theory behind this was both Marxist–Leninist and Maoist. Real learning was thought to be derived from the process of participation in the changing of reality—the experience of labour, via the process of production. One's state of consciousness was thought to be raised through a series of contradictions to a higher plane, through participation in class struggle and the struggle for production.

The bridge of philosophies supporting Maoist educational reforms spanned ages and cultures, reaching from Ancient Greeks to Daoists and from Marx to Mao, from dialectical argument to dialectical materialism, from Yin and Yang to 'contradictions'. In Mao's China it reached the limits of its structural endurance, being expected to support not only educational reform, but an entire Great Proletarian Cultural Revolution, in the guise of Mao Thought. It did not support this load, but it did produce experimentation and reform in the education system, and the Mao Thought propaganda teams exerted some influence after 1968 in maintaining the informal and experimental side of these innovations in the administration of schools and colleges.

Mao selected the Shanghai Machine Tools Plant as a model solution to the thorny problem of integrating work and study, which lay at the heart of his vision. The *Peking Review* published a crucial speech of Mao's in August 1968. He stressed that the length of schooling should be shortened, that education should be revolutionized, that 'proletarian politics' should be put in command of education, and that the policy of the Shanghai Machine Tools Plant, in training technicians from among its workers, should be emulated. Mao also stressed that college students should be selected from among workers and peasants with practical experience, who should return to production after some years of study. This policy was ultimately extended to university administration, with the result that enrolments were based not on examination results but on recommendations made by the revolutionary committees of the factories and communes where students had done a stint of work. Some work units recommended keen and intelligent applicants and some simply made full use of a golden opportunity to get rid of wet-behind-the-ears students who got in the way of a decent day's work, but the emphasis on integration between labour and education extended to the practice of schools running factories and factories running schools.

The programme of sending 'educated youth' (that is, secondary school students) into the countryside, was stepped up, and was known as 'going up to the mountains and down to the countryside'. This may well have been the result of Mao's vision of a spartan rural life, which would provide real physical and moral tempering for bookish youths. There were however, many who thought it may have been a modern version of 'burying scholars' since, unlike earlier movements to acquaint Party cadres with the realities of peasant life, this movement involved indefinite resettlement in the villages for youths who might otherwise have organized movements of their own in the universities. Students had already demonstrated that their revolutionary zeal could get out of hand.

So it was that millions of city youths went out for their first real taste of rural life. China's urban dwellers were inclined to prize the privilege of their registration as city dwellers because of the variety of physical and cultural comforts it conferred upon them, and country dwellers had looked upon education as a ticket out of the village. Now the products of the education system were flowing in the reverse direction. In December 1968 Mao called upon urban residents, including cadres, to send their sons and daughters, who had finished junior or senior high school, college or university, out into the countryside. He also called upon people in the rural areas to welcome these young people.

From 1969 to 1975 twelve million 'sons and daughters' were resettled in the countryside. The State paid the initial living costs of the 'educated youth', but they were expected to be financially independent after the first year, and were to be paid by the work-point system used in the communes—a system based on the contribution of each worker to the team effort. Because of their softness and inexperience the contribution of educated youth was often minute. Like factory workers suddenly confronted with raw schoolkids, peasants were often less than enthusiastic about the new arrivals, and were not always inclined to make them welcome, regarding them instead as a burden and a liability.

From the point of view of the youth themselves, the factories were at least located in the city, and it was possible to enrol in a university or college after some work experience. As a result many parents used the 'back door' to get their children into factories rather than rural communes. Few educated youths who went 'up to the mountains and down to the countryside' married there, because this decreased their opportunities of getting back into the cities. Large numbers of youth slipped back illegally into towns and cities and lived as 'blacks', that is, without household registration and unable to obtain food coupons legally. They were either sheltered by family or, quite appropriately, turned to the black market for a livelihood.

By 1973, Hsin-ping had formed the view that at last the Cultural Revolution had 'touched everyone's soul', as Lin Biao once put it. The endless campaigns and movements had always had their winners and losers, but now everyone was affected. Even those of respectable revolutionary pedigree could not avoid the consequences of this movement. And the children of cadres had to go and do their duty just like everyone else. To date, it had been possible to demonstrate one's revolutionary fervour by hating class enemies and loving Mao, but now it was necessary to receive 're-education' from the poor and lower-middle peasants, by going out and living among them.

Most of Hsin-ping's students went to the North-East, to a place called Beidahuang. No-one had lived there for years. Although it was a very fertile place, it had been used as a forced labour camp for prisoners of the old dynasty, and then for counter-revolutionaries under the new régime. With the benefit of her pro-Soviet education, Hsin-ping had always thought of it as 'China's Siberia'. Now it was to be a new frontier of student endeavour, under the guidance of the P.L.A. The families of these students were broken-hearted but there was little they could do or say about it. The back door was still ajar, but it was not so easy to push it open these days. In order to proclaim their love of Mao, these same secretly broken-hearted families pinned a large red flower to their front doors, celebrating the allocation of a son or daughter to the countryside.

Train-load after train-load of youths left Peking, and once again the station was the hub of a city's misery, as helpless parents bestowed last-minute clothing parcels on children whose life or death, return, or permanent exile, could only be guessed at. Hsin-ping knew a girl who had no one to see her off at the station. She was the daughter of a distant relative, who was very old and sick. The girl's brothers and sisters were not in Peking, and her parents could not make it to the

station, so Hsin-ping went along to farewell her. It was winter, and she
did not expect the station to be busy. She thought she could just buy a
platform ticket and wander down to the train and find the compartment
number she had been given. The bus could get no closer than a
hundred metres from the entrance and, when she got out Hsin-ping
heard a muffled roar that seemed to swell out of the station and seep
into the street like a fog. At the shock of this sound she thought of a line
from the poet Du Fu, who understood, best of all Chinese poets, the
joys and sufferings of ordinary folk. He had written about the departure
of conscripted soldiers for the Tang emperor's armies, and about the
grief of families as the soldiers left for the wars in the border regions:

> *qian yi dun zu lan dao ku,*
> *ku sheng zhi shang gan yun xiao.*
>
> [Clutching at clothing, dragging their heels
>   and blocking the way,
>   the sound of their anguish rose to the clouds.]

She had heard this poem so many times in high school, and knew it so
well. As had happened before during these years, she was hearing well-
known lines as if for the first time, as she trudged through a pall of
misery to the station.

To her surprise, she found that the girl's decrepit old father had made
the journey to see her off. He was over seventy, bent double upon a
gnarled pine walking stick the texture and colour of his own weathered
complexion. As the girl boarded, a row of P.L.A. soldiers, rifles at the
ready, pushed the milling crowd away from the train, to prevent a
tragedy that had by now become commonplace—relatives tumbling out
of the frantic crowd and into the path of departing trains. It was all just
as Du Fu had described a thousand years before. Curiously, in all the
din, Hsin-ping found herself wondering why Mao had never cared
much for Du Fu's poetry, preferring instead the eccentric wastrel Li Bai,
and she thought bitterly that perhaps Mao was no more sensitive to this
suffering than the Tang emperor had been.

Some did not go away, either because they had a medical certificate
exempting them, or because they were the sole sons or daughters of their
families, upon whom parents depended. Doctors were once more in
demand, but they could not save the vast majority of graduates of junior
and senior high school. Some went to Yan'an, to Shanxi, Hebei, Henan or
to Inner Mongolia. In poor districts the students could barely earn enough
money for food. Their parents might send money but a family on average
income, with two or three children, had little to spare.

In the North-East the land was covered in ice for five or six months of
the year and the young people had nothing to do. They were allowed
back into the cities to visit parents and relatives, but there was no

work or study to occupy them, and in many cases their energies were diverted to crime. The theft of food coupons became a feature of everyday life, and the incidence of rape, murder and robbery increased dramatically.

To make matters worse, many junior high school students were left alone in the cities by their parents, whose entire work units had also been sent out into the countryside. People knew that unoccupied rooms would be re-allocated by the Housing Bureau, so they left children behind, under the loose supervision of some nearby relative or neighbour. China's 'latchkey children' wore their badge of office round their necks, and had little to do but get into some sort of trouble, especially in the long vacation periods.

Many did not even return to the cities for a seasonal respite, and were worn into an ancient resignation, in which there was little place for tomorrow: 'A monk for a day must toll the bell for a day'. Others were able to employ their skills of literacy and organization, or worked as 'barefoot doctors', utilizing rudimentary scientific and medical knowledge for the benefit of villagers.

Stories of moral laxity filtered back into the cities, as young people who did not want to marry—because it would condemn them to permanent rural residence—shared their lives together. There was no contraception, and there was a 'bumper harvest' of illegitimate children. Hsin-ping knew of one girl who had agreed to live with a cadre in charge of work allocation, just so that she could stay at home and do domestic work instead of lugging great sacks of grain. There were stories of girls who were shared among several men, because of the shortage of eligible women in some production teams. Many women, who delayed thoughts of marriage in order to go to the countryside in answer to 'the Party's call', found on their return that they were likely to be passed over in favour of younger girls. Offered a choice of older or younger women, the men left their former classmates on the shelf, feeling embittered and exploited.

Old people, also, went out into the villages. Hsin-ping's aunt had a friend at the Agricultural College in Peking, a certain Professor Lin. He and her aunt's husband, the old entomologist who knew nothing about mosquitoes, had studied together in the United States. They had both, in consequence, been struggled against as 'stinking intellectuals' and had done a number of stints of labour reform since the beginning of the Cultural Revolution. With the advent of the 'down to the countryside' movement, it was argued that it was absurd to have an agricultural college located in the city and the whole institution was ordered off to Yan'an. The family's two daughters were sent to Inner Mongolia.

Sickness and frailty did not protect the old ones. The professor had very bad asthma and his wife had a terrible swelling of the legs, but nevertheless they both had to go. Their bourgeois intellectual lifestyle had excited some animosity, since they lived in one of the two-storey Western-style houses often allocated to academics in the past—especially to those who had studied abroad. When Hsin-ping went to visit them in 1972, they had moved upstairs and another family had moved in below. Hsin-ping greeted the old man, who was sitting in his chair, enveloped in a very large scarf, and wheezing his lungs out. He was surrounded by bundles of belongings. Hsin-ping had gone there to pick up a fur-lined coat which her aunt had bought some years before on a trip to Peking, and which she had left in their care, since she was going south into warmer weather. The old couple had asked Hsin-ping to collect it and arrange to send it on to her aunt, since they did not know when they would return, if at all. Hsin-ping asked the old man why he had not sought a medical examination, but he just said, 'The whole college has been ordered to go. How can I get out of it?' Eventually they did return—and on medical grounds. He had contracted one of the local countryside diseases.

After their return he and his wife applied to go to America to join relatives, and perhaps because of their advanced years, or because of the shift in foreign policy, they were given permission. But the old man died shortly after their arrival in America. His wife wrote to Hsin-ping, a very bitter letter:

> I remember when we were students long ago in America and we heard news of the communist victory. We could not wait to get back so that we could join in celebrations for the founding of the People's Republic. We were such ardent patriots. Then came movement after movement, campaign after campaign, and somehow it was always us and people like us who ended up the target. What on earth were we celebrating all those years ago?

Many families were broken up. Those who were lucky managed to keep at least two members in one place, like one family that Hsin-ping knew. The son had graduated from high school and was accompanied to the countryside by his sister—even though she was not yet of junior high graduation age—just so that they could stay together as members of a family. Often husbands and wives were separated by the allocation of their work units to different areas, and in some cases a family was scattered over three or four provinces. Hsin-ping's own husband was sent to Henan Province, while she remained in Peking, teaching a skeleton student population.

China's school system had been dismembered since the beginning of the Cultural Revolution. Students who left high school in 1966, 1967 and 1968 had a limited experience of formal class work, because of the call to wage revolution. Nevertheless these 'three old years', as they became known, were distinguished by at least some formal senior high

education, as well as a reputation for general *savoir-faire* and resource-
fulness, the product of their unique experience during the first years of
the Cultural Revolution. Like American intellectuals of the 1920s, they
came to be known as a 'lost generation'—an *avant-garde*, veterans in
exile, who would draw creative inspiration from their own sense of
waste, futility and shame.

After 1966, there were no further admissions to the old system of
senior high. Then, in 1969, graduates of junior high went out into the
countryside and, as a result, there were still no admissions to senior
high. In time the pressure of enrolments from primary into junior high
became intense, because of the baby boom just before the Great Leap
Forward of 1958. Some thought that the movement to the countryside
was Mao's way of releasing pressure on the school system. But when it
became clear that the rural areas could not cope with the influx of students, schools began to offer a four- or five-year course—one or two
years beyond the old junior high level. This was technically in accordance with Mao's wish that the old six-year system should be shortened,
but in practice amounted to an extension of the period of secondary
schooling, since students had for some time been leaving school after
only three years. Some thought these measures had nothing to do with
education, but were just part of a see-saw adjustment, first to keep students out of schools and then to keep them out of the villages.

Criticism of Lin Biao intensified by the summer of 1973 and, just as two
years earlier there had been an ominous silence preceding the October 1st
national holiday, suggesting that some kind of power struggle was going
on at the centre, all was still for some days before the Party's birthday
(1 July). Deng Xiaoping, the former 'number two person in authority
taking the capitalist road', had been rehabilitated as Vice-Premier in
April of that year. Lin Biao, who had formerly been considered
'ultra-left', was now an 'ultra-rightist' and was incorporated into the anti-
Confucius campaign, in a general attack on reactionary elements.

The campaign against Confucius became bewilderingly complex. It
seemed that the central leadership was promoting the anti-Lin Biao,
anti-Confucius line in order to destroy Mao's critics, who had compared
him with the tyrannical Qin Emperor, particularly in his treatment of
scholars and intellectuals. The gist of the campaign was that, in the
context of China's historical development, the Qin Emperor was progressive—because his was a feudal, rather than a slave-based society. If
Mao was a twentieth century version of the Qin Emperor, then Lin Biao
was Confucius, the chief advocate of a crueller and more primitive
régime. After all, the Qin Emperor had unified China and had initiated
many of the great hallmarks of Chinese civilization—including the
Great Wall and standardization of the script. Where would China be

today if he had not suppressed the reactionary clique of Confucian scholars? The Party organs stressed that a régime which suppressed certain groups in society was not necessarily wrong to do so—this was after all the inevitable result of class struggle, culminating in the 'dictatorship of the proletariat'. Certainly Mao had never been squeamish about the fact that one group will always use the power of the army, the police and the courts to suppress another. It was all a question of which group should be allowed to get on top—progressive or reactionary.

So the Cultural Revolution was approaching its finale in much the way it had begun, in a morass of abstruse literary and historical allegory, which for all its theoretical complexity represented the same simple and immediate dangers to teachers as the movements at the beginning of the Cultural Revolution. The Tenth Party Congress (August 1973) made the Lin Biao affair more public and set it in the context of a call for continuous struggle against revisionism. The Confucius debate re-affirmed achievements of the radical phase of the Cultural Revolution, including Red Guard activity in 1966. The Congress also emphasized Mao's view that the struggle against revisionism in the political and economic sphere must be reflected in the educational and ideological sphere.

Jiang Qing and two ideological helpmates, Chi Qun and Xie Jingyi, Chairman and Vice-Chairwoman respectively of Qinghua University's revolutionary committee, took up the challenge to root out Confucian authoritarianism in education. A student had suicided in Henan Province, allegedly as a result of harassment by her teachers after she had handed in a blank English examination paper. Earlier in the Cultural Revolution a student had been immortalized for just such a feat, which was acclaimed as a model response to reactionary educational methods.

In the case of the Henan girl, teachers had been so critical of her revolutionary spirit that she had committed suicide in feudal fashion—by leaping into a well. An enquiry was conducted by the principal and the Public Security Bureau, and they returned a finding of death by misadventure. They had discovered that the girl's mother and one or two highly-strung relatives had drowned themselves, and concluded that this was obviously a family trait. The file was closed—until Jiang Qing supervised a re-opening of the enquiry. Bourgeois intellectuals were still hiding in the class ranks it seemed, and a new purification campaign was needed. The principal and the Public Security Bureau investigators were arrested and charged with a cover-up.

This affair, and others like it, served the political objectives of the 'criticize Lin Biao, criticize Confucius' campaign. Teachers were once more put in the position of inviting, and even provoking, criticisms from their students. Classes which did not produce enough big-character posters were, by definition, under the control of revisionist teachers whose Confucian mentality had obviously led to the suppression of student opinion. Hsin-ping coaxed her apparently uninterested charges into criticizing her, in order to avoid the dreaded revisionist label. 'I am a very bad teacher', she instructed them, 'I have a lot of attitude problems. I'm just so backward. I'm greatly influenced by the style of thinking of Lin Biao and Confucius. You must criticize me. Come on, oppose me! Write big-character posters against me!'

One afternoon, her class—second-year junior high, class number nine—produced the fruit of their labours. Twenty-seven big-character posters opposing Teacher Wang! Not bad; almost one poster for every two students. Further analysis produced some interesting statistics. The twenty-eight boys in the class had written two posters between them, and the twenty-seven girls had written twenty-five. Hsin-ping forgot that she was supposed to be grateful to them. 'Heartless little bitches', she thought, 'How could they? After all I've done for them.' Recovering her composure, she began examining the content of the posters, doing her level best to look as if she really appreciated the spirit of constructive criticism that had inspired them. She had been bad tempered and fierce it seemed, and had once thumped the table with her fist and screeched like a wild beast, 'fangs bared and claws dancing'. Was this any way to treat successors to the revolution?

To add salt to the wound, that particular incident had resulted from Hsin-ping's attempt to prevent the boys from teasing them. She certainly had sharply rebuked a couple of the boys. 'Look what you've done. Making the girls cry like that! And what makes you think it's such a smart thing to do, to bully and victimize girls? You have to start now, to change your attitudes, so that you can respect women and treat them fairly. I want you to apologize to them and promise never to behave like that again.' And yes, she had banged the table and glared fiercely at the wrongdoers. So if anyone had been inclined to attack her it should have been the boys. She seethed at the injustice, as she pretended to be vitally interested in the details of their criticism. 'Well, I've learnt my lesson', she thought bitterly, 'from now on I'll just say "now, now boys, please don't be naughty. It's not nice". And if you little cats get tormented to death, it'll serve you right.'

The principal had started paying particular attention to physical training, and offered a 'red flag' award to the class which displayed the most zeal. Hsin-ping's class was skeptical about the wisdom of exercise on cold winter mornings. On one occasion she noticed that hardly any of the boys were present, although all the girls were lined up waiting. She knew perfectly well they would be hiding in the toilet and so she went knocking on all the toilet doors.

'Year two class nine boys, come out of there!'

'Teacher Wang. What are you doing here? You can't come in. You're a lady.'

'Well so what? What do you think you're going to do about it if I come in there after you?'

'You're a delinquent.'

This game went on for several days, until Hsin-ping decided that she had better take more effective action. 'If you can't do morning exercise,' she announced to the class, 'you must have a certificate. If you have a letter from your mother or father or some family member to say you are ill, or from a doctor, you can miss physical training for one or two months if necessary. You can stay behind in the classroom and work, or you can do hygiene duties, or wash the floors and clean the blackboard, that sort of thing. As long as you don't fool around in the classrooms.' Every day she kept a list of names of those who were 'exercising for the revolution'. She told the students that she would give copies to their families, indicating their record of attendance. Attendances improved as a result, but it was still winter, it was bitterly cold in the mornings and the wind was vicious.

One day she noticed that four or five boys and one or two girls were missing, and had not given her notes. She was not surprised about the boys, and decided she could talk to the girls later. So she started the lesson, and joined them in the routine as usual, unlike many of the other teachers, who shouted their instructions from a sheltered position. After this, she rounded up the missing students and sent them to the sports field for another session—trying to make it sound like a privilege, rather than a punishment.

During the drill, she reproached one of the girls for making her displeasure obvious, moving in a feeble, desultory fashion as if she were not long for this world. The girl burst into tears, and after suggesting that they discuss the problem later, Hsin-ping sent her back to the classroom. As she walked up the stairs to her room after lunch, Hsin-ping heard a terrible wailing. A colleague came scurrying up to her, squawking, 'Teacher Wang. Oooh, you've had it. You've really done it this time. Quick, get upstairs at once!' As Hsin-ping burst into the room, five girls were sitting together, sobbing hysterically, while the principal, the registrar and three other teachers looked on in panic.

'*Ai-ya*, we can't go on living, we just can't go on living', howled the girls.

'What the devil has got into them?' moaned the principal, wringing his hands.

'I don't know . . . I took them for P.T. as usual this morning in third period. That was the last I saw of them. They were all right then . . . Oh yes, there was one thing. One of the girls was a bit upset, I think

because I made her do the exercises she missed earlier.' Hsin-ping
walked over to the girl who had been listless that morning and asked
what the problem was.

'You still don't know? You still don't know?' screeched the girl.

'Last time I saw you, just before lunch, everything was fine. How am
I supposed to know what's happened since then? I can't read your
mind. You'll have to tell me if there's anything wrong. What is it?' The
principal was looking anxiously at Hsin-ping. He could see that she
was just as mystified as himself.

Finally, one of the other girls spoke up. 'She's got her period. She
couldn't do her P.T.'

'Oh', sighed Hsin-ping, with enormous relief, 'is that all? I've already
told you, that's perfectly all right. All you have to do is let me know.
Don't be embarrassed. After all, I'm old enough to be your mother. Just
tell me straight out, or if you don't want to do that, write something on
a piece of paper and hand it to me. It's nothing to be ashamed of.' She
turned to the principal. 'They never told me. How am I supposed to
know if they don't tell me?'

By now quite a throng had gathered. The party branch secretary
intervened. 'Did you girls tell Teacher Wang or not?'

'No, we did not. Why should we? It's embarrassing. She should have
known.'

'How am I suposed to know everything about all of you?' protested
Hsin-ping indignantly. 'So many students to look after. Next time this
happens you must tell me or write me a note. It's simple. I thought you
were just making a fuss because of the cold.'

The principal, or to give him his most recent title, the chairman of the
school's revolutionary committee, had the final word. 'All right. It's
nothing. Off you all go and have something to eat, and come back later
for this afternoon's classes.' As they left the room he whispered to Hsin-
ping, 'Typical, these little vixen can turn a fart into an opera'.

That afternoon the principal came to see Hsin-ping. He was even
more nervous than before. He had learnt to sense danger. He said, 'This
business today could get out of hand. We could all end up being some
kind of negative example. You'd better make sure you keep an eye on
that girl. Where is she at the moment?'

'I don't know. They're all in their activity groups this afternoon.'

'Well you'd better go and find her and see that everything is O.K.'

Hsin-ping went looking. She wasn't in any of the activity groups.
She went to her home. Not there either. She reported this to the
principal.

He shuddered. 'Oh my God, she's killed herself. I just know it. The
silly little bitch has thrown herself into a well or something, just like the
one in Henan. We're all done for when this gets out. Come on, we'll

have to go and look for her.' So the two of them set out on their bikes, searching the City Moat, which seemed an obvious place to start. Hsin-ping pedalled the entire length of the moat from the south wall of the Chinese City to Xizhimen Station, near the zoo, in the north-west corner of Peking. The principal followed the moat eastwards out past Taoranting Park and the Temple of Heaven. There was no sign of her.

The search party met back at the school, exhausted. It was late in the afternoon, and they rang the girl's parents at work. She had not been in to see them. Hsin-ping and the principal rode back to her home. No luck there either. None of the neighbours had seen her or her brother. They searched the whole neighborhood, several times. Not a sign of either of them. It was now about nine o'clock, and the streets were pitch black. They went back to the house again. The door was open and they found the girl and her brother sleeping soundly in their beds. They swooped on the startled girl and cuddled and stroked her, like doting grandparents. 'Ah, there you are pet', cooed the principal, 'At last we've found you. We've been out of our minds'. A little later, as they were leaving, he muttered to Hsin-ping, 'So the little shit isn't dead after all—and neither are we'.

That was the end of the matter. Fortunately the girl had readily admitted that Hsin-ping had not known of her delicate condition. It seems that she had been hankering after celebrity status, but she lacked commitment. As for Hsin-ping, at least she had plenty of fresh material for self-criticism. She made fulsome admissions that, as a teacher, it was her duty to pay greater attention to the personal needs of her students. 'Yes', she told herself, 'I'll get a special notebook and draw a whopping big red flag alongside the names of girls who are having their periods!'

9

回光返照

A Last Flash of Sunset

Hsin-ping had learnt enough survival skills to negotiate her last years in China without further serious mishap, although she had domestic problems when her husband was in Peking. There were times when this disharmony came to the attention of the school's administration. The Party branch secretary reproached her for her irresponsible attitude to the marriage. In his view, Hsin-ping had secured quite a prize, and should try harder to make things work, instead of badgering her husband about trifles. Hsin-ping protested that she was the one being badgered and that, in any case, she had not sought to make her grievances public, but this did not stop the Party branch secretary from reminding her of her duties as a wife. Not for the first time, the wife bit her tongue and refrained from making a speech about women in the 'new society'. Fortunately, the strains on the relationship were relieved by frequent separations, and life for Hsin-ping, Lulu and Grandma, who had now rejoined them in the architects' dormitory, was peaceful most of the time.

Hsin-ping often went to see her long-time friend Xun Linglai, just near the southern end of Tian'anmen Square. She, her husband Cui Weimin and her mother lived in a flat within sight of Qianmen. They often sat for hours in the flat, just listening to each other's troubles, and trying to make sense of things. Hsin-ping's husband would never intrude here, because he knew very well he'd be sent packing. Linglai had once thrown her shoes at him, on the occasion when he had complained about Hsin-ping spending eight yuan on some shoes of her own.

The old days were frequently relived, in a room full of old and beautiful furniture, which had survived the Red Guards. In pride of place on the red sandalwood altar-table there was a picture of four men in Western suits, their names signed under a title—'China's four most famous *dan*'. *Dan* were actors who played female characters in the Peking Opera, and these four—Mei Lanfang, Cheng Yanqiu, Sheng Xiaoyun and Linglai's father, Xun Huisheng—were considered the greatest exponents of the art. Other photographs showed Xun in his head-dress and embroidered silk gown, daintily holding a teapot and cup. This was his most famous role, Hong Niangzi in the Tang story, 'Tale of the West Wing'. Hong Niangzi was a servant girl, whose character Xun particularly admired. She was a free spirit, outspoken, rebellious and frank. She encouraged her mistress to resist her widowed mother's plans for her to marry into money, and urged her instead to marry the boy she loved—a poor, struggling scholar. It was a sad story, as was the life of Xun Huisheng himself. Hsin-ping had become involved in this sadness, too, at the end.

As a boy, Xun had tagged along with a local Hebei opera troupe of a style called *bangziqiang*, which used wooden clappers as musical accompaniment. He earned barely enough to eat, but he studied with his masters and became proficient in the skills of the Peking Opera. In time, he created a new style, combining elements of voice, movement and makeup which were normally featured in separate roles. Before 1949 he had already become the most famous of the 'four great *dan*'. After Liberation, the new government entrusted him with the responsibility for instructing young people in appreciation of this traditional art form, in an attempt to overcome the historical legacy of contempt for actors. In the old days of the temple fairs, the lion-dancers, stilt-walkers, boxers, magicians and all kinds of actors were frowned upon by authority and despised by respectable folk. Like most of his calling, Xun lived in humble circumstances near Qianmen, but under the new régime he was moved from Shanxi Street to a more prestigious northern address. He was even installed as deputy head of the Peking Municipal Culture Bureau. For a short time he enjoyed acclaim and status. Then, in 1968, during the campaign to purify the class ranks, he was re-cast as a remnant of the former privileged society.

Xun's whole family found itself in deep trouble. His wife, who had connections with the Nationalists, was detained at the Culture Bureau, and labelled an 'historical counter-revolutionary'. Two sons, drama-school teachers, were also detained at their workplace. Linglai managed to stay free, but could do little to assist her family. Every morning, before she went to work in the factory, she took her father to the Municipal Culture Bureau. Previously he had pleased himself whether he went into work or not, since he was really a figurehead, but now he was very much needed as a symbol of the bitter past. Linglai was unable to pick him up in the afternoons because she worked late, so she asked Hsin-ping to meet him and see him home every day after finishing school. Hsin-ping was amazed at the transformation since she had last seen him. Of course he was getting old now, but this did not acount for his appearance and bearing. She remembered him as Hong Niangzi. How lithe and dynamic and agile he had been on the stage. Now he seemed like a block of wood. Every day for a month she met him. He always came out last of all, walking-stick in one hand, lunch bag in the other. He was fat now and his hair had turned completely white.

Hsin-ping accompanied Old Xun home on the bus, and afterwards asked him what he would like to eat, and went out into the street to buy a few things for him. Every day he seemed to move more and more slowly, and to become more dull-witted. The supple hands of the servant girl were now rigid and clawed. Once or twice he asked Hsin-ping for a drink, and then dropped his cup to the floor. He was showing the effects of his recent interrogations.

'Recite from the Selected Works of Chairman Mao!'

'I can't remember.'

'You had no difficulty reciting your lines from the opera. How come you can't remember the words of our great leader, you old turtle's egg?'

'I learnt my lines from my master.'

'Well then, didn't he make you read and recite? You just haven't paid attention to the works of Chairman Mao, because you are a stinking old bourgeois intellectual, aren't you? You haven't written one word of self-criticism, have you? You haven't even written a single line from the Selected Works.'

'But I can't write, I never learnt', said the bourgeois intellectual.

'Then how did you manage to learn your lines for the opera?'

'I told you. I learnt my lines from my master. I recited after him. If I got a line wrong I was beaten . . .' His new masters needed no second invitation.

The old man was also severely criticized because he had on occasion instructed the young girls in his neighbourhood in how to make delicate, lady-like gestures. Whenever he saw a girl point at something in a natural, and from his point of view rough, gesture, he would stop and show her how to do it in a fetching and feminine manner, like a true little lady.

Finally, he was assigned to manual labour and sent to Fengshan County, on the outskirts of Peking, during the winter of 1968. There was very little he could do. His age and former occupation rendered him almost useless, but he was set to work pulling nails out of old wooden planks, until he got sick with bronchitis and developed a fever. Linglai wrote letter after letter to suburban and municipal revolutionary committees, begging for permission for her father to return to the city for medical attention. Finally she succeeded and he returned to Peking, but was unable to see a doctor. Healing the sick and healing class enemies were two different things, and doctors were acutely aware that they would very quickly be transformed from 'revolutionary medical workers' into 'bourgeois medical authorities' if they forgot the distinction. Those who refused to heed, and there were many, spent their time cleaning lavatories and sweeping floors, leaving only a handful of qualified people on duty in many institutions.

Linglai did not give up however, and eventually, by means of a back door, she managed to get her father into a hospital, despite the fact that he had been declared 'black'. He was given a bed in Beida Hospital, originally an annexe of Peking University. By this time he had an extremely high fever and great difficulty in breathing. He was panting in distress, and his heart was beginning to give out under the strain. On 26 December 1968, Hsin-ping went to see him. She, Linglai and Xun's daughter-in-law took turns to stay by his bedside. Hsin-ping took the morning shift, the daughter-in-law the afternoon shift, and Linglai maintained her vigil in the evenings. He seemed particularly weak that morning when Hsin-ping saw him. He was on an intravenous drip. Hsin-ping greeted him in her usual manner, 'How are things today, Uncle?' 'I will not come out of this', he rasped. 'Of course you will, and you'll be stronger than ever. But first you've got to get over your bronchitis, that's all.'

Suddenly a nurse came into the room. It seemed that all the beds had to be removed from the ward, in order to hold a meeting—not just any old meeting, but a celebration for Chairman Mao's birthday. The tubes were removed and Old Xun's bed was shoved into another ward. Hsin-ping asked him if he wanted something to eat, and offered him an apple, at which he nibbled briefly. Suddenly he sat bolt upright and clutched in panic at Hsin-ping's fingers. She responded by gripping his hands tightly, as he began choking and gasping. He seemed to be suffocating. She called out for a nurse, but nobody came. She pressed an electric buzzer, but still nobody came. She couldn't get free of his grip to go in search of help, and, in any case, she dared not leave him. His eyes were rolling and he appeared delirious for a moment, and then his eyes cleared and he looked astonishingly calm and lucid.

Hsin-ping had never actually been with anyone at the moment of death, but now she thought of the expression 'last flash of sunset.' They say there is a moment of brilliant clarity just before the end. She had the overwhelming impression that Xun was looking intently at something in the distance and that he wanted to let go his hold on life. She called out, in panic, 'Uncle, Uncle, don't go, please, don't go'. She clutched at him, as his eyes slowly began to close. She saw tears. She broke free of him and rushed out of the ward, calling for doctors and nurses—all of whom were at a meeting. After a very long time, long after she had given up all hope of assistance, two doctors came into the room, still arguing about the meeting and what should be done. Neither wanted to be the first to make a decision affecting the priority of Mao's birthday celebrations. When they saw Xun's condition they set to, massaging his heart, but it was too late.

Hsin-ping rang Linglai at work and told her the news. After some hours she was allowed to leave work and come to the hospital, but it was too late to see her father. They had already taken his body to the morgue. The next day Xun's wife was released from detention and told that she was being taken to see her husband in hospital. When she arrived she was left alone to search for the patient. She had assumed that he was seriously ill, but had no idea that he was already dead. She searched high and low throughout the wards and had given up in despair when two nurses called out to her. They wheeled over a body and asked her to identify it. '*Ai-ya!*' she shrieked, 'you've tortured him! You've frozen him to death!' She was dragged away screaming and placed back in detention at the Culture Bureau. A year later she was released.

Often, when Hsin-ping went to the flat, Linglai's mother would beg to be told again about Xun Huisheng's last moments. Hsin-ping obliged, partly out of pity and partly because she herself could not get it out of her mind. Often on a hot summer's afternoon, as they sat out on the balcony overlooking the street, the sound of the icy-pole man clacking out a tattoo on his sticks seemed to call up ghosts of the Hebei opera. But however many times she recalled it, Xun's death remained incomprehensible to Hsin-ping. Why had he not been left alone to live out the rest of his life with some dignity? He had all the right credentials surely? He had been poor, he had suffered abuse, discrimination and poverty during the old days. He had spent his youth, and his talents, giving pleasure to simple workers and peasants. Despite his illiteracy, he had made a great contribution to 'proletarian culture'. Surely trailing around from village to village performing for peasants could not be construed as 'élitist' or 'bourgeois?' Had he not portrayed women in a positive light, and shown the struggle of exploited servant girls against feudal morality and customs? In the very roles he had chosen and developed, he had portrayed the courage and wisdom of the oppressed classes—and all he wanted in his old age was the opportunity to pass on a hint of his craft to the young. He had not sought an important bureaucratic post, but had one thrust on him by the government. He could not even be accused of being contaminated with foreign ideas and lifestyles. What was foreign about the Peking Opera? Yet he had been bullied and beaten into a clumsy parody of himself.

Hsin-ping could not bring herself to talk about all the details, like those afternoons when he returned home after being beaten with belts and ropes, and kept asking, in his soft, mincing tones, 'I don't understand. Why has everyone become so evil-hearted? Where have all the good people gone?' That he had been sent out to do manual labour was bad enough. That he had developed bronchitis, and been unable to get a doctor and had been carted around in search of a hospital that would take him . . . above all, that even when he *did* get medical attention his condition was ignored in favour of a birthday celebration for the man who had immortalized Dr Norman Bethune!* It all seemed more fantastic, more melodramatic, more absurd, than anything in the opera.

In 1974, Hsin-ping made an application to visit her father in Australia. The official attitude to foreign contacts had changed dramatically since the Nixon visit and Australia's recognition of the People's Republic, and Hsin-ping had begun to correspond with her father again. In 1975, she was given permission to go. Before leaving China for her visit, she was asked to see the Party branch secretary. He warned her of the meretricious nature of Western bourgeois society, which he himself had never seen, and reminded her of her patriotic duty to watch for foreign capitalist spies and to give a good impression of the motherland at all times. 'Do not forget', he said solemnly, 'that you are a Chinese!'

While Hsin-ping was preparing for her trip, she saw quite a lot of her cousin, Fan Yuzhong. Fan had led a most interesting life. His mother, Grandma's second daughter, Wang Jieming, had studied Physical Education at Peking Teachers' University. There she fell hopelessly in love with a young man named Zheng. He was completely oblivious to her feelings and married another woman, after which Wang Jieming became chronically depressed. She never seemed to sleep, and all night long she could be heard pacing up and down in her room. In the morning the floor was littered with cigarette butts. After a while she went to Shanghai with her basketball team, and was seen in action by a man named Fan Chengchuan. His wife had recently died, he was lonely, and the grace and agility of Wang Jieming worked a spell over him. He bought a ticket for Peking, on the same train as the basketball team, and tried to strike up a friendship with her. Then he began calling on her family, and sending gifts. He got on very well indeed

---

* The Canadian doctor who died while treating wounded Communist soldiers during the anti-Japanese war. He was the subject of a eulogy by Mao on 21 December 1939, which became one of 'Three Constantly Read Articles' during the Cultural Revolution.

with Old Lady Wang, but was much less successful in his bid to win over Jieming's mother. She made no secret of her disapproval of his designs on her daughter, but she had little influence in the matter compared to the first wife of the household.

As Jieming slid deeper and deeper into inexplicable fits of depression, Lady Wang began to argue that marriage would be good for her, that it might bring her out of herself, and so on. Finally it was decided, and the marriage took place. Shortly afterwards Fan Yuzhong was born, and the family went to live in Hunan Province, in the city of Changsha, where Fan's father had come from. Wang Jieming's state of mind deteriorated sharply after the birth of her child and she never spoke at all. One day, after one of the servants found baby Fan lying on a chopping board in the kitchen, among the melons and cabbages that his mother was preparing, it was decided that the child should be put in the care of another woman. She was a widow who had lost her status as a family member after the death of her husband and had resorted to domestic work in order to survive. After the new woman came, Fan's mother was locked in her room, and had nothing further to do with the rearing of the child.

One day, Wang Jieming escaped from her room and was picked up by Japanese soldiers, who thought she might be an enemy agent. She was thrown into a cell, beaten and tortured, but never uttered an intelligible word. The Japanese thought she might be feigning madness at first, but were gradually convinced it was no act, and let her go. Her husband found her sitting alone in the street, filthy and bleeding, lice teeming in her hair—just sitting, tearing her clothing into small strips. She was taken back home and survived some years.

In 1945, both the Japanese and the Nationalists tried to woo Fan's father to their side. He was a textile scientist, an industrialist and a potential political leader who was known for his influential views on modernization. He was also a patriot and a liberal democrat at heart and refused a bribe of US$50 000 to go with the retreating Japanese. Then he refused the overtures of the Nationalists, soon to be in flight themselves, because he considered them to be corrupt and undemocratic. At one stage, when it seemed that the Nationalists might kill him rather than leave him behind to be useful to the new government, the Communists declared him an official 'war criminal' in order to trick the enemy into thinking that they might be able to persuade him to flee to Taiwan with them. This ruse kept him alive during a critical period. Eventually however, it became clear that he would never join the Nationalists, and that his sympathies were with the Communists, whom he regarded as progressive and patriotic. He was pursued by Nationalist agents, who intended either to abduct or murder him. During a search of his textile mill, the workers hid him in a boiler until the danger passed. After the flight of the Nationalists, he was recognized by the new government as a progressive and patriotic element, and made a member of the Political Consultative Committee, an advisory group of Party-approved non-communists.

Wang Jieming was by now hopelessly insane, and Fan wanted to marry again. He went to Peking with his intended, who had been his secretary, in order to explain the situation to Grandma, now head of the household since the old lady had died. He wanted to seek her blessing, not for a second wife but for annulment and remarriage, modern style. Grandma did not approve at all, since her daughter was still alive. If she died and her husband remarried, that would be another thing. If he took other wives, that would be perfectly normal too, and nothing to get excited about, provided Jieming maintained her status in the family. The thought of her daughter's rejection alarmed Grandma, but in the end she was forced to accept the inevitable.

After the remarriage, the Fan family moved to Qingdao, and Fan Yuzhong grew up as a 'little prince', accustomed to horse-riding, being chauffeured about in limousines, and travelling in aeroplanes, as a result of his father's high status and income. He matured very quickly and began to take an interest in girls by the time he was thirteen or fourteen. After junior high, he went to Peking. Grandma would have been perfectly happy to have him stay with her and Hsin-ping in Toufa Lane, but Fan preferred to live in at his school, and visit them for holidays and weekends. By this time young Master Fan had begun to develop an almost religious devotion to communist ideals. He contemptuously rejected the temptations of his birthright and passed up an opportunity to go to the famous Peking Number Four Secondary, in favour of the humble and unassuming Hebei Secondary. He began to make a point of rejecting out of hand any suggestion of privilege or advantage, and to cultivate an ascetic air, suggestive of revolutionary heroes and martyrs.

On one occasion, Fan and Hsin-ping were walking past Tian'anmen Square together when suddenly Fan dropped to the ground and lay on his back, overcome with the ecstasy of being there in that Holy Place where the People's Republic had been born. Hsin-ping was mortified, and yelled at him to get up before she died of embarrassment, but he just lay there, waving his arms about as if he meant to embrace the sky itself, and singing a hymn of praise to the Revolution. Finally, Hsin-ping could stand it no longer. She cursed him for a madman and walked quickly away, leaving him prostrate in the square.

Then Fan began to grow his hair long, in the manner of Soviet intellectuals and revolutionaries, whom he worshipped. Once, when he was staying with Hsin-ping, he snatched a picture from her bedroom wall and began screwing it up into a ball. How could she bring herself to

Hsin-ping approaches (top) and enters the courtyard of Grandma's house in Toufa Lane, 1987

The courtyard of Grandma's house in Toufa Lane, 1987

The Sleeping Dragon Pine at Jietaisi in the Western Hills near Peking, 1987

take part in the slavish adulation of some bourgeois American flib-berty-gibbert actress? Fan became almost demented when Hsin-ping explained, with acid restraint, that it was, or had been, a picture of a famous Soviet actress who had played the heroine in a film about a woman leading a group of orphans out of Nazi-occupied Poland to the safety of the Soviet Union. Since she seldom held the moral high ground from which to lord it over her pious cousin, Hsin-ping took full advantage of the moment. She delivered her lines and strode from the room leaving the devastated Fan to contemplate his sacrilege. When she returned she found him engaged in a great work of reconstruction, attempting to iron out the wrinkles from the violated icon.

Fan read everything he could lay his hands on about the Soviet Union. He made strenuous attempts to look Russian, and was forever lecturing Hsin-ping that she should not read bourgeois foreign literature, such as Shakespeare, when there was Pushkin and Tolstoy to be read. He dreamed of sacrificing himself for the Revolution. He renounced food almost completely and seemed to require negligible sleep. This was the regimen of the revolutionary, tempering himself for the heroic deeds which would sustain and inspire the next generation.

However, Fan soon began to realize that not everybody who professed communist ideals was as sincere as he was, and that some of the displays of love for the Party were contrived. By the end of high school, he had come to despise the 'phoney activists' who pledged themselves to a spartan life in the countryside, serving the peasants, while secretly conniving to get themselves into some élite city college. He decided to stay on in his school, and do valuable propaganda work as a secretary for the Communist Youth League, rather than go on to university. He also became a prolific writer of articles on youth and revolution for magazines and newspapers.

These activities did not preclude a number of tempestuous love affairs; in fact many girls found his passionate idealism quite intoxi-cating. To add to his attractions, his reputation as a literary figure grew with the publication of Chinese translations of foreign children's stories, such as *The Golden Apples* and *The Black Arrow*. He had studied English with his father as a small child, and then in primary school, and he now began to put this skill to use, sometimes sitting up all night to write out English translations of Chinese works in long-hand, because he had no typewriter. He continued to publish polemics until the time of the Hundred Flowers movement, when he, like so many others, over-stepped the bounds of permissible criticism of the Party.

Like his cousin, Fan came to grief over the issue of Chu Anping and the 'Party kingdom' article in 1957. Unlike Hsin-ping however, Fan had jubilantly put pen to paper on this theme, hardly able to contain his joy and enthusiasm at this precious opportunity for unfettered literary and political debate. He was, of course, fervently committed to communism, and did not for a moment deny the Party's role as the 'vanguard' of revolution, but he expressed concern that persistent remnants of feudalism might survive and prosper under a monolithic, one-party state, unless certain safeguards were built into the system. In very short order he was denounced as a rightist, as was his father, and they were both sent to the countryside for manual labour.

This set-back turned out to be a blessing in disguise. Fan learned to lie low, so that when the Cultural Revolution came, he did not draw any more attention to himself than was absolutely necessary. He endured suspicions and investigations as a former 'rightist' but he managed to avoid cultivating too many rivalries and animosities. Above all, he learned to curb his tongue and his pen. He went on studying English in secret, with all the intensity of the fanatic and, when it was safe to do so, suddenly produced a bewildering array of excellent translations of English stories, including Agatha Christie novels.

During his period of labour reform, he survived partly as a result of his own youthful preparations for a future ordeal, and partly because of the devotion of a young woman whom he had helped to join the Communist Youth League. She had been a student in the school when he was the League secretary. Like many others, she was infatuated with Fan, and throughout his period of exile she made regular visits, and took him food and clothing parcels. After his release, they married. Fan married her largely out of sincere gratitude for what she had done for him. She may well have been the difference between life or death for him. He was also extremely attracted to her beauty and her charming mannerisms, but Hsin-ping sounded an ominous warning in this regard: 'Never mind what she looks like now. Take a good long look at her mother. that's what she'll end up like.' Her mother was large, aggressive and coarse. She was also highly critical of her daughter's choice of a husband—not entirely without reason. She did not trust the lady-killer for one thing, and soon after the marriage she began to hear a litany of complaints from her daughter about his impossible ways—his moods, his passions, his abominable untidiness, his habit of staying up all night, his resentment of any distraction from his private thoughts and dreams, and his frequent inexplicable absences.

Above all, both women were baffled and frustrated by his 'romantic' nature. The word was a reproach in itself, redolent of those ridiculous foreigners and their childish drivel about love and longing. But what kind of 'romantic' was Fan? Was he, like the poet Li Bai, in love with nature itself? Li Bai was supposed to have drowned in the Yangtse, trying to embrace the moon's reflection in the water. Or was it his own? One could easily imagine Fan doing something like that. A mystic perhaps; someone whose aesthetic sensibilities were beyond all understanding or expression. Was he an idealist and a visionary, dreaming noble dreams? Or was he a slave to unutterably sophisticated and decadent fancies? Fan had some characteristics which were disturbingly reminiscent of his grandfather, Wang Jinfang. Perhaps he just had his head full of stuff and nonsense from reading too many books. This was certainly the theory favoured by Grandma. Whatever the case, Fan was an overwhelmingly 'romantic' figure. Although small, he had great presence. He always cut a dashing figure, despite a chronic disregard for the normal conventions of grooming—and he had an extravagant shock of wavy hair which made him look rather like one of those busts of European composers which lay crumbling away in the cupboards of college music departments. There was something else. Fan had the air of an internationalist, Bohemian, and sexually liberated intellectual of the 1930s. Many women were attracted to this quality—a sad reminder, perhaps, of what the Revolution should have done for them.

During the early 1970s, Fan made frequent urgent requests of Hsin-ping to borrow her flat in the architects' dormitory. The first request began with unaccustomed solicitude for Lulu, and her lack of fresh air and recreation. He urged, with great persistence, and eventual success, a day at the zoo. The following Sunday they set out, Grandma complaining bitterly that it was far too cold to be going out, and Lulu moaning that she felt sick. Their mutterings of discontent rose to a crescendo after lunch, when Hsin-ping announced that they would have to stay out until four because Fan had guests in the flat. After one or two more such requests, Hsin-ping made him tell her what was going on. She agreed to be a sport and co-operate as much as possible, but drew the line at staying out all day.

The arrangement came to an abrupt end when Fan's wife and her mother came to the flat one Sunday and demanded to know where Fan and his slattern were hiding. Fortunately, this was one occasion when Hsin-ping was genuinely unaware of Fan's whereabouts, but there was a great deal of shouting and name-calling before the two women accepted this. Shortly afterwards, Fan confided to his cousin that he had been involved in a number of affairs, some of them simultaneously. Hers was not the only acommodation he had used. 'No wonder so many people in Peking go out on Sunday afternoons', said Hsin-ping.

Fan and Hsin-ping remained close confidantes throughout these last years in Peking, as they had been all their lives. Each regarded the other as a soulmate, the one person who would always understand and never betray, no matter what. One warm and windy spring evening in 1975 they sat together in the flat, discussing Hsin-ping's imminent departure for Australia, and the times they had lived through together. Hsin-ping recalled the night Fan came knocking urgently at the door, and burst breathlessly into the room. They laughed as Hsin-ping mimicked the

way he had darted to the window, pulled it shut, whipped the curtains
across and then dashed back across the room to lock the door. She
remembered the impact as he told her that he had heard some sen-
sational news from a prohibited foreign broadcast. It was September
1971 and the news, which had not been released in China, was that Lin
Biao had died in a plane crash en route to the Soviet Union, after an
unsuccessful assassination attempt on Mao. As they recalled the way
revelations came to light about Lin Biao and his family, and the widespread cynicism this had caused, the discussion turned to 'China's
Khrushchev', Liu Shaoqi, and the way *he* had fallen.

'Did you see that newsreel about Liu's wife in Indonesia?' asked
Hsin-ping.

'Yes, I did. And did you see what the students did to her at Qinghua?
I hate things like that. It's just primitive, barbaric. Women as witches
and . . . It seems to bring out all the worst fears and superstitions, even
among educated people, like students.'

'They say when she was dragged out on to the campus she was
jammed into a tight Western evening gown, and had high-heeled shoes
like stilts.'

'Yes, and a necklace of ping-pong balls, with skulls painted on them',
said Fan, with revulsion. 'Maybe that'll happen to Jiang Qing herself
one day. You know, I can't help thinking about all this business of our
leaders and their power struggles. Liu Shaoqi and Lin Biao and Mao. I
don't know what happened . . . but I can't help wondering . . . do you
remember how Lin Biao suddenly appeared on the scene in the 1960s
and the hunt was on for counter-revolutionaries? Was he really ill before
that? Or was he just lying low, waiting for his chance to . . . '

Hsin-ping burst in. 'Do I remember? You must be joking. You know
that nitwit friend of mine . . . Tang Ling? She almost got us killed. Cui
and Linglai and I were watching a newsreel, in the picture theatre. Must
have been 1966. Suddenly Lin Biao appeared on the screen. He looked
really white, like a ghost. Do you know what that stupid fart Tang Ling
did? She thought Lin Biao's face was so white he looked like that
turtle's egg landlord in the opera. So she bawled out at the top of her
voice 'Hey, look! Who's that? It looks like the landlord . . . what's his
name . . . ' Thank God, Cui managed to clap his hand over her face
before she got any further, or we'd all have been for the Vegetable
Market. We all sat shaking in our shoes for some minutes, wondering
who might have heard.'

'Well, now you can say what you like about Lin Biao. He was a bourgeois careerist, a renegade, a traitor, a counter-revolutionary double-
dealer, a conspirator—and a dirty old man.'

Hsin-ping shook her head in bewilderment. 'Why do we fall for it?
Is it our national character? Are we just too trusting of our leaders?

We're very patriotic, and maybe that's a weakness as well as a strength.'

'A modern socialist country should tolerate ... encourage ... criticism and debate. But you know, it's not just us Chinese who are gullible. In the West ...'

'Yes, that's true', agreed Hsin-ping. 'The Fascists in Europe and so on. But, I just wonder, you know—if our leaders say we can have forty yuan a month, that's O.K. with us. If they say fifty, that's O.K. too. If they tell us we must eat less, we eat less. If they say we should die for the motherland, then we die. In the Great Leap Forward, they said ...'

'I know exactly what you mean', said Fan, sadly, 'but what I'm saying is we are all human beings and we *all* fall for it, somewhere, sometime. There's no shortage of examples, in this century alone, of political leaders all over the world telling outrageous lies, and people believing and fighting each other and dying in millions ...'

'But Fan! China! Has any place ever been like China these last years? One slogan after another. 'Four clean-ups', 'five reds', 'two lines', 'three red flags'—no wonder we Chinese invented the abacus. And how many innocent people have died for it all? Our leaders just use us, to fight against each other, for their own reasons.' Hsin-ping paused and pointed slyly at her chin, a mute reference to the Chairman, who had a large mole on his chin.

'Hsin-ping, it is *people* who torture and kill and hate each other, not just leaders. Some do it for a cause, some do it for their own ambitions ... and some do it just because they enjoy it. Sometimes political leaders start things for a particular reason—as a diversion, let's say—and they just get out of hand. As for Mao, well ... certainly he was a genius of guerilla warfare and tactics. Look at the way he went on his rest cure in 1966, left Liu to deal with the work teams, and then made a spectacular comeback, bobbing up and down in the Yangtse to show how fit and virile he was. Liu was done for after that. But that's not to say that even Mao knew everything that was going to happen.'

'But what about our country? What about China?' protested Hsin-ping indignantly. 'What about production and progress? Don't leaders care about that sort of thing? We were in a desperate, backward condition in 1949, thanks to the Nationalists—and the warlords and the Japanese. Then, in the 1950s, things seemed to be going really well, we were developing. China stood up. Then we got the Great Leap Forward ...'

'I wish you'd stop telling me about the Great Leap Forward! Do you think I need reminding? I was doing all right myself until then, you know.'

'Oh Fan. You were an idiot in those days. You drove us all crazy with your speeches and articles ...'

'Oh yes, and you were so damn clever too, weren't you? Remember the "Party kingdom"?'

'At least I only got myself into trouble. What about you, Mr Intellectual? What a great idea, to send me a copy of Liu Shaoqi's *How To Be A Good Communist* for my birthday. You might as well have sent me *How To Cut Your Own Throat*'

'Well', said Fan, when their laughter had subsided, 'at least I learnt my lesson after the Hundred Flowers.'

'Whatever happened, we can both honestly say that our attitude to workers and peasants has always been good', said Hsin-ping soberly. 'Anyway, the point is, our leaders made fools of us all, stirring up campaigns to take our minds off famine and economic crises. Foreigners get bread and circuses. We get "continuous revolution".'

'That doesn't explain much really', said Fan, a little irritated with his cousin's cliché. 'You know, cynicism is a kind of naïvety, too—if you are too easily satisfied with a simple explanation. It's the cruelty and violence I can't really understand. It terrifies me, not because I'm afraid for myself, but because it exists.'

'I know. I will never forget those screams at night. I often heard horrible screams, outside in the street. Why do people . . . how can they . . . I remember that old man, who criticized the students for beating their teacher. They doused him with boiling water . . . first scalding hot, then cold, then hot . . .' Hsin-ping stopped, shuddered violently, and then covered her face in her hands. Fan reached out gently and drew her hands away. Hsin-ping looked up. 'You can't deny what Jiang Qing did. That scheming slut, spraying shit all around, like a dung beetle sneezing. She certainly knew how to handle Mao, the dirty old . . .'

'Or did Mao handle *her*, Hsin-ping? I'm not denying she had all her enemies done away with, but you can't just say she was the one responsible for it all, or that she was the only one who had designs on power and needed to get rid of a few rivals. And anyway, she couldn't manage all that without supporters could she?'

'Do you think Mao used *her*?'

'I don't know', mused Fan, 'I just don't know. Sometimes Mao was right . . . about getting rid of all that Confucian rubbish, and attacking bureaucrats. He urged youth to question, to agitate for change, to condemn vested interests . . . and yet, nobody could criticize him. Who knows if that's what he really wanted or not? Maybe he heard so much about himself he began to believe it.'

'That proves he is only human', said Hsin-ping, grinning sheepishly now.

'Maybe, cousin, maybe. But you went out and bought a wax mango for your altar-table, didn't you?'

Hsin-ping cackled as she dried her eyes.

Shortly after, Hsin-ping left for Australia, and was re-united with her father. One day, as he was showing her around the Victoria Market in Melbourne, she saw her first real mango.

'What's that?' she asked.

'It's a mango, you hick. Haven't you ever seen a mango before? It's a native of Africa, very popular in . . . What on earth are you laughing at?'

In time, Hsin-ping's visit turned into permanent residence. Lulu and Grandma also came to join her. Her husband came too, but they divorced shortly after his arrival. Then Hsin-ping married again—this time to a 'foreigner'. She and her new husband, Steve—and Lulu, and Grandma—went into the restaurant business.

Epilogue

In July 1987, Hsin-ping went back to China. Steve and Lulu and I went with her—and Grandma, in the form of ashes in a little black box, going home for good. As we talked about Grandma, I recalled the way her tiny face would suddenly appear through the frosted glass of an adjoining door, like a floating head at a seance, as Hsin-ping called up the past for us on those Saturday mornings in Moorabbin.

Occasionally, after the apparition vanished, we would hear a distant, plaintive moan, as Grandma sought some nameless comfort from her grand-daughter, in the manner of a child calling for her mother in the night. The old lady could be a frightful pest sometimes, but everyone liked her just the same. She would be missed. I thought of the time I had asked Hsin-ping whether Grandma ever expressed surprise that Ron and I, two long-noses, spoke Chinese. 'Of course not', she said, giggling, 'You look funny, but you are still human beings. Human beings speak Chinese, don't they?'

Grandma used to hoard every conceivable foodstuff and medicine in her room. Cicada skins, snake-bile powder—it would not have surprised me greatly if she had a kilo of pangolin scales under her bed along with her innumerable jars of fruit and pickled vegetables. Occasionally, during one of her nocturnal foraging expeditions, she tripped over something and woke the household. Finally, she did it once too often and broke her hip. Even in hospital she seemed as durable as an ancient coin, and defied any hint of extinction by devouring remarkable quantities of food. She would not stay in bed, so they had to restrain her, to prevent her from dislodging the pin in her hip with another fall. This seemed to be the last straw for Grandma, and she died soon after, although the doctors said her heart was still as sound as a bell.

The old woman was cremated after a service by an Australian Buddhist priest. Hsin-ping consulted him about Grandma's wish that her ashes should be scattered on the waters somewhere in her homeland. This presented some difficulties at the time, because Hsin-ping had no plans to go back to China. The priest explained that in the Buddhist cosmology, all the waters of the universe are one, and flow together ultimately, like the immersion of the self in the Great One-ness. Hsin-ping was not entirely convinced that Grandma would appreciate the finer points of religious philosophy, so she put her on the shelf, literally, for the time being. Then, in 1987, Grandma got her wish.

As I sat in the plane, my thoughts were a jumble. I really wanted to savour the significance of this journey—for Hsin-ping, and for me. I tried to recall my feelings during that first flight to China in 1975. I just could not concentrate. I was allowing myself to be annoyed by a party of senior high school kids, bouncing their coke-ad energy all over the plane. What on earth were they doing here? What would they get out of a trip to China? I realized I had become a snob about China, but still, they irritated me. Short back and sides and dangling forelocks, they looked as if they were on a trip to the 1950s as well—another affront to me because I had spent a lot of time there too, once.

All of the people on this plane would see a very different China from the one experts inspected twelve years ago. In those days there were slogans everywhere, and children in kindergarten singing about tractors and pigs and hydraulic presses. There were great white statues of Mao, and loudspeakers in the streets crackling with martial music and revolutionary operas. Visits—not to temples, but to schools, factories and communes. Meetings with revolutionary committee members—and fairy tales, not about the Monkey King, but about production statistics. No free markets, no coca-cola, no 'disco', no Doris Day hits played with piano accordion, no 'I climbed the Great Wall' T-shirts. The trouble is that all these will seem like the quaint efforts of a backward country making an earnest attempt to be modern and sophisticated. People will point out the Disneyesque characters in the children's bookshops, or the huge plastic Father Christmas used to advertise a 'Western-style' restaurant, or the girls with their knee-length nylon stockings, or the sunglasses worn with the brandname stuck in the middle of the lens. It will simply look as if China is a land of ersatz and kitsch, a little behind, but well on its way to being like everywhere else. MacPeking.

Some might perhaps notice that modernization is not the only issue in China these days. The one-child policy may attract some attention. Some will find it too harsh, because people should be free to decide how many children they want; some will find it is not harsh at all, because there are too many Chinese anyway; and almost nobody will get any insight into how it feels to be on the receiving end of a 'policy'. They are a disciplined and conformist nation anyway, they are used to that sort of thing, it's part of their culture ... we shouldn't judge from a Western point of view. Maybe somebody will remember an older stereotype about Chinese and their strong family orientation, but after all that's not the 'real' China these days. That's only in the movies.

We watched an in-flight Chinese movie, as it happened. The film was in shocking condition, and since the Chinese character sub-titles were superimposed over the English sub-titles, it was not possible to read either. The soundtrack gave the general effect of a microphone placed inside a bag of potato chips. It was a contemporary love story.

A boy sees a girl, a fellow worker, in the shipyard one day. He follows her home after work, and the girl, afraid that he is a delinquent, tells her mother about it. The mother tells a policeman, who confronts the boy, contacts the shipyard, finds out that he is a model worker and a member of the Communist Youth League, and then lets him off with a warning. One day the Communist Youth League calls a meeting to elect office-bearers. Those who wish to be nominated make speeches—all of which are pretty much the same, about working for the good of the country, not pursuing individual profit and so on. When the boy gets up, he delivers a quite different sort of speech. He is controversial, and argues that it is not a crime to make money, or want a better standard of living. These are essential elements of modernization and progress and democracy. The girl is absolutely captivated by his inspiring speech and his romantic and idealistic approach to getting filthy rich. In a sort of foolish, lovesick gesture she doodles the name 'Mike' in English on her nomination paper, never intending to hand it up. She considers him dashing, exotic, sophisticated, debonair—a vision of the future and modernization, just like the people in those foreign movies—so she dubs him 'Mike'.

Unfortunately for her, however, her nomination slip is gathered up while she is day-dreaming and, to her horror, is read out to an astonished meeting. Who is this foreigner? Who on earth would nominate a bloody foreigner for office in the Communist Youth League? The branch secretary calls for the culprit to own up. The girl stands up, defiantly. Yes, she did it—because to her the name seemed to suit his breadth of vision, his imagination. This is not received well, but there are no recriminations, and the whole thing seems to pass without too much fuss. The strange affair of Mike is put down to her state of infatuation, and the two begin seeing a lot of each other.

After a suitable interval, the pair decide they would like to marry. First, they must meet each other's family. The boy's family are simple, humble folk who live in average urban accommodation in Shanghai. The girl's mother, however, is a high-ranking cadre. She lives in a very plush apartment, facing south, with a fridge, colour television and a very large foreign-style cabinet with roman letters on it. In pride of place in the cabinet are a red glass dolphin, a large vase of artificial chrysanthemums, a huge four-speaker Sanyo cassette recorder, a bottle of X.O. brandy, and several cartons of Marlboro.

Mother expresses opposition to the marriage, because she does not feel that the boy can provide her daughter with the life to which she has become accustomed. With a touch of Chinese self-deprecation, she puts it a different way. The girl is a little soft, a little spoiled, useless around the house. On the other hand, the boy's parents are delighted. The mother takes the girl, whom she has just met, into a very grimy kitchen and says, 'I am old and tired. You are young and strong. You must take over the responsibilities of this household.'

The characterizations are beginning to take shape, to lend themselves to the message of the film. The boy is controversial in his ambitions for prosperity, but is starting out from nothing, has no connections, is using his own initiative to improve himself, and so on. No wonder he reminded his girlfriend of characters in foreign movies. He wants to make money, but he is not of the corrupt cadre class. He sits up all night in his garret, writing technical textbooks of great social use, and sells them to publishing companies who report that they are selling like hot cakes, helping people who cannot go on to further formal education. He is clearly a goodie. The girl's mother, on the other hand, is clearly a baddie—a menace to progress and modernization as well as being a snob. After all, while the boy is economically ambitious in a socially useful sort of way, the mother is socially ambitious in an economically useless sort of way. What kind of contribution is she making to the 'four modernizations?' She is interested only in preserving her own influential network, or 'back door', by means of a judicious marriage.

In order to underline the point that there are worthy and unworthy ways of creating wealth, the boy has a sister. She and some typical Shanghai spiv run a match-making business. It is not that the business is unsavoury. After all, the government has been urging people to use their initiative—what a thing to tell the Shanghainese—and there's no doubt that being a go-between is a time-honoured occupation in China. No, the problem is the way she spends her money, her objective in running the business. She likes fancy food, fine clothes and a good time, and she has no socially worthwhile purpose in mind. She is just a little bourgeois dolly bird. But, there is hope for her. She admires her brother so much—she often gets up in the middle of the night to mop his sweaty back as he slaves over his textbooks—that she begins to see the error of her ways. He also points out to her that her notion of match-making, based on advantageous alliances, is a backward and destructive influence on China.

Just as we were approaching the denouement, there was a blue flash. The movie had been aborted, because we were coming in to Peking. Nobody reacted, because nobody was watching. Why should they? Soon they would see the real China.

Among a sizeable throng of people waiting outside the luggage collection area were several who were calling out to Hsin-ping and darting about in an attempt to keep her in view. Hsin-ping pointed out a little button face among the crowd—Tang Ling. Next to her was Xun Linglai, and her husband Cui Weimin. The old gang. Outside, after frenzied greetings and unheeded introductions, a mini-bus took the party to our hotel in the Eastern Archways district.

Next morning Hsin-ping and I got a cab down to Qianmen—the 'Front Gate'—which used to provide access from the northern, or 'Tartar' city into the southern, or 'Chinese' city. As we drove past Qianmen, now stripped of its walls and looking like a piece of another world left standing where it fell on Tian'anmen Square, Hsin-ping talked about the old southern walled city—and the streets her grandfather used to frequent, the suburbs which were disreputable even in Marco Polo's day and which Grandma had put off-limits for little girls. What a place this must have been when it was alive with teahouses and theatres and little drum-and-gong bands; a *demi-monde*, a 'low-life' district, where magicians and medicine-men and circus acrobats mingled in the teeming streets with fortune-tellers and barbers and cricket-cage sellers; a world of pimps and and pickpockets and coney-catchers and dandies out for a lark with the sing-song girls. Prostitution has long since disappeared from these streets, and so has the poverty and filth. Nevertheless, Qianmen these days is a rather sorry sight, overlooking a barren and soul-less 'Chinese City'.

The 'gate' itself is a remnant of the city built by the Ming emperor, Yong Le. Only two towers now remain of a beautiful structure finished in 1419, just before the Ming moved their capital from Nanking to Peking. In the past there used to be an inner gate, surmounted by a tower, and a half-moon wall with an outer tower and gates, which enclosed some little temples and a garden. The outer gate was opened only when the emperor issued forth to worship at the Temples of Heaven and Agriculture, as at the winter solstice. The inner and side gates provided access for ordinary traffic but were closed with some ceremony at night, after residents of the northern city had been given sufficient warning to return inside or stay out all night on the tiles. Both towers were burnt down in 1900, during the Boxer Rebellion. They were rebuilt, but in 1916 the whole outer half-moon wall was torn down to make room for twentieth-century traffic. Now, since the inner walls have recently met with a similar fate, only the two towers remain, like sentries, one on each side of the road at the southern end of Tian'anmen Square.

My dreams were dispelled by the robust voice of our taxi driver, and I began to listen in to more modern tales of Peking. He was actually a plumber, who had an interest, with his three brothers, in a taxi company. He was at present however, driving us in the 'company car', belonging to his work unit. Apparently he was doing us a favour in return for some help he had received from a friend of a friend of Hsin-ping after some nasty business about a building accident and an enquiry into alleged company negligence. Still within sight of Tian'anmen Square, we pulled up outside a block of flats. We walked up two flights of narrow concrete steps, and were admitted through a pair of padlocked iron doors with an iron grill, squeezed past several parked bicycles, and filed down a narrow corridor into a kitchen area shared by two or three families. A young woman was cooking—one of the increasing number who earns her living as a domestic in middle-class Chinese families. Then we saw Tang Ling, Xun Linglai, and her husband Cui Weimin.

We ate almost immediately. The atmosphere was uproarious and stories flowed. Hsin-ping was very relaxed, despite her twelve year absence. She looked as if she had just dropped in on the family in the usual Sunday afternoon way. In fact she spent most of the time talking to Tang Ling and Xun Linglai out in the kitchen, helping to prepare dishes. A diamond-shaped paper-cut stuck on the kitchen door displayed the character *fu* (riches, happiness, success) turned upside-down—because the word for 'upside-down' sounds similar to the word for 'arrive'. Reaching one's destination, coming home, is a kind of upside-down happiness.

That afternoon Hsin-ping and I went to the Western Archways district. Near here are some of the oldest of Peking's temples, including the Guangji Temple, where Big Grandma's funeral took place in 1944. They say it was a prison for Buddhist monks in recent times. From the Western Crossroads we drove south down past Xidan Market towards Xuanwumen, which used to be one of the western gates leading from the south wall of the Tartar City. This area has had markets since ancient times, and storehouses of hides and firewood, and handicraft stalls. The southern side of Xidan Market became an area of bookshops, libraries, stationery supplies and shops which sold the 'treasures of the study', such as inkstones and brushes. This was an old scholar–bureaucrat neighbourhood.

The commercial atmosphere has been revived these days, with the advent of free-market policies, and there was a profusion of clothing and fruit stalls, as well as a few tradesmen, such as cobblers and carpenters. There were watermelons everywhere. Before we reached Xuanwumen, we turned right from Xidan Street into Toufa Lane, where Hsin-ping used to live. *'Toufa'* means 'hair', and Hsin-ping has always assumed that this is because it is a narrow lane, a 'hair's-breadth' wide. A much more interesting explanation links the name to an arsenal on the site. In 1625 it exploded, and the only remains of thirty men, who had been unloading kegs of gunpowder, was a pile of human hair.*

We stopped the car at the entrance to the lane and walked. Toufa Lane probably hasn't changed much in appearance in the last hundred years or so. The houses are made of neat little bricks smeared with grey plaster, and the roofs have segmented cylindrical tiles. Despite the greyness, the overall effect is not at all dull, especially in the houses with red lattice windows opening onto the lane, and two-leaved wooden doors with great inset iron rings. Now and then one of the houses has an ornate iron grill in front of the doorway. The only obvious indication of modernity in the lane is the shabby electric wiring and the collection of metal rubbish bins gathered beneath a notice from the Hygiene Bureau, advising that the bins will be emptied between six and seven a.m. daily.

Hsin-ping stopped at a little brick shed adjoining the south wall of a house. This was the rickshaw man's shed, the place where Old Zhou used to sit, temporarily free of his own five brats but unable to guess what Miss Wang had in store for him during the day. Near the shed, on the wall of the house, was the plastered outline of an old arched doorway, now bricked over, which used to be the front entrance. We turned down Little Toufa Lane, which winds past the east wing of the house, and approached a narrow wooden door, which had been left open. Screwed to the right-hand-side of the door was a metal plate, declaring that this was a 'civic-minded and courtesy-conscious' household, certified by the Hygiene Bureau to have maintained high standards of sanitation and consideration for others in the neighbourhood. In the background a huge block of white cement flats towered over the old lanes. We entered the courtyard.

The space which once was a courtyard is now almost entirely filled with a ramshackle conglomeration of rooms, inhabited by former neighbours. A woman peered from the doorway of the first house on

---

*See L. C. Arlington and William Lewisohn, *In Search of Old Peking*, Oxford University Press, 1987, pp. 162, 163.

our left as we entered. Inside was a family group, sitting in their kitchen, eating noodles and cabbage. The woman, who was middle-aged, called out to Hsin-ping by name and greeted her with interest, but with no great surprise apparently. Her manner suggested that Hsin-ping was returning from a holiday. Gradually the whole family emerged and everybody chatted about relatives. They remembered that Hsin-ping's Third Aunt, the one who had studied nutrition, had dropped in a few years ago.

Rooms lead off in all directions from the courtyard, making it hard to visualize the former layout. Brocade quilt covers hung on bamboo coathangers dangling from the eaves. There were washbowls, stools, birdcages, rag mops, and rows and rows of balsam in pots. The family who had greeted us were living in one of the old reception rooms. We spoke with them for some minutes, declined the ritual offer of a meal— even a stranger in a public toilet will preface his conversation with an enquiry as to whether you have eaten yet—and then walked along a narrow path where the garden used to be. We passed the rooms of the east wing, which once contained the library and the study, and entered the old altar room in the north wing.

On our right was Grandma's bedroom, and inside was the sleeping form of its present occupant. The old four-leaved doors—behind which Hsin-ping spent so much time 'kneeling a little, hurting a little'—have been replaced with dilapidated yellow doors with glass panes. Another former neighbour came out of an adjoining area, which used to be servants' quarters and furniture storerooms, and recognized Hsin-ping almost immediately. As they chatted, I tried to invoke the spirit of forty years ago. I thought of the whole household, including staff, sitting together in the courtyard on warm evenings during the Mid-Autumn Festival or Spring Festival, drinking wine and eating crabs, or enjoying fireworks and lanterns in anticipation of Grandma's celebrated dumplings. I thought too of Grandma's sense of foreboding about the shape of the house. Because the north wing had a kitchen and servants' quarters which protruded beyond the extent of the south wing, the house had the overall shape of a short-bladed chopper, or axe, rather than a square. Grandma had always warned that someone in the family was bound to die prematurely as a result of living in a house which resembled an instrument of execution.

Grandma herself had not succumbed to the curse of the axe. Her ashes were floating on the lake out beyond Fuxingmen, where Hsin-ping and Lulu had scattered them that morning, in accordance with her wishes. Characteristically, Grandma's ashes had refused to stay put while Hsin-ping was getting a good swing up, in order to throw the box out into the current. As a result, some of Grandma opted for earth and some for water. Hsin-ping had made a resolute effort to look horrified as she told me what had happened, but all to no avail, as her self-conscious grin gave way to unrestrained laughter. However, despite Grandma's longevity, her suspicions about the shape of the house appear to have been well-founded. Her husband had died young and so had two of her daughters. Another—Fan's mother—had gone mad and had ceased to live in any real sense soon after her marriage.

We walked through the altar room and reception area into Hsin-ping's old bedroom. A young woman got up from her bed and greeted us casually. After a few words of introduction, she invited us to sit down, have a cup of tea, and so on. Hsin-ping would not linger in the room, and seemed anxious to dispel any impression of a claim on this place. But perhaps there was something of herself lying around here in spite of all the changes—an old book, or a mark on the wall. We walked back, peered in once more at Grandma's bedroom, and then went round the corner of the house to a little room which had been sealed up. It was about twelve square metres, and had been locked up and left empty three years ago, after a period in which it had been used as a storage shed. This was the property of Hsin-ping, guaranteed to her by the Chinese government. Other rooms may also revert to her ownership if they become vacant. A number of other people greeted Hsin-ping, and she stopped to chat briefly. Finally, as we left the house and stepped out into the lane again, a sizeable group gathered to fare-well us.

We went in search of the other houses which used to belong to Hsin-ping's grandfather, Wang Jinfang. Number 60 Shi Fu Ma Street had been home to Wang Jinfang, Lady Wang, Grandma, and five children. After Grandfather took ill from his exertions, the family moved around the corner into a 'Western-style' house, in Shoushuihe (Sullage) Lane—where they lived for a time before returning to Toufa Lane. We walked through the front gate of Number 60 Shi Fu Ma Street into—a restaurant. The place was empty except for a few people working in the kitchens, but a cook came out to greet us in the area which used to be a courtyard. The kitchens were located in the old reception rooms and bedrooms, and the courtyard has been roofed in. The rear of the house has been demolished.

After a brief discussion with the cook, we left the house and made our way on foot to Shoushuihe Lane. This house was almost unchanged, although shabby and dilapidated. Grey brick walls and red wooden windows faced the street, and the main doorway was a striking feature, giving the house its air of importance. There was a decorated facade over the large brick archway, flanked by two imposing pillars—the kind of Chinese–Western style you often see in a Chinatown Masonic Lodge, or some such building. Huge iron double-doors decorated with lace-work opened into a sort of porch, and we walked through to the inner side, from which four red wooden doors opened on to the courtyard. Above us the eaves were faced with carved wooden arrow-heads pointing to the ground.

A pudding of a boy, aged about seven or eight, bowled out to meet us. We asked if anyone was at home and he shoved the door open and bustled us inside the building. We had seen quite a few very fat and very pampered little boys in the city. Fancy counting this kid as only 'one child'. And from the way he threw his considerable weight around, he looked as if he would be perfectly at home drinking fermented mare's milk from the skulls of his enemies. He chivvied us inside and bawled out for his mother, who emerged from one of the rooms on the ground floor, and invited us in to have a look, after Hsin-ping explained what we were doing there.

As we walked into the living room, the woman motioned to us to sit down on a bed in the corner. Hsin-ping declined, but the boy made a rush at her, and pushed her down on to the bed. Despite Hsin-ping's good natured laugh, the woman was embarrassed and harried her son out of the room. After a few minutes idle chat about the past, we returned to the corridor, and picked our way among bowls and dishes and steamers and bottled-gas stoves belonging to several families on this floor. An unlit wooden staircase, varnished with generations of cooking oil and grease, led to the second floor. At the top of the stairs an old man in a ragged singlet was cooking rice. We exchanged pleasantries and, after peering about uselessly in the gloom, went outside into the harsh sunlight of the courtyard, which was almost overgrown on one side with tangled sinews of melon vine. As we walked through the grand faded doorway into the street, I thought of little Hsin-ping, passing on her way to school, and playing in these alleys, or as a teenager chattering with Tang Ling on her way to Xidan Market, or riding home from work after she herself had become a teacher. In the lane, in the narcotic heat, I fancied I could hear other children, calling out to Hsin-ping that the Red Guards were at Grandma's house.

We drove on to Shoupa (Handkerchief) Lane, to Hsin-ping's old primary school, now Peking Number Two Experimental Primary School. Its old status has been maintained in this new title, and it is designated a 'key' or 'priority' school, with allocation of superior staff and resources. China's educational policies of the late 1970s and 1980s have put the clock back to the days before the attack on examinations and bourgeois intellectuals. Now, as the education system gears itself up for the 'four modernizations', there is a generation of casualties, caught between old snobs who believe they are superior because they went to school before the Cultural Revolution, and new snobs who believe they are superior because they went after. There is only a token, and irrelevant, acknowledgement that some things can be learned without schools—and without snobbery. Now more than ever, more even than in Hsin-ping's day, it is important to get into the system of 'priority' primary, secondary and tertiary institutions.

Just inside the school gate were a dozen or so little kids, cavorting about in a state of delight, their exams finished. This was the second-last day of the school year, and the spirit of the summer holiday was abroad in the playground. As we stood inside the gate, waiting for someone to notice us, a swarm of boys and girls burst out of a nearby corridor, squabbling over who was to wheel a barrow in which they were collecting portable blackboards for holiday storage. This was obviously one of those exquisite little responsibilities which not only got the workers out of the classroom, but symbolized the summer holiday itself. A pile of blackboards fell to the ground, there was shrieking and yelling and pushing and shoving. A middle-aged woman walked in their direction, looked as if she might be about to intervene, and then obviously thought better of it—it would soon be holidays for her, too.

The woman approached us, and Hsin-ping introduced herself as a former student. She asked the woman if any of the old staff were there, and reeled off a list of names of her teachers. One or two were still on the staff, but were on leave. A big poster in the entrance to the court-yard had rockets and stars on it, and a slogan about science and progress. After a while the woman went off to look for the principal, to tell him he had foreign guests. In the meantime, Hsin-ping struck up a conversation with the gate-keeper, who remembered a name or two.

The principal told us that many former students come from overseas to visit their old school. He seemed a cordial, relaxed person, and was happy enough to spend time showing Hsin-ping around. I followed along behind, as she pointed at this and that—'That's where they put the mop so that it would fall on teacher Jia's head'. She blushed to be recalling such wickedness in the presence of the principal. The old classrooms were still there, between the playground and some new multi-storied buildings. They were still quite attractive rooms, and still in use, although terribly run-down. In the new building we observed some lessons in progress. The kids sat bolt upright in their seats, eager to answer the teachers' questions. Out in the corridor some were stacking completed examination papers. The ones we saw were English papers, in which the kids had to translate from Chinese into English, 'We love our socialist motherland', and 'Beijing moves swiftly forward in modern socialist reconstruction'.

The blackboard gang were still quarrelling out in the playground. The girls had broken away into a 'chasey' game, and the six boys who remained were pulling at the barrow, all in different directions it seemed. Sometimes socialist reconstruction gets held up by 'narrow egalitarianism'. We walked round a crumbling old wall overhung by a glorious Persian Silk Tree (*Albizzia Julibrissin*) in full bloom, with pink, feathery puffballs all over it. On the other side was a pretty little court-yard, a playground and kindergarten. There was a miniature water-wheel in a shallow pond, some much newer climbing frames, and some tiny seats in a sheltered courtyard watched over by a pair of ginkgos and a white-barked pine. So this was where Hsin-ping had gone to kindergarten.

As we were leaving, Hsin-ping encountered an old man who was wandering aimlessly about with a filthy old rag mop. She greeted him with delight, as he had been the caretaker when she was here. They chatted excitedly for some time until Hsin-ping began asking about her old teachers, and the atmosphere changed. She said goodbye to the old man, and as we walked away, she shook her head. She had asked about the 'old maids'. One had been beaten to death by Red Guards. One had suicided by jumping from the roof of a nearby building. And one had hung herself—Great Aunt Yin Quan. It was she who had kept on asking, 'Why is every place a courtroom?', and whom Hsin-ping had not seen after leaving with Grandma for the village in 1966.

Next morning we drove to Erlong (Second Dragon) Street, to Hsin-ping's old high school. The sign above the gate read 'Peking Teachers' University Experimental High School'. This place also had maintained its old privileged status. The billboard inside the main gate declared that education is geared to the needs of modernization, and beneath it some cloth squares read 'Wishing you success'. The meaning of this became apparent as we saw, through the windows of the classrooms, the bowed heads of examination candidates. I thought of the persistence of examinations in China, and of the continuity of its make-or-break significance in people's lives. In Ming and Qing times candidates who had passed the provincial examination went to the Public Halls in the south-eastern part of the Tartar City to take part in the triennial metro-politan examinations. Success in this crucial ordeal meant qualification for an official post, and for entry to the palace examinations. For these, candidates were locked into sealed cubicles for days at a time. Some-times they died there, but the seals on the doors could not be broken and bodies had to be removed through a hole in the wall. The examin-ation was then almost the only means of selection of officials for the civil service; the only means of admittance to power and privilege. Today again, examinations are the ladder to the clouds for millions of Chinese. The badges of rank are more subtle than the old peacock feathers and embroidered cranes and pheasants, but the 'back door' of unofficial privilege is as great an advantage as any of the old sumptuary laws. Once more the tragic tales of failed candidates and suicides and ruined lives are the stuff of everyday life in China.

A gate-keeper went to get the principal. He was one of Hsin-ping's old teachers—her history teacher, whom she used to call 'Metternich', because of his obsession with nineteenth-century European political figures. I wondered if the principal of a school gearing itself to the needs of modernization would thank Hsin-ping for such a name. A plump, silvery-haired fellow of about sixty waddled towards us. Hsin-ping introduced herself, and he made a most unconvincing fist of remembering her. An anxious young man ushered us away from the window of the examination hall, but the principal seemed no more concerned for the comfort of the candidates than a farmer for battery hens. He took us on a tour of the school. A huge billboard in the sportsground read, 'We have idealism. We have morality. We have culture. We have discipline'. Above these words a shining jet aircraft rose almost vertically into the sky.

Hsin-ping's old classrooms were all European-style buildings, pleasantly situated behind a little garden. In a darkened building, a Temple of the Four Modernizations, we were shown an extraordinary array of video cameras, sound equipment and computers. The equipment was being put to good use, and we watched some boys manipulating mathematical tables in the computer room. In schools like this the chaff of waiters, clerks and department store attendants is winnowed from the wheat of university students.

What a world of difference between these keen, absorbed faces and the worn, grimy faces of boys and girls we had seen sleeping on sacks of grain in the back of trucks hurtling through the suburbs early that morning. Or the faces of the temple attendants, with boredom and futility etched on their features like acid scars. I thought of the young girl at the Palace Museum, in the Hall of Clocks, her broom fallen from limp fingers and her head tilted grotesquely in sleep, her mouth agape like a dead carp. 'Let the past serve the present', say the posters.

Posters around the hotels and tourist spots indicate that the staff have won awards, such as the 'five-star smiling service award'. This does not fool young workers into taking their jobs seriously, or 'serving the people' as an older message put it. They know too well the value society places on their work, and that they must look out for themselves. As for tourists, if they want something better, they can make an offer. In our hotel dining room, 'five-star smiling service' consisted of standing around where nobody could possibly catch your eye, occasionally sortying forth to scatter cups and bowls like frisbees, and then disappearing before the guests could demand something to put in what was left of their crockery.

The past and the present. Out in the villages it would seem that the children are as unimpressed with education as any Qing dynasty peasant, except for the few whose families see some prospect of a change of registration from rural to urban household as a result of a child's academic prowess and elevation to some government job. Among the others, there are many who are getting very rich these days as a result of the new economic measures, and need many sons to manage their present wealth and take care of their future needs. Education, science and technology, population control—these are only new slogans as far as many peasants are concerned, and soon they will be as faded and irrelevant as 'learn from Dazhai'. They are still learning from the past.

Among middle-class urban families, education is opening doors again, and it is a high-pressure business. Cultivation of talent is the catchcry in Chinese homes and schools these days. China must foster the abilities of fewer but better babies and, paradoxically, the more single-child families there are, the less choice China's children will have as to how, or if, they want those abilities developed. Popular psychology, of the kind that deals with the stimulation of intelligence, is the theme of innumerable magazines and periodicals, and has thrived on the one-child family.

Did a 'Cultural Revolution' ever happen? Looking at the school where Hsin-ping went, listening to Metternich, it began to seem a fantasy. The visit was an anti-climax really—for me at least. We drove away from the school in silence. As we approached the Guangji Temple, Hsin-ping told me that near here was Number Three Girls' Secondary School, where a girl, also named Wang Hsin-ping, had become a legend overnight. During Red Guard rallies in the school, the principal had been hounded to death. At one of the rallies after his death, they say the other Wang Hsin-ping cut out the heart of the principal and held it up for the mob, screaming 'Is this a red heart, or a black heart?'

In Fuchengmen Road, just a little west of the Western Archways, are two ancient temples. The Temple of the White Dagoba (Baitasi) was built in the eleventh century, during the time of the Liao Tartars. It was restored in the thirteenth century by Kublai Khan, burned down and restored during the Ming, and restored again by the Qing emperors, Kang Xi and Qian Long. The Guangji Temple stands where temples have stood since the twelfth century, but it was enlarged during the Ming and Qing, and in modern times became the headquarters of the Chinese Buddhist Association, of which Big Grandma was a solid member. The characters inscribed above the arched entrance give an important clue to the history of the place, although they are not readily decipherable to modern Chinese, and there is no attempt at explanation. It appears that the Emperor Kang Xi changed the temple's name slightly to include the element of compassion—or to include the element of himself—in the aura of the place. He was a good deal more subtle than the present caretakers, who don't care much what the place stands for as long as we know who is in charge. On the right side of the archway is a marble plaque establishing that the temple falls within the jurisdiction of the Peking Municipal Ancient Institutions Aministration Bureau.

Presumptuously, we drove in through the gateway and parked our car in the courtyard, which contained a number of signs declaring 'entry prohibited'. An old man got up from his stool and advanced on us in a highly agitated state, fanning his hand violently across his face in the Chinese gesture of prohibition. Hsin-ping smiled benignly at him and kept gazing around, while he remonstrated with our driver—no doubt inwardly cursing rude, pig-headed foreigners. The driver took the brunt of it all, and Hsin-ping stood silently by—an incongruous figure in sunglasses, a Dior handbag dangling from her arm, and a coloured Balkan Sobranie in her mouth. We were not allowed any further, and did not even see the famous 'iron trees' (cycads) which had excited Hsin-ping's attention more than forty years ago, or the statues of the Goddess of Mercy—if they are still there. But we did see quite a bit of the sour old sentinel who watches over the temple these days. We gave up our quest, and went in search of food.

Our driver Zhao was a Buddhist, and sympathized with the old man at the temple. He felt that he was not just bored and grumpy, but also resentful of visitors. He had probably seen places like this pillaged by teenage zealots in the 1960s. Even now, although the temple was safe from the more obvious forms of destruction, it was hardly being preserved in any genuine sense. Even if there were services again some day, this place would be like the others, a tourist attraction, staffed by public servant monks, selling Kiwifruit Soda and cloisonne thermometers. I asked Zhao about his religious beliefs, in particular his dietary strictures, and was told that two of his brothers ate meat, but that he and a fourth brother, who had been raised by a Buddhist grandmother, did not. We were in a Xinjiang Muslim restaurant at the time and had ordered lamb, on huge sword-like skewers. With obvious relish, Zhao helped himself to three or four skewers. I asked how come he was eating lamb, and he said it was because he liked the taste. I offered him some lamb meatballs from another stew-like dish and he recoiled in horror. 'But I thought you could eat lamb?' I said, in some confusion. 'Yes, but not *that* kind!' he replied, almost indignantly. At the risk of offending him, I just had to know what ritual had been violated in the preparation of this dish. 'Why can't you eat *this* lamb?' I asked. 'Stinks like sheep-piss', he said.

Over the meal we discussed foreigners. Zhao told us of his abiding dislike for Japanese, Vietnamese—and Southerners. Southern Chinese are not *quite* a different race, but they certainly are different, according to northerners. 'Cantonese are only interested in their bellies and their pockets', declared Zhao, 'As for those sly, stuck-up Shanghainese . . .

they think even their farts are perfumed ... you know, even people who marry Shanghainese don't really *like* them'. The meal ended in some hilarity when Hsin-ping pointed out that she was born in Canton and had married a man from Ningbo—everyone knows they are even worse than the Shanghainese.

We spent a lot of time driving around the suburbs of Peking. The city was much more lively than I remembered, especially at night. On several occasions in the past I had walked around the city—and on one memorable occasion though the Forbidden City—at night, and seen hardly another soul. Everybody was indoors by nine o'clock in 1975 and 1976, even in the spring and summer. Things have changed now of course, but this was always a striking difference between the dour north and the jaunty south. On one or two occasions, when I was lost near Qianmen late at night, there simply was nobody to be seen, except the occasional shift worker on a bus. In 1987 there were free markets everywhere and things going on till late at night.

There were a surprising number of private motor vehicles in the streets. We saw several private cars and vans, including two or three with 'pin-up' pictures of children in the back window. These were not photographs of the driver's children, they were cut from magazines—and there were two pictures, not one. Chinese 'bumper stickers' perhaps, proclaiming an opinion about the one-child family policy. Trees have been planted in great numbers in Peking, and this compensates a little for the startling ugliness of the new roads and freeways. Small scholartrees line the streets now, but you have to go to a temple or some such place to see a great, old one.

We visited two of Peking's dwindling supply of genuine ancient temples, and marvelled at their trees, on a visit to the Western Hills with Cui Wemin. These temples were just far enough out of the city to have been neglected by the Red Guards. Near them is the kind of countryside in which Grandma had grown up, and where she went to work again after the Red Guards came. The roads into the hills were lined with poplars and birches, and as we climbed we noticed that there were many new houses in almost every village. These were not ugly concretè affairs, but stone cottages with tiled roofs. There were chickens and pigs, an occasional dog, lots of donkeys and mules, and fields of wheat, barley and sweet potatoes. I thought of Grandma sorting the sweet potatoes, sometime after the wheat harvest.

About fifty kilometres out of the city we pulled up near a small roadside market. There was construction work going on, a restoration of Tanzhesi (the Monastery of Deep Pools and Wild Mulberries). The wild 'mulberry' (*Cudrania Tricuspidata*) is not a mulberry at all, but a thorny little tree, the leaves of which were used for feeding silkworms before the real mulberries were ready, or when leaves were scarce. The bark was also used, for yellow dye. This is an enchanted place—terraces and courtyards, hill-side dagobas, a thousand-year ginkgo, twisting pines, persimmons and walnuts, heady scents and gorgeous white peonies. There is only one old wild mulberry, at the front of the temple. We climbed several flights of steep steps and stood looking out over the beautiful blue Western Hills, then wound our way back along an over-grown path. When we reached the bottom again we stopped at the ginkgo, which is known as Di Wang Shu (Tree of Emperors and Kings). According to legend, this tree foretold the passing of the old emperor and the advent of the new, by means of shoots sprouting from its massive trunk. Cui Weimin and Wang Hsin-ping sat beneath the ancient oracle like a couple of Tang poets celebrating an exquisite moment.

A few miles south-east, another ancient temple, Jietaisi (Ordination Terrace Temple), has also been in use for over a thousand years, and is also undergoing a facelift. Within the walls of the temple is a giant scholartree, as old as the temple itself. Inside the temple grounds are some very large and unusually forked white-barked pines and two near-horizontal trees called the Protecting Pagoda Pine and the Sleeping Dragon Pine—the same entities noted by travellers in ancient times. These days they are likely to be photographed, as background to the visitor. Photography seems to have blunted the sensibilities of many Chinese to their own treasures, and despite the stylized poses of the subjects, draped in their Sunday best around the trees and rocks and stone tablets of temple gardens, all the photographs end up looking like passport shots. They are, after all, just travel documents.

But there are many trees which defy photography, which defy even the eye, and those who want to remember them must try to touch their spirit. Such trees are often twisted, stunted affairs, not at all like their kin, but they compel our attention. Hsin-ping's cousin, Fan Yuzhong, has taken root in my mind like the pines of Yellow Mountain, ever since I met him in Peking in 1980 and, as I lingered over the Sleeping Dragon Pine, I found myself paying my respects to that probing, restless spirit which could never be confined to the perimeters of the temple court-yard, but chose to take its own path, over the wall. Like the Sleeping Dragon too, he has jutted out impossibly over my attempts to define 'The Chinese'. I must do what the ancients did, and simply make a hole in the wall for him to grow through.

In the spring of 1980, while travelling in China, I wrote to Fan from the Stone Forest, near Kunming, explaining that I was a friend of Hsin-ping, that I would be in Peking in a couple of weeks and would like to meet him. I was a little concerned that my action might cause him trouble, but things seemed to have changed and I felt that the political climate might allow him to meet a foreign tourist without incurring suspicion, especially since I brought news of a relative. In fact, there *were* great changes in the air. In Chengdu I had seen a portrait of Liu Shaoqi in a museum of revolutionary heroes. He had been posthumously rehabilitated, and portraits were appearing all round the country. So I sent my letter, telling Fan that I would try to contact him in two weeks time.

In Peking, I asked a China Travel Service guide to phone his school and ask him to ring me at the hotel. This seemed a good way of testing the water. If there was going to be trouble, the guide's reaction might forewarn me and Fan could escape gracefully from a tricky situation with a harmless phone call made in public. The guide, who had compiled a glossary of Australian colloquialisms so preposterous that not even an American film-maker would regard them as authentic, telephoned me in my room and asked why I wanted to see Fan.

'Because he is a friend's cousin.'

'Who is his cousin?'

'His cousin is a friend of mine.'

Later that same day I received another call. 'Mr Trevor. I see you are in your room. You have not shot through.'

'That's right. What can I do for you?'

'I want to ask you. Why do you want to see Mr Fan?'

'I told you, because he is my friend's relative.'

'Who is his relative?'

'His relative is my cobber.'

I had one more phone call of this nature, and I resorted to the universal language of the bureaucrat, a mixture of arrogance and obscurantism. I also asked him if he knew the expression, 'You couldn't organize a piss-up in a brewery'. He hung up and apparently made the necessary arrangements, because next day I had a call from Fan, who said he would come to my hotel.

That evening at about half-past seven, Fan came to my room. He had been required to leave his name with a security guard at the entrance to the hotel. After a brief conversation, in which he expressed some anxiety that we might be overheard, he invited me to his room—Hsin-ping's old room in the architects' dormitory near Yuetan—so that we could talk freely. He said I was welcome to go there 'on one condition'. I suspected some kind of cloak-and-dagger precautions, but not a bit of it. 'Don't tell Hsin-ping about the mess', he said, 'I haven't got around to tidying up lately.'

He put me on a bus, and rode his bike home. He must have set a cracking pace, because he pulled up at my stop within one or two minutes of my arrival, and we walked over to his building. He wheeled his bike inside and locked it; theft was very common, he told me. Then we sat in his room and talked, for two hours or so, in English. The only light was a small bedside lamp, and the conflagration of our rough Qianmen-brand cigarettes. The atmosphere lent itself to sedition. He told me that the dust was driving him mad, blowing in his window, and that the government was trying to fool people into thinking this was just the usual dust from the Gobi Desert. He believed it was the result of erosion, of mismanagement of the environment. 'They know perfectly well what damage is being done', he said, 'And what should be done about it. But they don't want us to know that they know. Our water is polluted with industrial waste, and no one is allowed to mention it. Can you imagine what will happen to China if our waterways are poisoned? Sometimes I think they are actually *proud* of our pollution. They regard it as a symptom of progress. Do you know, when we have Japanese industrialists here, to visit our factories, do you know what they do? They bring ducks and fish from the countryside and put them in the water near the factory, so that our foreign guests will think we have no pollution. That dust all over this room is typical of what's wrong with China. Our leaders tell us what we may think, and to think anything different is heresy. Tomorrow we may be allowed to discuss pollution, but it'll be too late.'

We discussed a few examples of Western governments which were not above telling the people whoppers, and which seemed to thrive on secrecy. None of my revelations were new to Fan. Judging by the titles of books on his shelves, there was not much going on in the world which had escaped his attention. He told me that friends were always sending him books, and he took the view these days that it was better to publicize the fact that he knew many foreigners, who were extremely interested in him, than to conceal it. The government might just realize that if anything harsh were to happen to him, it would cause an unpleasant fuss. That was why he had not hesitated to come to my hotel. He told his school that the head of a foreign education delegation had asked to see him.

Our discussion turned to Hua Guofeng and Deng Xiaoping, and the extent to which criticism of Mao was permissible since the arrest of the 'gang of four'. Suddenly there was a very loud knock at the door. Fan jumped up in alarm. He went very apprehensively to the door, and heaved a sigh of relief as he let in a tall, balding, middle-aged man—a friend, it seemed, or a colleague. The three of us sat for another hour-and-a-half, until Fan warned me that the last bus would leave for Qianmen at about midnight. I felt very privileged to have sat in on what I thought was an extremely frank discussion, and I said as much to Fan as we walked to the bus-stop. He jerked his thumb over his shoulder at the departing figure of the visitor and said, 'I couldn't tell you the things I wanted to with him in the room'.

'But I thought you seemed at ease, and the conversation we had about Mao was pretty frank.'

'It's O.K. to say some things', Fan replied, 'and that one knows exactly *which* things. He knows which way the wind is blowing and he blows along with it. He would start praising Mao again, if necessary. While his sort are around, it will always be possible for our leaders to whip up another Cultural Revolution if they want to. Thank God they don't want to.'

I caught my bus and waved to Fan, standing alone in a bleak landscape of grim and silent buildings, with the wind and dust binding him to the barren street. I felt a profound admiration—and guilt—that I could speed away from his life so effortlessly, after visiting hours. I felt a coward, a deserter, a voyeur—and yet I knew he would just get on with things. The wind was bitterly cold and reached in like claws through the open windows as the bus hurtled through the empty streets. When I arrived in the vicinity of Qianmen, I got off one or two stops too early and was lost. Strangely enough, as I struggled to find my way about the dark and deserted streets, I felt much more cheerful than I had on the bus. You can smell hope in China when you get down from your carriage.

I never saw Fan again, but I got a letter from him, to tell me that he was in America. 'I am free at last. I love China, but China does not love me.' For some time I heard from Hsin-ping that he was struggling to exist in the United States. He had no money, couldn't get work, had no friends and was leading a miserable life. Suddenly the tide turned. He won a scholarship. People were interested in his translations. He was going to do a doctorate. Then one Saturday morning Hsin-ping told me that he had been killed in a freak accident—run down on the footpath by a car out of control. There was some hint that he had recently been approached by secret agents of some sort, and had sent them packing.

On our last morning in Peking, Hsin-ping and I set out for the architects' dormitory, to pay a visit to her old room—and Fan's. The taxi driver had some difficulty finding the place, much to Hsin-ping's disgust, and we went back and forth across Yuetan for some time, past the Children's Hospital and Lulu's old school, until we found the right place. The road where I had caught the bus that night was all chopped up, and pipes were being laid. We found the building and went inside. I remembered the porch on the first floor. Hsin-ping knocked on a door and a young woman responded to our introductions quite readily, almost as if we were expected.

We were invited into her room, which I thought must have been Fan's. It seemed very different, and I put this down to the fact that the furniture had changed, there was a good deal less clutter and mess and, of course, it was broad daylight. Nevertheless, I was disturbed that I could not remember anything. After twenty minutes or so of conversation with the woman, who was a relative of Fan's wife, we got up to leave. As we went back through the porch, the woman pointed to a door I had not noticed on the way in. She opened it and went in, Hsin-ping following. I heard her saying 'There were so many books, I didn't know what to do with them . . . '*This* was the room. It all came flooding back. There was the desk in the corner, under the window through which the dust had blown in on his life. I turned to tell Hsin-ping . . . but she dropped to the sofa as if she had been pole-axed.

She covered her face in her hands and after a while her sobs became audible, despite desperate attempts to stifle them. 'I've seen the back of his head so many times as I came into this room, sitting just over there reading at his desk. Just now I could see him.' The woman stood quietly in the corner, and made no attempt either to console or to interfere in Hsin-ping's pain. She just waited. After a little while, we said our goodbyes and walked back to the car. Hsin-ping seemed all right for a while, but in the car she started crying again. 'He was the brightest of us all, he could have done anything, been anything. It's such bad luck, such really bad luck.' Whenever Hsin-ping thinks of Fan these days she says the same thing—'*Zhen daomei, Zhen daomei*'. It is stronger than 'Bad luck'. It is more like cursing fate.

That afternoon, Cui Weimin, Linglai, Tang Ling and a variety of friends and relatives gathered at the airport to see us off. There were not too many tears shed, but Hsin-ping and her old gang called each other names, slapped each other playfully and clutched hands until the last minute. Somebody once told me that the Chinese are used to farewells.

Index